KATHARINA AND MARTIN LUTHER

The Radical Marriage of a Runaway Nun and a Renegade Monk

Michelle DeRusha

BakerBooks
a division of Baker Publishing Group
Grand Rapids, Michigan

Published by Baker Books
a division of Baker Publishing Group
P.O. Box 6287, Grand Rapids, MI 49516-6287
www.bakerbooks.com

Printed in the United States of America

Library of Congress Cataloging-in-Publication Data is on file at the Library of Congress, Washington, DC.

ISBN 978-0-8010-1910-4

Scripture quotations are from the King James Version of the Bible.

Interior design by William Overbeeke

17 18 19 20 21 22 23 7 6 5 4 3 2 1

For my dad
the most Lutheran Catholic I know

CONTENTS

LIST OF ILLUSTRATIONS

FOREWORD

The five hundredth anniversary of the Reformation, marked by Martin Luther's public disputation against papal indulgences (later known as the *Ninety-five Theses*) made on October 31, 1517, will certainly bring revived interest in the life and legacy of one of church history's most influential figures. And justifiably so, for few have had as much impact on the world both inside and outside the church as Martin Luther. The Protestant Reformation that Luther set into motion ushered in the modern age, an age of world-changing developments. These include the Enlightenment, widespread literacy, the rise of the individual, and innumerable shifts in culture, education, and the arts. In fact, one cannot study literature (my own field) without at least a passing familiarity with Luther's writing because his impact on the world, including the world of letters, is so far-reaching.

But until I read this fascinating account by Michelle DeRusha of Luther's marriage to Katharina von Bora, I knew nothing about this central part of Luther's life and work. It's a shame, really, that when we study history, even church history, scant attention is usually given to domestic life. There are various reasons why that's so, but one is our lingering embrace of a sharp—and artificial—division drawn in the nineteenth century between the public sphere and the private sphere.

Biography, whether the reading or writing of it, can go a long way toward correcting this error. The examination of a person's whole life, one placed within the context of his or her work and times, offers a crash course in a myriad of subjects, as well as a powerful demonstration that one thing always touches on another. Public and private cannot be separated in a person any more than hydrogen and oxygen can be separated and still be water. A person's public works are shaped and formed by his or her private life, and vice versa. This biography of a marriage, then, goes even further in reconciling the public and private parts of a life that has left such a legacy.

In the case of Martin Luther, marriage—both his theological views of the institution and his own marriage—was central to his work as a reformer. Luther's decision to marry played a pivotal role not only in his private life, but in the public impact of his ministry in reforming the church and its teachings on marriage. For it is one thing to preach a doctrine; it is another to practice it. This truth is particularly applicable to Luther's situation because he took considerable aim at the contemporary church's teaching on sex, marriage, and celibacy. Luther's controversial marriage allowed him to take a heretofore abstract doctrinal topic into the realm of lived experience. Luther's marriage extended his efforts at reforming orthodoxy to orthopraxy. Simply by marrying, and thereby embodying the doctrine he was teaching, the power of Luther's reforms was magnified. Luther's theology of marriage, one refined by practice, changed the way Christians thought about marriage and thereby shaped the very institution of marriage in ways that continue today.

But it wasn't just getting married that allowed Luther to influence the institution of marriage. As the account that follows in these pages shows, Luther's decision to marry Katharina von Bora specifically also contributed to the Protestant understanding of marriage because of the particular ways these two particular people shaped one another and the life they created together. For one thing, Martin's decision to marry out of obedience to God and service to the imperiled Katharina (as opposed to mere affection) serves as a model for us today, an antidote to our overly romanticized view of marriage as centered on personal compatibility and fulfillment. Martin and Katharina did find compatibility and fulfillment in their marriage—but only as these resulted naturally in their pursuit of marriage's nobler offices.

It is these nobler offices of marriage, those for which God established the institution and still blesses it today, that shine so brightly in this story of one marriage formed so long ago. Those times were so very different from ours, and much about Katharina and Martin's betrothal, wedding, and life together seems strange to twenty-first-century readers: convent life, heresy trials, a marriage bed of straw, the requisite eyewitness to the consummation, and the devastating hardships of labor, disease, and early death that were part of life in those days.

Yet, from within all this strangeness, an astonishing familiarity emerges. Strip away the veneer of the differences between the Luthers' marriage and the typical modern marriage of today, and what shines forth is a picture of what God has always intended marriage to be: an obedience to him and to each other that glorifies him and is a picture of Christ's relationship to the church.

In such a time as this—when marriage seems to be at once despised and idolized, both within the church and outside it, and when the very definition of marriage has been challenged, chastened, and changed—the radical marriage of Katharina and Martin Luther serves as a timely remembrance for the church. In both its strangeness and its familiarity to readers in a world five hundred years away from theirs, this story of a husband and a wife reminds us that marriage was designed to serve the other, not ourselves, and to advance the kingdom of God here on earth, not our personal kingdoms.

In other words, the biblical vision of marriage has always been radical.

Karen Swallow Prior
Professor of English
Liberty University

PREFACE

The morning I began my research for this book, I stood amid the library stacks at the University of Nebraska–Lincoln and nearly wept as I gazed at the hundreds of books by and about Martin Luther lining the shelves. A large number of them were written in German. Most were tomes of five hundred pages or longer. Many of the works comprised multiple volumes. Given the breadth and depth of the scholarship already available, I couldn't possibly see where there was room on the shelf for yet another book in the extensive Luther repertoire.

As it turned out, there *was* something important left to say about Martin Luther. Most of the scholarship covered his theology, doctrine, politics, and many aspects of his career and life in great detail. Few books, however, offered much more than a cursory glance at his marriage or his domestic life.

Even less has been written about Katharina von Bora, the woman who became Martin Luther's wife. She comprised half of what is arguably one of the most famous marriages in Christian history, yet it seems history has largely forgotten her.

Their marriage was radically revolutionary and arguably one of the most scandalous and intriguing in history. Yet five centuries after they said "I do," we still know little about Katharina and Martin Luther's life together as husband and wife. That's why there is room on the shelf for this book.

While this biography largely offers an admiring look at the Luthers, it's not an entirely uncritical perspective. I occasionally question both Luther's and Katharina's actions, but because history is more replete with information about Luther, my critiques tend to be directed his way. Together, this legendary couple encountered tremendous adversity and persevered in the face of hardship. They experienced joy and grief, triumph and travail in their twenty-one years together. In short, they were human, which means they were flawed and fallible, just like the rest of us. This book aims to paint a well-rounded picture of Katharina and Luther's life together as husband and wife.

A Word about Research and Sources

As I mentioned, finding information about Martin Luther is not difficult. The challenge was sorting through the vast number of resources to uncover the information most relevant to this book. The American Edition of *Luther's Works* (identified in the notes as LW) spans fifty-five volumes. I focused primarily on Luther's letters and his *Table Talk* for insights into his personal and domestic life. I also studied his theological works—particularly his treatises on marriage (*A Sermon on the Estate of Marriage*; *The Estate of Marriage*; *Marriage Matters*) and his most famous works, including the *Ninety-five Theses*, the *Babylonian Captivity of the Church*, *To the Christian Nobility of the German Nation*, and the *Judgment on Monastic Vows*—with an eye toward how his theology was or was not reflected in his own daily life. I supplemented these primary sources with several contemporary biographies and commentaries. Richard Marius's *Martin Luther: The Christian between God and Death*, Heiko Oberman's *Luther: Man between God and the Devil*, and James Kittelson's *Luther the Reformer: The Story of the Man and His Career* were especially helpful, as was Susan Karant-Nunn's and Merry Wiesner-Hanks's *Luther on Women: A Sourcebook*, which offered insightful analysis and commentary on how Luther's works reflected his views on women and the role of women in the home and in society generally.

Researching Katharina von Bora offered the opposite challenge. The dearth of primary source material (only eight of her letters survive today, none of which were addressed to Luther) compelled me to get a bit creative in my research and, at times, formulate educated hypotheses based on the experiences of some of Katharina's contemporaries, whose letters and journals have been preserved. I also relied on sources such as Wiesner-Hanks's *Convents Confront the Reformation*, Charlotte Woodford's *Nuns as Historians in Early Modern Germany*, and James Anderson's *Daily Life in the Reformation*, among many others, to construct a picture of what life might have been like for Katharina, both as a nun and as a wife and mother in early modern Germany. Finally, I relied heavily on the only two biographies of Katharina Luther available in English (a handful of others have been published in German): Ernst Kroker's *The Mother of the Reformation: The Amazing Life and Story of Katharine Luther*, and Rudolf and Marilynn Markwald's *Katharina von Bora: A Reformation Life*.

In addition to the endnotes, a selected bibliography of the sources I used in researching this book, organized by theme, can be found on page 311.

M. D.

ACKNOWLEDGMENTS

Writing the acknowledgments section is always my favorite part of writing a book, because even though it's my name on the cover, the truth is, a whole community of people helps to birth a book. I am so grateful to all those who have held my hand, prayed, cheered, encouraged, and helped all along the way.

Chad Allen, editorial director at Baker Books and editor of this book—thanks for asking me, "If you could choose only one out of the *50 Women* to write a book about, who would it be?" From that question—and my answer: Katharina von Bora—this book was born.

The Baker Books editorial and marketing teams—you are the consummate professionals. I am so grateful for your creativity, your energy, your attention to detail, and your smarts. Thank you all for helping to make this book the best it can be and for shepherding it into the world.

My agent, Rachelle Gardner—you never give up, do you? Thank you for your faith in me as a writer and for your unwavering confidence that there will be another book project for me around the next bend.

Karen Swallow Prior—thank you not only for your insightful words and for so graciously agreeing to write the foreword to this book during one of your busiest seasons, but also for your kindness and encouragement. Your positive attitude put a spring in my step on the days I needed it most.

The staff at the Lincoln City Libraries and especially the University of Nebraska–Lincoln Love Library. A lot has changed since I was in graduate school. Thanks for helping me locate the books and articles I needed and for guiding me to those mysterious in-between floors.

My blog readers—thank you for reminding me again and again that you really are eager to read this book. Your encouraging words, cheerful comments, and kind emails kept me focused and determined.

Pastors Greg, Michael, Beth Ann, and Karl-John and my church family—you live out Luther's vision for the church every day as you quietly love your neighbors and faithfully serve others. I am so grateful to be part of the Southwood Lutheran community.

Deidra Riggs, Shelly Miller, and Jennifer Dukes Lee—you were the ones who convinced me that I was the person to write this book. I wouldn't have said yes if it hadn't been for you. Thank you for having faith in me, especially when I didn't have faith in myself.

Maureen and Buzz DeRusha and Jeanine DeRusha—thanks for always asking how the book was coming along, even when you knew it meant I'd ramble about it for far too long.

Noah and Rowan—I know, I know, you want me to write fiction. Maybe next time . . .

And finally, thank you, Brad. In the early stages of research, when I was overwhelmed and afraid, you said everything would come together. I didn't believe you at the time, but you were right. Thank you for always being a steady voice of reason, an encourager, the very best brainstormer, and my very own personal editor. I told you this already, but I'll repeat it here for the record: this book should have your name on the cover too. I love you!

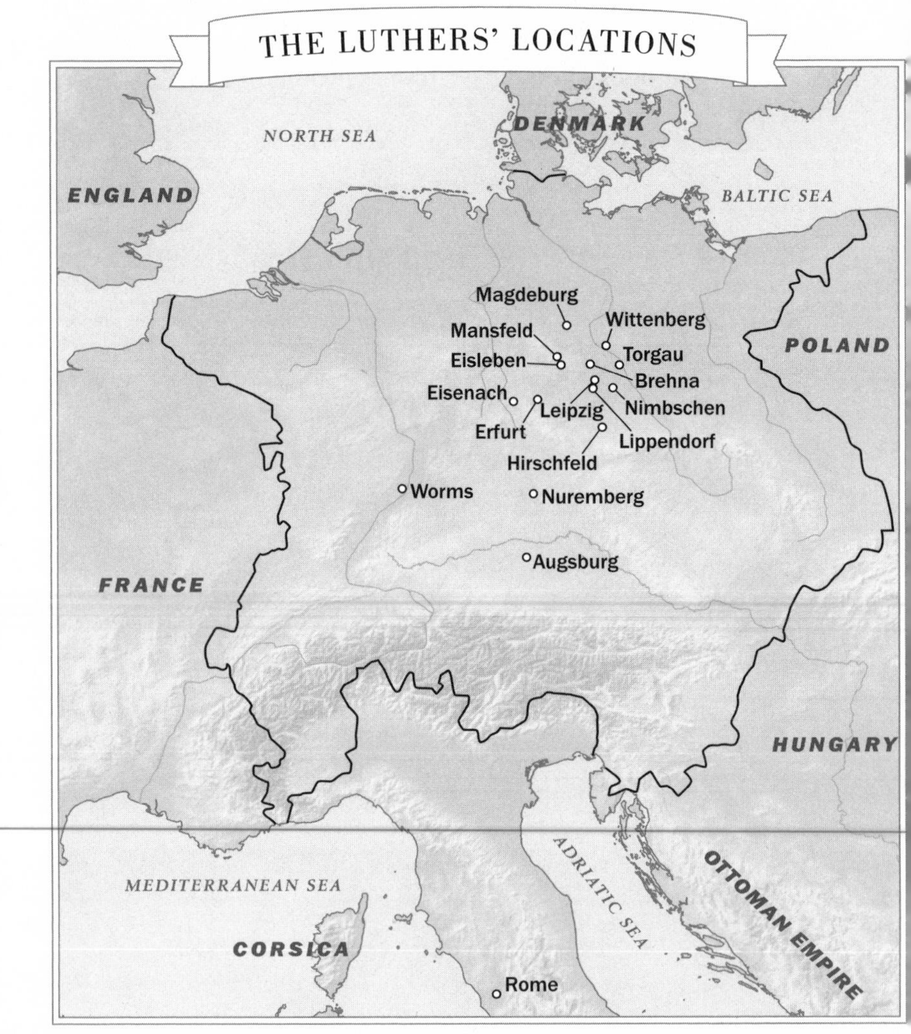
THE LUTHERS' LOCATIONS
NORTH SEA
DENMARK
BALTIC SEA
ENGLAND
Magdeburg
Wittenberg
Mansfeld
Eisleben
Torgau
POLAND
Brehna
Eisenach
Leipzig
Nimbschen
Erfurt
Lippendorf
Hirschfeld
Worms
Nuremberg
Augsburg
FRANCE
HUNGARY
ADRIATIC SEA
OTTOMAN EMPIRE
MEDITERRANEAN SEA
CORSICA
Rome

KEY

Brehna: location of the Benedictine cloister school Katharina attended as a child.

Eisleben: Luther's birthplace and place of death.

Erfurt: Luther attended the University of Erfurt and planned to enroll in law school there.

Hirschfeld: possible birthplace of Katharina.

Lippendorf: possible birthplace of Katharina.

Mansfeld, Magdeburg, and Eisenach: locations of Luther's elementary and secondary schools. Magdeburg is also the town Katharina and her children fled to during the war after Luther's death. Wartburg Castle, where Luther hid disguised as a knight after his excommunication, is in Eisenach.

Nimbschen: location of Marienthron, Katharina's Cistercian convent.

Torgau: the town Katharina and the other runaway nuns stopped in after they escaped from the convent. Torgau is also the place of Katharina's death.

Wittenberg: location of the Black Cloister, the Augustinian monastery where Luther lived as a monk and where he and Katharina later lived as husband and wife.

Worms: town where the Diet of Worms took place.

INTRODUCTION

The Story of an Unlikely Life

As night turned to early morning and it became clear the end was drawing near, a small group gathered in the bedroom, their shadows flickering across the walls in the dim candlelight. They hovered over the figure lying prone beneath the bedclothes, his breathing slow, rasping, labored. As Martin Luther drifted in and out of consciousness, his longtime friend, his three sons, and a local minister knelt by his side. They draped his body in warm towels and blankets, dabbed the pulse points on his wrists with herbal water, and smeared his chest with a healing poultice specially prepared by his wife. They held a cup of wine mixed with grated "horn of unicorn" (narwhal tooth) to his lips and offered him words of comfort and prayers for peace. Luther writhed, his face gray and pinched in the faint light. "Reverend father, are you ready to die trusting your Lord Jesus Christ and to confess the doctrine which you have taught by his name?"[1] Luther's friend whispered in his ear. "Yes," Luther replied, his declaration cutting through the darkness with resolute clarity.

It was in many ways a typical deathbed scene, with one critical exception: Luther's wife of nearly twenty-one years was not present at his bedside. Four days earlier Luther had penned what would be his last two letters, one to his wife, Katharina, the other to his longtime friend and fellow reformer Philip Melanchthon. Neither letter hinted at the dire turn of events to come. To Melanchthon, Luther mentioned the death and burial of Pope Paul III and other brief bits of political news and gossip. His letter to Katharina, on the other hand, exuded a discernible lightness and exuberance not evident in his correspondence to his friend. Luther told his wife he planned to return home later that week. His business in Eisleben was finished, his health was much improved, and he was sending ahead a gift of trout. "We have plenty to eat and drink and [live like] lords," he said jokingly of him and his travel companions. "We are well cared for, even too well, so that we might easily forget about you people in Wittenberg."[2]

Luther, however, would not return to Wittenberg and to his wife as planned. On the evening of February 17, 1546, the sixty-two-year-old reformer complained of a headache and chest pains during supper. Although he rallied for a few hours, by the middle of the night he was racked with pain and experiencing both tightness in his chest and shortness of breath. His friend Justus Jonas sent for the physicians and the castle preacher, and they, along with Luther's three sons who had traveled with him, kept vigil at Luther's bedside. "Father, into your hands I commend my spirit. You have redeemed me, faithful God," Luther whispered, his last coherent words before slipping away between two and three o'clock in the early hours of February 18.[3] As Martin Luther took his last breaths in his hometown of Eisleben, Germany, his forty-seven-year-old wife Katharina slept seventy miles away in Wittenberg, unaware.

Katharina had tried to convince Luther not to travel. He had been suffering from poor health for months, and that winter had been particularly hard on him. No longer strong enough to walk to the town church to preach, he was driven there each Sunday by wagon instead. He was often forced to cut his sermons short due to dizziness and shortness of breath. He suffered from kidney stones and gallstones, depression, difficulty breathing, digestive distress, ear infections, weakness, and exhaustion.

Katharina was filled with a sense of foreboding as Luther prepared to travel to Eisleben. She'd wanted him at home, where she could keep a close eye on him and nurse him back to health, but Luther, ever obstinate even in illness, would not be deterred. He insisted on traveling by carriage to his hometown to help mediate an ongoing dispute that had erupted and intensified between local political leaders in the area. Katharina couldn't accompany Luther herself, so she did the next best thing: she insisted that three of their sons—Hans, Martin, and Paul—travel with him, and she prepared a package of healing herbs, poultices, and medicinal remedies to send along with them. Still, when she bid him farewell, Katharina couldn't possibly have imagined her husband would never step across the threshold of their home again.

Unfortunately, very few of Katharina's letters have survived, but we can infer a great deal about her personality, her state of mind, and her affection for her husband from Luther's correspondence to her. We know, for example, she worried incessantly about him during his last trip and others. We also know from the number of his replies to her that she wrote him frequently during his three weeks in Eisleben. In his February 1, 1546, letter to Katharina, Luther admitted he had experienced vertigo and weakness en route, which he attributed to a frigid wind that blew so forcefully into the carriage it seemed it would "turn my brain to ice."[4] While he assured her he had recovered fully, Katharina clearly was not comforted, because six days later Luther wrote her a longer letter, insisting that she cease worrying.

"Free me from your worries," he pleaded on February 7. Luther tempered his request with his trademark humor, addressing his letter lightheartedly: "To my dear mistress of the house, Catherine Ludher [the original spelling of Luther's name was Luder, though Luther used several other variations during his lifetime, including Ludher; he also frequently called Katharina "Catherine," among other nicknames], a doctor, the lady of the pig market at Wittenberg [a reference to the fact that she owned pigs]—placed into the hands of, and at the feet of, my gracious lady."[5] He urged Katharina to read the gospel of John and his own *Small Catechism*, and then joked, "For you prefer to worry about me instead of letting God worry, as if he were not almighty and could not create ten Doctor Martins, should the old one drown in the Saale, or burn in the oven, or perish in Wolfgang's bird trap" (a reference to his servant Wolfgang Seberger's hobby of trapping birds in the backyard).[6] Turning more serious, Luther reminded Katharina that the situation was out of her control, as it should be. "I have a caretaker who is better than you and all the angels," he consoled his wife, "he lies in the cradle and rests on a virgin's bosom, and yet, nevertheless, he sits at the right hand of God, the almighty Father. Therefore be at peace. Amen."[7]

Luther was clearly distressed by his wife's suffering and sought to ease her mind with both comforting words and playful teasing. Three days later he teasingly blamed the power of her worrying for the fact that he'd had several brushes with death, including a fire in the hallway that tried to devour him, a stone that just missed falling onto his head, "nearly squash[ing] [him] as in a mouse trap,"[8] and mortar crumbling around him while he sat in his "secret chamber"[9] (i.e., the toilet). "I worry that if you do not stop worrying the earth will finally swallow us up and all the elements will chase us,"[10] he continued in jest. Although his tone was playful, his message was clear: Luther did not want his wife to worry about him. He could not stand by and allow her to fret, not only because such anxiety indicated a lack of faith and trust in God, but also because he cared too much about her to allow her to suffer, especially on his behalf.

Martin and Katharina Luther loved and cared deeply for one another. This is evident from both the tone and content of Luther's final letters and the many others he wrote Katharina throughout their marriage, as well as from the bits and pieces of their conversations that were recorded by guests who sat with them around their table. Theirs was not simply a marriage of convenience, nor was it a marriage lived out in political or theological name only. Rather, Martin and Katharina Luther shared a mutual and abiding love. Theirs was a partnership founded and strengthened on shared joy and grief, triumph and travail.

Yet what an unlikely union it was, this marriage between a runaway nun and a renegade monk—she, unknown and destitute; he, one of the most famous and powerful men of the time. Their relationship could be written into the pages of a romance novel. But this love story, one of the most scandalous and intriguing in history, is not fiction but fact. How did this most unlikely, most radical union come to be? How did Martin Luther the monk and Katharina von Bora the nun come to wed in the first place? And even more importantly, how did such a union not only survive but thrive in the face of the most daunting odds?

This monumental moment in the history of marriage was born out of a dramatic set of circumstances. For a variety of reasons, Katharina von Bora and Martin Luther each determined that marriage—the most radical of options—was also the best one. Not only did that choice impact them personally as individuals, it also had a powerful and lasting effect on their own early Renaissance culture and society. Today, five hundred years later, the impact of their choice continues to reverberate in the lives and faith of Christians across the globe.

Yet behind the historical significance of their marriage is also the story of a man and a woman who met, married, and raised a family together. True, Martin and Katharina Luther were radical revolutionaries, but they were also simply two people who shared twenty-one years together, until death did them part.

This is the story of their unlikely life together as husband and wife.

1

To the Cloister School

The young girl gazed at the countryside as the wagon jolted over the rough roads. Since she was more than one hundred miles from the home where she was born and raised, nothing in the unfurling landscape looked familiar to her—not the fields and farms she passed, not the bustling town marketplaces, not the faces she saw along the way. Neither the girl nor her father who sat beside her said much during the two-day journey. Each was distracted by a swirl of thoughts—a mix of fear, trepidation, and doubt. Each dreaded the moment the wagon would arrive at its destination, knowing that when they parted ways, they might not ever see each other again.

Birth

Most historians concur that Katharina von Bora was born on January 29, 1499. According to one of Katharina's earliest biographers, she wore a commemorative medal around her neck—a gift from Luther—inscribed in Latin: "Dr. Martin Luther gave this symbol to his Katharina who was born on the 29th of January in the year 1499." One side of the medal pictured the bronze serpent Moses carried on a pole in the wilderness, along with the Latin inscription "The lifted-up serpent is a type of crucified Christ." The reverse side depicted Christ on the cross, along with the words "Christ died for our sins."[1] If we accept this account as reliable (the medal has since been lost), which most scholars do, then we can be fairly confident that January 29, 1499, is indeed the date of Katharina's birth.

From here, though, details get sketchy. The truth is, despite the fact that she married one of the most famous men in history, we know very little about Katharina von Bora's early years, and we hear even less about her life in her own words. While volumes of Luther's correspondence, particularly his letters to politicians, theologians, and friends, have been preserved, a scant eight letters written by Katharina are extant today, most of them dealing with legal and economic issues after Luther's death. Any diary or journals she may have kept, as well as her letters—and we know she wrote many to Luther, because we have his replies to her—were lost or destroyed, including some of the family papers, which were destroyed in 1945 at the end of World War II.[2]

This is not surprising. Women who lived during the Middle Ages and early Renaissance (also known as the early modern period) were considered second-class citizens. In fact, most unmarried women during that time were not granted citizen status at all. German cities required that individuals fulfill three criteria in order to be granted citizenship: military obligation and an oath of allegiance formalizing it; an honorable means of support; and property ownership—or as historian Merry Wiesner puts it, "war, work, and wealth."[3] As one might imagine, for a single, working woman to meet even one of these requirements would have been challenging; to meet all three was nearly impossible. There was, however, a loophole: for women, marriage was the only surefire way around the citizenship requirements. "Though women were never categorically excluded from citizenship in German towns and villages," Wiesner notes, "notions of women's proper place within the family and community increasingly made the only type of female citizenship that was acceptable a derivative one."[4] In other words, the fact that she had a husband made a woman eligible for citizenship.

In addition, most women did not have the opportunity to attend school and were thus illiterate. The few, like Katharina, who were educated in convents and could read and write were not valued in the same way men were valued in society. Most women (with rare exceptions, as we will see in a subsequent chapter) simply did not have a voice during this time. Their thoughts and opinions were not considered. Aside from their responsibilities as wives and mothers, their role in society was regarded as unimportant. Thus, while it's disappointing that no one deemed Katharina's correspondence worth preserving, it's not unusual for the time.

That said, primary sources like city ledgers and government and historical documents have allowed scholars to piece together what they believe are the basic facts of Katharina's early years, although even the most rudimentary details, like her birthplace and her mother's name, are still debated. Most scholars agree that Katharina descended from Saxon nobility, although her exact ancestry remains controversial, due largely to the fact that Bora (the "von" signifies nobility) was a popular name during the time. Research is further complicated by a coincidence: two noblemen by the name of Hans von Bora—Katharina's father's name—lived in close proximity in Saxony (a small area located about halfway between what are now Berlin and Prague) around the same time.[5] Historians question which Hans von Bora was Katharina's father.

Biographer Ernst Kroker, author of *The Mother of the Reformation: The Amazing Life and Story of Katharine Luther*, cites Hans and Katharine (maiden name unknown) von Bora of Lippendorf as Katharina's parents, basing his theory on a claim that a Hans von Bora assigned his wife a manor at Saale, in Lippendorf, as her retirement property (this typically happened on the day a couple married, which was the husband's way of ensuring his wife's livelihood after his death).[6] Katharina von Bora biographers Rudolf Markwald and Marilynn Morris Markwald, on the other hand, claim Katharina's parents as Hans von Bora and Anna von Haugwitz of Hirschfeld, citing a 1998 official statement by the Saxon State Archive at Leipzig, German Central Office for Genealogy. However, they also concede that after the village of Lippendorf was bombed in a World War II air raid, a plaque inscribed "Katharina von Bora was born here on January 29, 1499" was discovered in the rubble.[7]

We could dedicate a significant number of pages to the disparate theories about Katharina's lineage, but this fact would still remain: Although her marriage to Martin Luther and her role in helping to define clerical marriage and Protestant family life makes Katharina an important contributor to the Reformation, scholars can't be absolutely sure of even the most basic facts about her early life. Everything that transpired between her birth and her arrival at the convent school in Brehna is unknown. The best we can do is to paint her early years in broad brushstrokes, employing educated guesswork and our imaginations.

To a Distant Land

While confusion about Katharina's ancestry persists, scholars agree that her mother died in 1505, and that her father remarried a woman by the name of Margarete, a widow, within the year. We also know that Katharina's father, Hans, was in debt. Although the von Boras were members of the landed gentry, meaning they owned land and were considered nobility, they were what we might call "house poor" today. Hans was a "gentleman farmer"—a knight, indicated by the title "von"—but his relatively small parcel of land, combined with an agricultural crisis in the early 1500s, did not produce enough to pay the bills. In addition to Katharina, Hans had three sons and perhaps another daughter with his first wife, and his second wife brought several children of her own, and no dowry, to the marriage in 1505.[8] Katharina's father simply couldn't support his expanded family on his income. Something had to give, and that something was Katharina.

Shortly after her mother died in 1505, Katharina von Bora's father packed up his six-year-old daughter and her paltry belongings and traveled from their rural home in Saxon Germany to a Benedictine convent in Brehna. There she bid goodbye to her father and the only life she had ever known. When she entered the cloister school, Katharina was still reeling from her mother's death. She would remain behind convent walls for the next eighteen years of her life.

It's tempting to criticize Hans von Bora for a decision that seems heartless and more than a little selfish. But there are additional factors to consider: it was not unusual for families in the Middle Ages and early modern period, especially the nobility, to send their young daughters off to cloister schools and even to the convent for life. For example, twelfth-century German mystic Hildegard of Bingen, the tenth-born child in her family, was sent by her parents to the convent at age eight as a tithe (as the tenth child, she represented 10 percent of their assets) to the church and to God.[9] In many cases convent schools were the only opportunity for girls to receive any education at all. Most medieval villages had only one school, which typically enrolled only boys, so many parents did what they had to do to ensure their daughters' education. Furthermore, schools connected with Benedictine cloisters were noted for their stellar academic reputation. As Kroker notes, "Katie certainly received a better education with the Benedictine nuns in Brehna than she could have received otherwise as a young girl of the nobility anywhere else in the country at that time."[10]

Hans von Bora may not have initially intended his daughter for the religious life when he enrolled her in the cloister school in Brehna; the decision may have been a temporary measure, the best solution to a difficult situation. Enrolling Katharina in a convent school at the age of six resulted in one less mouth to feed for Hans von Bora, along with the assurance that his daughter would be well cared for.

Regardless of Hans von Bora's intentions, the decision undoubtedly had a tremendous impact on young Katharina. Imagine, for a moment, that long, uncomfortable, one-hundred-mile journey via horse-drawn wagon from her rural childhood home to the cloister school. The trip would have taken the better part of two days, and just a few miles into it, the familiar, comforting surroundings would have given way to new and unfamiliar terrain. We can't know for sure the thoughts that tumbled through her young mind, but we can try to put ourselves in Katharina's shoes, imagining what it must have been like to bounce along those rough roads. The route took them across fertile fields and meadows and into the bustling city of Leipzig, where Katharina would have experienced an overwhelming array of new sounds, sights, and smells. Perhaps these experiences distracted her from the hard truth of what she was leaving behind and the fear of all that lay ahead. Or perhaps young Katharina was simply too terrified and grief-stricken to notice much at all. Perhaps her father tried to soothe her fears; or maybe he sat silently at her side, wrestling with remorse and regret. There's a chance Katharina was excited about the new experiences that awaited her, but it's far more likely the six-year-old girl, still grieving the sudden death of her mother and now leaving behind everyone and everything she'd ever known, sat small and quiet on the wagon seat, trembling with dread, sorrow, and fear.

Known for its high-caliber curriculum, the Benedictine cloister school in Brehna primarily attracted the daughters of nobility who were there to be groomed as nobles' wives. The remainder of the Brehna students were orphans. Such was the case of Klara Preusser, daughter of the Leipzig magistrate Dr. Johann Preusser. Klara entered the Benedictine cloister school when her parents died, around the same time Katharina arrived, and perhaps because of their shared history, the two became friends. Many years later, when Katharina was married to Luther and Klara was living in Halle as the wife of Magdeburg chancellor Lorenz Zoch, Klara wrote to Katharina, reminiscing about their years together in the cloister school. She promised to visit Wittenberg so the two could renew their friendship. Unfortunately, this letter is the only factual information we have about Katharina's four years at the cloister school, and we don't know whether the two friends ever reunited in Wittenberg.[11]

Katharina was likely schooled in reading, writing (in Latin and German), and arithmetic, as well as in morals, manners, and religion. It's not known how often she saw her family or if she was allowed to visit home during her four years at the cloister school. Given the distance between her father's estate and the school and the arduous travel required by horse-drawn wagon, it's unlikely Katharina saw her father or siblings very often, if at all. We do know her uncle, Baron von Rachwitz, lived near the cloister school—Katharina and her father stopped at the baron's estate on their initial trip to Brehna—so she may have found some comfort in the proximity of extended family. But it's also very possible that the day Katharina kissed her father goodbye at the entrance of the cloister school was the last time she ever saw him.

A Sudden Change

Four years later, on a summer morning in 1509, an emissary stepped down from a horse-drawn carriage, knocked on the door of the cloister school, and presented a letter to the prioress. Unbeknownst to her, Katharina's father had made arrangements with the abbess of a Cistercian convent in Nimbschen, forty-two miles south of Brehna, for his ten-year-old daughter to become a nun. Hans von Bora had put aside a small amount of money to support Katharina's enclosure in the convent for the rest of her life. The letter delivered by the emissary was an announcement of this plan, as well as details and instructions for Katharina's transfer from the cloister school to the Cistercian convent *Gottes und Marienthron* (Throne of God and St. Mary) in Nimbschen, effective immediately.

As far as we know, Katharina was not consulted about this decision. Not only had she no say in determining the course of her life, she hadn't even been privy to the particulars—for example, which convent and which order she would enter as a novitiate. That said, the news of her transfer to Marienthron may not have come as a huge surprise. After all, it was common for families to place their young daughters in the convent—at least temporarily—as the nunnery was one of only two viable options (the other being marriage) for noblewomen like Katharina.

"The nunneries of the early Middle Ages not only offered women the chance to pursue the ascetical life; they performed an important social role in providing a haven for the daughters and widows of the aristocracy for whom no suitable marriage [could] be found," explains medieval historian C. H. Lawrence. "The women who entered them, and the families that placed them there, expected them to enjoy the society of their own kind. They were thus aristocratic and socially exclusive communities."[12] Katharina's contemporary, the Spanish Carmelite nun Teresa of Avila, for example, was first placed in the convent by her father in order to protect her virginity and prepare her to lead a devout domestic life. But for Teresa of Avila, the convent life was hardly the stringent, austere existence one might assume. For the first twenty-six years of her life as a nun, Teresa lived in a two-floor suite in the convent, complete with fine furniture and its own kitchen. She spent much of her time entertaining friends and relatives, was encouraged to leave the convent when she needed to, and was even referred to as "Dona Teresa," a nod to her social standing.[13] In other words, life in a sixteenth-century convent didn't necessarily entail dire poverty and hardship but was often more of an exclusive, women-only aristocratic society in and of itself.

For all we know, Katharina may have desired to become a nun on her own accord (although the fact that she would later escape from the cloister suggests otherwise). On the other hand, she may have assumed that once she reached the proper marrying age—which, in the early modern period, was anywhere from the late teens to the early twenties for women—she would be matched with a suitable husband. Given the fact that she was only ten years old when the decision was made, it's likely Katharina hadn't given the matter much thought at all.

While we can't know Katharina's thoughts and expectations regarding this life-altering decision, consider this question: If Hans had enrolled his daughter at the cloister school in Brehna so that she would receive a proper education and grooming for marriage, as was posited earlier, why this sudden, dramatic change in course? Why transfer Katharina to a convent for life?

According to most scholars, there is one probable answer to this question: money. While some young women did feel an authentic religious conviction and a call toward the contemplative life, many had their future determined for them by their parents or guardians simply because it was cheaper for a daughter to become a nun than to be betrothed to a man in a particular social stratum.[14] The fact was, the entrance fee to a convent was markedly lower than the dowry needed to attract a husband of Katharina's social order. Katharina would have been expected to marry a nobleman, and thus come to marriage with a substantial dowry. Hans von Bora, whose financial troubles had only worsened in the four years Katharina was enrolled in the Brehna cloister school, may not have had any choice but to send his daughter to the convent.

But why transfer Katharina to a different convent? Why did Hans von Bora have his daughter removed from Brehna, where she could have entered the Benedictine cloister along with some of the girls she had grown close to during her four years there, and lived out her life in a place that was familiar, a place that had become home? Again, the answer is likely money. The entrance fee—called a "cloister dowry," symbolizing the fact that a nun became the bride of Christ when she entered the convent—for the Benedictine cloister at Brehna was much higher than the fee to enter the Cistercian convent in Nimbschen. Hans von Bora paid thirty *Groschen*—the lowest possible fee, and a pittance—for his daughter to live at the convent in Nimbschen for what he assumed would be the rest of her life.

The price was low for a reason. The Cistercian convent in Nimbschen was Spartan, even by medieval standards. At the Benedictine cloister school in Brehna, each building was well designed and aesthetically appealing, and the monastery's refined architecture served to enhance the entire town, note the Markwalds.[15] After four years there, Katharina was accustomed to the abbey's impressive complex of airy, light-filled buildings, including a large cloister church; ample sleeping quarters for the nuns; a bakery and kitchen; root, apple, and wine cellars; and an infirmary, a guesthouse, and the school buildings, in addition to outlying barns and extensive land. In contrast, Marienthron, the Cistercian convent at Nimbschen, was simple and bare to the point of severity. Constructed of dark rock extracted from the local hillsides, the rough exterior gave the entire convent a somber, gloomy feel. The walls were not plastered, making the buildings seem crudely or hastily

Linda Bushkofsky

The ruins of the Marienthron convent in Nimbschen, Germany, where Katharina lived as a cloistered Cistercian nun for fourteen years.

constructed, and the church was unadorned and indistinguishable from the other buildings. Neither decorations nor artwork were allowed in the church or elsewhere in the convent, save the occasional simple wooden cross. Windows were made of clear glass, not colorful stained glass, so as not to be distracting. Only ruins of the convent in Nimbschen remain today, but even in those one can see the starkness and austerity of the structures.[16]

Unlike fellow nun Teresa of Avila, Katharina wouldn't enjoy high-society convent living and a two-floor suite. Instead, she would sleep in a bare-bones dormitory with the other novitiates. And unlike Teresa of Avila, who frequently entertained guests and was allowed to leave the convent to travel, Katharina lived in silence; saw no one save the prioress, her fellow novitiates, and the priest assigned to the convent; and was not allowed to leave the walled enclosure.

The Cistercians

The Cistercian Order was founded in 1098 in the village of Cîteaux (Latin name, *Cistercium*),[17] France, when a Benedictine abbot by the name of Robert of Molesme left his monastery in Burgundy, France, with twenty-one supporters to found a new order that would more strictly adhere to the Rule of St. Benedict. Robert's successor, Stephen Harding, established the first female Cistercian convent in Le Tart, France, in 1120.[18] These early founders of the Cistercian Order yearned to return to the poverty, simplicity, and isolation that were hallmarks of the original Benedictine Rule, established by St. Benedict of Nursia in 529. "The early Cistercians wanted to roll back the centuries of monastic development to revive what they believed to be the pure simplicity of St. Benedict's plan," says C. H. Lawrence. "It was applied to everything—to dress, food, buildings, and furniture. It was simply a question of getting back to the Rule of St. Benedict, which was to be observed to the letter."[19]

For Katharina, this meant that her significantly limited life in the Benedictine cloister school became infinitely more limited when she crossed the threshold of the Cistercian convent. For starters, the location of the convent at Nimbschen was intentionally isolated. According to regulations of the Cistercians' General Charter in 1134, monasteries were to be constructed in remote, rural locations, far from towns, villages, or castles.[20] Marienthron was set deep in a valley and protected by a hill on one side and dense woods on the other. Beyond that were the fields, planted with wheat, rye, barley, oats, hemp, flax, and hops. The buildings were modest and built low to the ground (especially compared with the soaring cathedrals indicative of other orders); towers, steeples, and any other architectural accoutrements were not allowed by the order.

The buildings were divided into two main sections. The *Propstei* (provost's section) housed the provost, a Cistercian lay official who oversaw the convent, along with two monks from the nearby Pforta Abbey, who were responsible for hearing confessions and for the overall spiritual supervision of the nuns. The *Propstei* also included an underground room where many of the convent's craftsmen and laborers, such as the blacksmith, the cook, the baker, the furnace man, and the miller, lived and worked. Between forty and fifty workers supported the lives of forty-three nuns. Behind the *Propstei* was the *Klausur* (cloister), where the nuns lived. A deep ditch ran along the bottom of the hill, and the entire complex was surrounded by a stone wall—both features were intended to keep the nuns separate from the world outside.[21]

"Cistercian foundations were located with an eye to the preservation of seclusion and strict enclosure," Lawrence notes. "The sites they accepted were generally on deserted or uncultivated lands, far removed from inhabited settlements."[22] A watchman was positioned at the convent's gate at all times, and even the entrance to the convent itself was partially hidden, sending a clear message to "all would-be intruders: *Zutritt verboten!* ('Off limits!')."[23] Inside the church, a screen in the shape of a cross divided the nuns and postulants (the candidates, like Katharina, seeking formal entrance to the convent) from anyone else who might be visiting the convent and attending worship services, although pilgrims and visitors were not typically allowed into the church.

As far as we know, neither her father nor her stepmother accompanied Katharina from Brehna to Nimbschen. At best she made the journey with a guardian from the convent school; perhaps she even traveled the forty-two miles alone, with only the driver of the carriage by her side. In his biography of Katharina von Bora, Ernst Kroker paints an idyllic picture of the Nimbschen convent and the surrounding land, describing it as "situated in the midst of a quiet lovely landscape," complete with "wooded hills," a "calmly flowing river [bordering] the meadows and fruitful fields," a "shady forest and sunny fields."[24] But the harsh reality of her situation undoubtedly tainted how Katharina received such a picturesque view. The fact is, Katharina knew that as a cloistered nun, she wouldn't have the freedom to experience this landscape, however beautiful and tranquil, in person. Knowing that a lovely landscape lay just beyond the convent's walls would only serve to deepen her sense of isolation.

One can only imagine Katharina's apprehension, how her heart must have sunk when she glimpsed the ugly, low-slung buildings from the carriage as the convent came into view. One can only imagine her dread and dismay as she walked through Marienthron's gates, knowing that once she stepped inside, she wouldn't be allowed to leave. Once again Katharina had been plucked from her familiar, comfortable surroundings and deposited into a foreign environment. Once again she was required to live among strangers. Once again she was forced to adapt to a new, unfamiliar routine. But this time was worse because this move, she knew, was to be her last. Here in this remote countryside, behind these formidable walls, Katharina would live out the rest of her life.

2

A Nun without a Choice

The bell rang sharply, cutting through the predawn stillness and rousing the nuns from sleep. Katharina did not linger under the warm blankets. She rose, dressed quickly in her white robe, and scurried in silence down the chilly hallway toward the convent church. She had only been at Marienthron a few weeks, but already she was accustomed to the daily routine, which rarely varied.

The first bell of the day tolled at 2:00 a.m. to awaken the nuns for Matins (from the Old French word *matin*, meaning "morning"), or Night Vigils, as they were sometimes called—the first phase of the seven-part Daily Office the nuns performed. As a postulant, or candidate for the nunnery, Katharina most likely did not have her own cell but slept in a dormitory with the other young candidates. She rose with the other postulants and nuns, donned the white robe indicative of the Cistercian Order (other cloistered nuns wore black robes, but the Cistercians wore a coarse habit of undyed sheep's wool, keeping in line with their emphasis on simplicity and austerity), and proceeded in silence to church, where she took her place in the choir section.[1] There she recited the prayers, psalms, and Scripture readings and sang the hymns specified for the Matins hour.

Lauds (from the Latin imperative *laudate*, meaning "praise ye!") followed Matins at daybreak. There were five additional hours performed throughout the day: Prime (6:00 or 7:00 a.m.), Terce (9:00 a.m.), Sext (noon), Nones (3:00 p.m.), and Vespers (4:00 or 5:00 p.m.), with Compline closing the day before the nuns retired to bed at 7:00 or 8:00 p.m. Each of the hours followed the set of prayers, Scripture, and hymns prescribed by the Divine Office for that particular hour on that particular day. All work ceased at the sound of the bell; the nuns were required to stop whatever they were doing and attend services in the church.[2]

In the early Middle Ages, a day in the convent (and the monastery) was measured by the movement of the sun, which meant that a nun's day was much shorter in the winter, since the sun rose later, than in the summer. During the summer, for instance, Lauds would have been celebrated at 5:00 or 6:00 a.m., rather than 7:00 or 8:00 a.m., and Compline would have closed out the day around 9:00 p.m., rather than 7:00 or 8:00 p.m. during the winter. However, by the late thirteenth century, the invention of the mechanical clock had standardized timekeeping in the convent. By the time Katharina entered Marienthron in 1509, the day was no longer measured in twelve parts, as it had been previously according to canonical law, but in twenty-four equal hours.[3] The convent at Marienthron likely owned a mechanical clock, which tolled at the appropriate hours to rouse the nuns or call them to prayers. Earlier in the Middle Ages, the Cistercians, who were "sterner and more strict with themselves," forced themselves to stay awake between Matins and Lauds and either read in the cloister or spent time praying privately, but by the time Katharina entered the convent, some of the earlier rules had been relaxed, and the nuns were typically permitted to return to bed and sleep until daybreak.[4]

As one might imagine, getting adequate sleep was a challenge, especially for the new postulants, who were unaccustomed to such a rigorous schedule. "Sleep, like food, was regarded as a physical need and self-deprivation was a mark of holiness, showing one's mastery over the senses," says medieval monastic historian Julie Kerr.[5] Cistercian abbot Bernard of Clairvaux deemed sleep a waste of time for himself—he was known to spend the entire night in vigil—but he also considered it potentially dangerous, "as the sleeper who was dead to the world might also be dead to God."[6] Likewise, the thirteenth-century Scottish monk Adam of Lennox slept only a few minutes at a time, either sitting upright or lying prostrate before an altar dedicated to Mary. It's said the "straw over which his sheets were placed remained in the same position" during all twenty years he was a member of the monastery, implying that he slept so little he didn't even rumple his bedsheets.[7] Most monks and nuns weren't expected to achieve this level of control, but they were advised to sleep lightly so they could be easily awakened for Matins and Lauds.

Some abbots and abbesses were more lenient than others. Richard Fox, sixteenth-century bishop of Winchester, England, for instance, "clearly appreciated the difficulty of rising during the night and advised the nuns in his diocese that those who were up first should rouse the others by making a soft and somber stirring with their mouths or feet, but might knock upon the bedstead of any who were sluggards."[8] We don't know for sure how strict or lenient Katharina's abbess was when it came to sleep, but we do know that according to the Daily Office, at the very least, Katharina awakened in the middle of the night for prayer and began her day before dawn, a habit that would stick and one that would later prompt Luther to nickname her affectionately, "Kathe von Bora, the Morning Star of Wittenberg."[9]

A Quiet Life

Between thirty-five and thirty-nine nuns lived together at Marienthron during Katharina's years there, which was considered an average-size convent for the time. Yet despite the number of nuns and the close living quarters, daily life within the convent's walls was conducted almost entirely in silence. The nuns were not allowed to speak in the choir—the section in the church where they sat for worship, which was separated by a wooden or iron screen from the public space—nor was talking allowed in the dining hall during meals or in the dormitory. Katharina and her peers likely relied on a form of sign language to communicate with each other. The only time verbal communication was allowed was when a nun read from Scripture during mealtime and when the nuns recited prayers and psalms and sang hymns during the Office.

One can imagine how difficult it was for Katharina to pursue connection and friendship within such tight communication restrictions and how lonely and isolated she must have felt, especially coming from the comparatively convivial atmosphere of the cloister school in Brehna. Yet we also know she wasn't entirely alone in Nimbschen. Margarete von Haubitz, a distant relative of Katharina's mother (according to the Markwalds), served as the recently elected abbess at Nimbschen when Katharina arrived in 1509.[10] Her paternal aunt, Magdalena von Bora (who would later live with the Luthers in Wittenberg), was also already a nun there.[11] We also know that Katharina did, over time, forge a close friendship with at least one other nun. Eva Schonfeld arrived at the convent shortly after Katharina and escaped with her in 1523.[12] The two were friends for many years, even after they left the convent.

Meals at the convent, like everything else, were simple. While the Rule of St. Benedict suggested that only one meal be consumed per day during the winter (summer, because the days were longer, allowed for a light supper as well), the rules were relaxed in the late Middle Ages, allowing the nuns at Marienthron three meals a day. Breakfast consisted of a slice of bread and either a cup of water, wine, or beer (wine and beer were commonly consumed at all three meals during the Middle Ages and early Renaissance). Lunch was the heartiest meal, featuring either fresh fish from the cloister pond or salted herring, along with vegetables, raisins, almonds, or figs. Supper was often soup, bread, and a cup of water, wine, or beer.[13] Meat was not typically part of a Cistercian nun's diet, unless she was ill, in which case she was allowed a bit of meat for nourishment and fortification and to aid in the healing process.[14] On special occasions, such as feasts and anniversaries, the nuns might enjoy what were called *pittances*—treats that often included eggs, fine white bread in place of the grainy black bread, and spiced wine rather than ale.[15]

There was a reason for such basic fare. "The restrictions imposed on the monastic diet, like those imposed on other aspects of their life, were a way to master the senses and suppress physical desires such as greed, lust and torpor," explains Kerr. "This would ensure that the mind stayed focused on lofty matters and was not a servant to bodily wants."[16] As Bernard of Clairvaux said, "The body, but not the soul, is fattened by frying pans."[17] Second-century Benedictine monk William of St. Thierry put it bluntly but succinctly: "Black bread and plain water, mere greens and vegetables are assuredly no very delectable fare. What does give great pleasure is when, for the love of Christ and the desire of interior delight, a well-disciplined stomach is able to satisfy itself with such fare and be thankful."[18] It was important that the nuns stay focused and alert during the repetitive, hypnotizing chants, prayers, and hymns of the Daily Office. A spare but healthy diet helped the nuns stay awake. As Bernard of Clairvaux warned in the 1100s, "Anyone who attended Vigils before having fully digested his food would yield a groan rather than a tone."[19]

However, the reasons for dietary restrictions and other practices—like wearing rough, floor-length wool habits and keeping their hair shorn under their veils—went deeper than their effect on singing or even prayer. Chastity, one of the three vows taken by the nuns upon installation (the other two were obedience and poverty), was a huge concern for both cloistered men and women. Abstaining from particular foods, especially meat, was believed to be an effective means for suppressing the libido and keeping carnal desires in check, which, as we'll see in later chapters, was a major point of discussion during the early Reformation.

The White Nun

During her first six years at Nimbschen, Katharina practiced the religious rituals of the convent; continued her education in German, Latin, mathematics, and canon (church) law; and prepared for consecration. She attended classes with a group of girls enrolled in the small convent school at Nimbschen. The nuns referred to Katharina and the other candidates as "the adolescent virgins," to distinguish them from the nonmonastic school girls.[20] In addition to attending the daily eight Offices, higher expectations and stricter rules were placed on the candidates. There was no wiggle room for the girls who expected to become nuns.

Katharina became a novitiate in 1514 and was officially consecrated on October 8, 1515, at the age of sixteen. She took the vows of obedience, chastity, and poverty, and donned the floor-length white habit, over which was placed a black scapular attached to a wimple (a garment worn around the head and chin) and veil that covered her neck and cropped hair. Only her face and hands were visible. A cincture made of rope or fabric was tied around her waist over the habit and scapular. Like her sisters, she would be called a white nun of the Cistercian Order, a title she expected to hold for the rest of her life. Although her consecration was an important ceremony and a monumental event in Katharina's life, her father and stepmother were likely not present. Like most of the milestones in her life up to this point, Katharina marked the occasion alone.

By the time Katharina was officially consecrated as a nun, she was well adjusted and accustomed to daily life in the convent. In addition to performing the Daily Office, she likely had specific tasks assigned to her by the abbess. While the nuns never stepped foot off the premises, there was still plenty of work to do behind the convent's walls. For example, nuns during the Middle Ages often translated religious texts, illuminated manuscripts with elaborate artwork, or did embroidery or other handiwork. Even if Katharina didn't participate in this kind of work, she most certainly had a number of daily chores assigned to her by the abbess, including house-cleaning, food preparation, or gardening.

Prioress of the Cistercian abbey of Saint Mary of Rieunette near Carcassonne (France). While this image depicts a contemporary Cistercian nun, the habit, scapular, and wimple are similar to what Katharina von Bora would have worn.

Zelfgemaakte fot in de abdij van Rieunette nabij Carcassonne in Frankrijk; Willy Leenders, 2006.

"Convent life provided women with the opportunity to hold many different positions of responsibility," says German Reformation historian Charlotte Woodford. For instance, the fifteenth-century Dominican reformer Johannes Meyer listed twenty-five offices for nuns, in addition to the abbess, including "the sacristan, infirmaress (nurse), chantress (singing mistress), portress (door-keeper), teachers for the pupils and novices and librarian. Other nuns were responsible for supervising the lay sisters while they prepared the meals, made clothes, or carried out their other daily tasks. . . . One of the most important offices for a professed nun after the abbess was that of cellaress. She was the convent bursar, responsible for the economy. . . . She presided over the convent's income from its farms and estates, both in kind—grain, livestock, and wine—and money, be it from trade, taxes or elsewhere."[21]

As a recently consecrated nun, Katharina probably wouldn't have held any of these supervisory positions, but she undoubtedly did the work required in most, if not all, of these particular areas.

Katharina must have taken her vows seriously, because in the fourteen years she lived at Marienthron, not one complaint or reprimand was registered against her in the *Urkundenbuch*, the official record of the cloister.[22] In fact, twenty years later, on Pentecost in 1540, we know by Katharina's own testimony (some of only a handful of her own words that have been preserved) that she prayed "feverishly, diligently, and frequently" while in the convent, a fervent zeal she seemed nostalgic for all those years later.[23] What we don't know anything about is Katharina's inner state of mind during her years at Marienthron. Did she suffer from doubts and depression like Luther did during his monastic years? Did she resent the fact that she was forced into a life she might not have chosen for herself, had she been given any say in the matter? Did she struggle with feelings of abandonment or loneliness? Did she succumb to feelings of despair and hopelessness in the face of such utter powerlessness? Or was she content and relatively satisfied, comforted by the daily rituals and grateful for sustenance, shelter, and community? We can't know for sure.

We do, however, know of one critical fact in Katharina's personal history, perhaps *the* most important fact. We know that when she was twenty-four years old she escaped from the convent. She fled. She was not released from Marienthron by her parents; she was not dismissed against her will; she was not cajoled out of the cloister. Rather, Katharina escaped from Marienthron in the middle of the night under cover of darkness, by means of an elaborately orchestrated plan. Katharina von Bora abandoned the only existence she'd ever known and risked everything to step into life outside the convent walls. That fact alone speaks volumes about her desires for the future.

3

A Family Rift

At the same time Katharina von Bora was living her childhood and early adult years as a cloistered nun, one hundred miles away in Erfurt, Germany, her future husband was living a markedly similar life as a monk.

Like Katharina, Martin Luther never expected to enter monastic life. In fact, his father, Hans Luder,[1] had lofty expectations that his firstborn would pursue a career in law, and for the first twenty-two years of Luther's life, the plan unfolded accordingly. Luther spent four years at Erfurt University, first studying liberal arts and then law. He took his academic work seriously, completing his bachelor's degree in one year (ranking thirtieth out of fifty-seven students) and two years later his master's degree (improving his rank to second out of seventeen students).[2] His father was proud of his son's accomplishments and immediately began to address Luther with the pronoun *ihr*, the more formal and respectful "you," instead of the familiar *du*, to demonstrate that he considered Luther a professional.[3] Hans also presented Luther with an extravagant gift: a complete edition of the *Corpus juris*,[4] a not-so-subtle hint at his expectation that Luther would continue on to earn a law degree at the university. That was the plan, and Luther seemed willing to go along with it, until the fateful evening of July 2, 1505, changed everything.

That night, twenty-two-year-old Luther was caught in a violent thunderstorm as he traveled on foot back to Erfurt from the village of Stotternheim. Fearing for his life as lightning flashed and deafening thunder rolled across the countryside, Luther cried out to St. Anne, patron saint of miners[5] and mother of the Virgin Mary, promising that if she protected him, he would become a monk. "Suddenly surrounded by the terror and agony of death, I felt constrained to make my vow," he later wrote in the introduction to his treatise *On Monastic Vows*.[6] Luther kept his promise, in spite of his father's protestations and in spite of the fact that he himself questioned whether he should spend the rest of his life as a monk.

Great Expectations

Hans was furious. As Luther himself put it, his father had paid "bitter sweat and toil" to put him through the university in order to launch a respectable career in law, not to spend the rest of his life chanting psalms and praying in a dank cell.[7] Hans undoubtedly worked hard to fund his son's education; however, the picture Luther liked to paint of his family as destitute farmers wasn't entirely accurate. Although in his later years Luther emphasized that he was born of peasant stock—for instance, he mentioned more than once that his mother gathered firewood and carried the sticks home on her back—the truth was, the Luders were not peasants or farmers, nor were they exceedingly poor.[8]

Hans was the son of a farmer, but he was not a farmer himself. According to German tradition, the youngest son, not the oldest, inherited the land, so when Hans came of age he was expected to pursue his own profession. Soon after their marriage, Hans and his wife, Margarethe, settled in the county of Mansfeld, an area rich in mineral resources, particularly copper. The Luders first lived in Eisleben, where Luther was born, and then later moved to the town of Mansfeld. There Hans worked his way up in the local mining industry from pickman in a copper foundry to business partner in a series of small shafts. He also had a leaseholder's interest in three smelting works. Together these business ventures, while not hugely lucrative, allowed him to purchase a house for his large family (Luther was one of eight children) and fund his oldest son's university education.[9]

Some scholars speculate that Luther invoked the image of agrarian peasant beginnings in order to present himself as a person who had overcome great hardship on his path toward achievement and success.[10] Biographer Richard Marius adds that Luther was not unique in rewriting his past: "A whiff of hardship hangs over the family history as Luther told it—though like many successful men recounting their autobiography to adoring disciples, he may have exaggerated his youthful rigors."[11] Biographer Peter Manns, however, is more overtly critical of Luther, implying that the Reformer may have intentionally reworked the details of his personal history in order to deemphasize a middle-class upbringing:

> He would have obtained the same effect had he emphasized with equal vigor his origin as the son of a "poor miner." Oddly enough, Luther did not do this, or did it only infrequently, and not with the same insistence. For compared with that of a farmer, his father's profession was difficult, interesting and quite modern. In other words, due to his father's profession, little Martin grows up in a nearly modern ambiance yet makes nothing of that fact.[12]

Regardless of the reasons for Luther's revisionist family history, one detail is consistent in all his accounts: almost from the start of Martin's life, Hans Luder intended that his firstborn would become a skilled lawyer, holding out hope that the career choice would raise the Luder family to the highest status open to them. Plus, adds Manns, "Smelters always found themselves embroiled in some legal dispute and constantly needed cash. It was expected that little Martin would come to the aid of the firm in the quickest possible way through the study of law and a wealthy marriage."[13]

Birch Branches and Dunce Caps

Toward this end, young Martin was sent to school, beginning with grammar school in Mansfeld at age five, and then private school at the age of thirteen—first in Magdeburg, which was about forty miles from his parents' home, and then, a year later, in Eisenach, nearly one hundred miles away. Luther did not have fond memories of primary school, particularly the eight years he spent in Mansfeld, which he later referred to as "an 'asses' stable and devil's school,' run by 'tyrants and jailers.'"[14] Luther compared his primary education to purgatory and hell,[15] and recalled a morning in which he was beaten fifteen times with a birch branch for failing to decline and conjugate his Latin verbs properly.[16]

Such corporal punishment was not unusual for the time. In addition to the birch branch, wooden horse halters were hung around the students' necks as a form of punishment,[17] and the student who had performed least well during the morning was forced to wear a dunce cap and was "addressed as an ass"[18] for the rest of the afternoon. As biographer Richard Friedenthal points out, "A birch the size of a garden broom, as the scepter of every schoolmaster, is proudly displayed on the title page of all the pedagogic tracts of the day."[19] Yet one wonders if Luther, who was always sensitive in nature, found these disciplinary measures especially humiliating and harmful. The fact that decades later he mentioned the punishments he endured as a schoolboy suggests that though common, these physical disciplinary measures left a lasting impact on him.

Although Luther had relatives in Eisenach, when he arrived there at age fourteen to attend the parish school of St. George, they couldn't afford to have him live with them. His father had scrimped every penny in order to fund his eldest son's education, but Luther was left to fend for his own room and board. Initially Luther probably found lodging at a hostel or in a school, as these places often provided rooms for students without family or housing. Later the wealthy matron of the Schalbe family offered him free board at her house when she heard him singing in church and noticed how devout he was.[20] Luther also joined some of his classmates as they roamed the streets in the children's choirs, singing door-to-door for money. "These were the origin of the modern practice of caroling," says biographer James Kittelson, with one critical difference:

these boys caroled all year long. "Far from Christmas revelers, they were beggars who became adept at using this accepted means for students to acquire food and drink."[21] This wasn't altogether unusual. As Richard Friedenthal points out, begging for alms was not seen as disgraceful and was even considered standard practice for boys who were more financially secure than Luther.[22]

Put aside, for a moment, the Luther you know from the history books and think about Martin Luther the young boy, left to make his own way in an unfamiliar city. It's hard to envision this Luther, the meek young teenager, begging on the streets for money and food, struggling financially, sleeping in hostels and unfamiliar homes. Like Katharina, Luther was forced to rely on the kindness of strangers and forge his own way in the world. Not only were these lean years an important part of Luther's personal history, they also helped to shape the Reformer and theologian he was to become.

Familial Friction

Like Katharina, we don't hear much from Luther about his family life and boyhood years, but not because his words weren't preserved. Oddly, he simply didn't seem to have much to say about his nuclear family. Richard Marius points out that in the 7,075 entries that comprise what's known as Luther's *Table Talk*—the copious notes students transcribed during their dinnertime conversations with him—Luther mentions his father a scant twenty-seven times, as well as only occasionally in his letters and theological works.[23] Was it because, having left home at a young age, Luther, like Katharina, simply didn't have much of a relationship with his parents? Or was there perhaps a deeper reason for the distance between parents and son?

Some scholars have drawn radical conclusions about Luther's relationship with his parents, particularly with his father. In 1958 biographer and Freudian psychiatrist Eric Erikson suggested that Luther's frequent use of slang and his propensity for scatological humor, as well as his revolt against the patriarchal fathers of the Roman Catholic Church, were all the result of Hans's excessive discipline. "Hans beat into Martin what was characteristic of his own past, even while he meant to prepare him for a future better than his own present," Erikson states.[24] He also declared that the root of Luther's theological questions and rebellion could be traced back to his tenuous relationship with his father.

While Freudian literary and historical theory isn't as popular as it once was, and Erikson's theories should be vetted against more contemporary analysis, we do know from Luther's own admissions that both of his parents used physical punishment to discipline him as a child, a practice not uncommon in early sixteenth-century Germany. "My father once whipped me so severely that I ran away from him, and he was worried that he might not win me back again," Luther recalled. "I wouldn't like to strike my little Hans [Luther's own son] very much, lest he should become shy and hate me. I know nothing that would give me greater sorrow."[25] Luther's writings contain few mentions of his mother, but the little he does share about Margarethe does not reflect well on her. He recalled in his *Table Talk*, for instance, that his mother once beat him until he bled for stealing a nut off the dining room table.[26] While corporal punishment was common both at school and in the home during Luther's time, his comments, though brief, suggest that he believed his parents and teachers may have overstepped their bounds. In fact, Luther even went so far as to suggest that his parents' severe discipline drove him to seek comfort and refuge in the monastic life.[27]

Relations between parents and son did not improve as Martin matured. As was mentioned earlier, Hans Luder was livid when Martin abandoned law school just a few weeks after he'd begun. He considered the monastery a waste of Martin's education—the education Hans had worked so laboriously to fund—and his future. It seemed, though, that by the time Luther celebrated his first Mass in 1507—a momentous occasion, his first act as a priest following his ordination—Hans had recovered from his anger and forgiven Martin. After all, Martin postponed the event by a month, just so his father, whom he hadn't seen since his university days, could attend, and when Hans arrived for the ceremony with twenty horsemen and much fanfare, he made a generous contribution to the monastery, which seemed like a positive sign.

But Hans, it turned out, was still seething with resentment beneath his seemingly generous and gracious exterior. After the Mass, when father and son sat down to dinner, Hans turned to Martin with an accusatory question. "You learned scholar," he fumed, "have you never read in the Bible that you should honor your father and your mother? And here you have left me and your dear mother to look after ourselves in our old age."[28] Imagine Luther's disappointment in this moment, one of the most celebratory milestones in his life thus far. Initially pleased by his father's decision to attend his first Mass, Luther must have been crestfallen when he realized Hans hadn't altered his opinions a bit. Hans's acerbic words undoubtedly cut his son to the core.

Luther assured his father that he could do more for his family by praying for them as a monk than by remaining out in the everyday world, and he reminded Hans that he had been called to the cloister by a sign from heaven. "What if it were only a delusion of Satan?" Hans shot back at his son, a response that both angered Luther and watered the seeds of doubt buried deep inside him.[29] "'On hearing these words of my father's,' said Luther, . . . 'I was so shocked that I felt as if a sword had pierced my heart—to think that I needed him to draw my attention to the Ten Commandments. After that I could never get what he said out of my mind.'"[30]

The fact that Luther reiterated his father's caustic words about his monastic call not once but twice in his testimony before the Diet of Worms nearly fifteen years later attests to the fact that Luther truly could not get his father's words out of his head. Hans's criticism angered and offended Luther, but it also deeply hurt him.

There are hints, both in what Luther chose to say about his parents (his father in particular) and in what he left unsaid, that his decision to enter the monastery carved a chasm between Luther and his father. It's possible that chasm was never entirely bridged, the rift never entirely mended. Although he did confer with Hans before asking Katharina to marry him, and Hans and Margarethe did attend Martin and Katharina's wedding, Luther admitted that it was only the possibility of a grandson to carry on the Luther name that ultimately softened his father and eased the tension in their relationship. "Then my father restored me to his favour and I became once more his dear son," Luther said, in reference to the birth of his first son, whom he named Hans in honor of his father.[31]

But even a grandson and the continuation of the family name could only help so much. The truth is, the relationship between Luther and his father remained strained at best. Unlike some of his siblings, who settled near Mansfeld and carried on the family mining business, Luther lived his adult life in Wittenberg, more than seventy-five miles away from his childhood home. He saw his parents very little. Even when Hans lay on his deathbed in 1530, Luther did not visit him, but instead wrote him a letter, citing dangerous travel conditions and a politically unstable environment as the reason for his absence. However, these conditions didn't stop Luther from traveling a much longer distance just a few months later to take care of some business.

Luther wrote to his closest friend Philip Melanchthon that the news of his father's death at the end of May had "thrown [him] into sadness," yet he mentions his father's death only after first complaining about a lack of letters from friends and then communicating several bits of news and gossip.[32] He then briefly mentions the possible public reaction to his recently published *Exhortation to the Clergy Assembled at the Diet of Augsburg*, before finally, in the second half of the letter, announcing his father's death.

Luther begins by reflecting on "the very kind love [my father had for me]," but then in the next breath implies that his father was simply a vehicle through which God conveyed his love: "for through him my Creator has given me all that I am and have."[33] A few lines later Luther writes, "Seldom if ever have I despised death as much as I do now," acknowledging that "the pity of heart and the memory of the most loving dealing[s] with him have shaken me in the innermost parts of my being."[34] Yet at the same time, his comments to Melanchthon are distant and seem more preoccupied with the thought of death itself, rather than grief over the personal loss.

> Yet "the righteous man is taken away from calamity, and he enters into peace;" that is, we die many times before we die

> once for all. I succeed now in the legacy of the name, and I am almost the oldest Luther in my family. Now it is up to me, not only by chance, but also by law, to follow [my father] through death into the kingdom of Christ.[35]

On June 19, Luther's friend Veit Dietrich observed, "Within two days [Luther] has gotten over [the death of] his father, although it was very hard for him."[36] Dietrich also reported that upon hearing the news, Luther picked up his Psalter, went into his room, and "wept so greatly that the next day his head [hurt]," but "since that time he has not betrayed any further emotion."[37] That his first reaction was to weep suggests that Luther began to accept his father's death right away. He didn't exhibit denial, anger, or any of the other typical five stages of grief, but instead slipped almost immediately into acceptance, which could imply that the loss did not as profoundly affect his emotional state as one might have assumed.

In short, it seems evident that Luther did not have a particularly close relationship with his parents and may have even been estranged from his father for several years following his entrance into the monastery. As Richard Marius notes, "The least that can be said is that Luther's recollections of both mother and father but particularly of his father are ambivalent,"[38] which leads one to consider the possibility that Martin and Katharina may have had more in common than is readily obvious at first glance.

A close look at Martin and Katharina's family histories reveals unexpected commonalities. Although Luther spent his elementary years enrolled in a nearby village school, like Katharina, he was separated at a young age from his nuclear family and relocated one hundred miles away among strangers. From about the age of thirteen on, Luther lived independently in an unfamiliar town and attended an unfamiliar school that was at least a day's wagon ride from his parents and siblings and his hometown. Like Katharina during her years in the cloister school, and later in the convent, Luther likely didn't have much contact with his immediate family during this time. Likewise, he didn't have much money. His father paid for his schooling, but Luther was forced to fend for himself to survive.

Katharina's plight as a virtual orphan surely resonated with Luther, who had also experienced familial distance and subsequent feelings of isolation, abandonment, and perhaps even betrayal as the result of his tenuous relationship with his father. Luther may have recognized his own imperfect childhood and his own strained familial relationships in Katharina's challenging personal history and circumstances. Perhaps, in spite of their many differences, the fact that they were both unmoored and unattached and in many ways wayward souls served to connect Luther and Katharina in a powerful way. Though their paths were by no means identical, Martin and Katharina did share a surprising number of similar experiences, particularly in their formative teenage and early adulthood years, which may have offered them unexpected common ground.

4

The Good Monk

After the danger of the thunderstorm had passed and Luther had made it safely back to Erfurt that infamous night, he immediately began to regret the vow he'd blurted to St. Anne in the midst of his panic. In addition to contending with his father's anger, Luther had to fend off his opinionated friends, who tried to talk him out of the decision to enter the monastery. Truthfully, Luther himself was appalled that with a single, brief declaration made in a moment of fear, he had irrevocably altered the course of his life. But in spite of his reservations, Luther honored his vow. He sold his law books, and after arranging his affairs and hosting a farewell dinner—complete with raucous singing, dancing, and revelry that went on late into the night—he walked to the Augustinian monastery the next morning, knocked on the formidable wooden doors, and entered. With one last look over his shoulder, Luther crossed the threshold, leaving his friends protesting in the street and the rest of the world behind him.

To modern-day readers, Luther's decision to honor a vow spoken in a single moment of drama might seem rash, even irrational. We wonder why he didn't simply recant his statement. We are curious as to why Luther felt compelled to honor what looks to us like a flimsy promise blurted in panic and fear. In order to truly comprehend the weight and ramifications of his commitment that stormy night, we need to put ourselves in the social, cultural, and especially the religious context of sixteenth-century Germany. Men and women in pre-Enlightenment Germany were typically much more superstitious than today. They frequently prayed to the saints, believing the saints had the power to bestow favors or ward off evil. To make a vow to a saint was akin to making a commitment to God himself, which in Luther's time was no minor matter. Once Luther vowed to St. Anne that he would enter the monastery if he lived through the thunderstorm, he was committed to his promise. The fear of sin (and lurking beneath that, the fear of death and damnation) was a significant motivation behind his decision.

Religion and Superstition

In Luther's day, the Roman Catholic Church was *the* church, and not only was it a weighty spiritual presence in the lives of early modern Germans, it permeated nearly every facet of everyday life, from politics and law to love and marriage. "Its bells sounded the hours," writes Marius. "Its sanctuaries—especially its great cathedrals—sent spires and domes heavenward on almost every street in large cities, and the parish church threw its protective shadow over tiny villages in remote places. Its chapels dotted the wilderness. The familiar old rituals of its liturgies channeled people along the difficult pathway of life from birth, through happiness, suffering, and death, providing ceremonial enrichment to daily existence."[1]

In Erfurt alone, a city with a population of about 18,000 during Luther's time, there were more than ninety churches and chapels, as well as thirty-six monasteries and convents.[2] The Roman Catholic Church was the center of communal life. It impacted the everyday lives of men, women, and children across every social stratum in ways that are nearly impossible for those of us living in the twenty-first century to comprehend. The Church was everything: law, order, morality, and eternity, all wrapped into a single powerful entity.

"Religion and superstition made up an important part of most aspects of Catholic daily life," adds Reformation historian James Anderson. "Church and monastery bells continually reminded the inhabitants of towns and villages of the presence of God and the danger of committing sins."[3] *Sin* is the key word here. Sin, with its power to damn a person to hell for eternity, was a terrifying force during Luther's time, and most people, Luther included, did everything within their means to avoid it and repent of it. Priests who listened to confessions often referred to detailed handbooks that catalogued sins of thought, word, and action (including acts against God and neighbor and the seven deadly sins); sins committed with the senses or various parts of the body—including sins of the head, neck, ears, eyes, nose, mouth, tongue, gullet, hands, stomach, genitals, heart, knees, and feet; as well as sins committed specifically against the seven sacraments; sins against the seven virtues; sins against the seven gifts of the Holy Spirit; sins against the fruits of the Holy Spirit; and sins against the eight beatitudes of the Gospels.[4] There was a potential sin connected to virtually every body part, every thought, and every action.

Death, Death, Everywhere Death

Driving the fear of sin was a pervasive fear of death, the presence of which was unavoidable as people witnessed wave after wave of the plague decimate their cities and towns. Originating in China, the Black Death reached Europe's shores in 1348, and by the time the first wave of the pandemic played itself out three years later, it's estimated that 25 million people—almost a third of Europe's population—had fallen victim to the pestilence.[5] The disease was gruesome, virulent, and frighteningly efficient. People who went to bed healthy were often discovered dead the next morning; entire families were killed in a matter of days. "In men and women alike," wrote fourteenth-century Italian poet Giovanni Boccaccio, who witnessed and survived the Black Death, "at the beginning of the malady, certain swellings, either on the groin or under the armpits waxed to the bigness of a common apple, others to the size of an egg, some more and some less, and these the vulgar named plague-boils."[6] Blood and pus seeped from swellings, followed by multiple, worsening symptoms—fever, chills, vomiting, diarrhea, terrible aches and pains—and finally, death. In short, death by plague was a horrific way to die and a horrific way to watch someone die.

No one knew what caused the Black Death or how it was transmitted. Some suggested the disease took on the form of a spirit: "Instantaneous death occurs when the aerial spirit escaping from the eyes of the sick man strikes the healthy person standing near and looking at the sick," claimed one medieval doctor.[7] Others were convinced it was God's punishment for sins like greed, blasphemy, heresy, fornication, and worldliness, and thus sought to rid society of those they considered heretics and sinners. As a result, some people reasoned that if they punished themselves thoroughly enough, they might be spared God's wrath. Upper-class men, for instance, joined processions of flagellants that traveled from town to town and engaged in public displays of penance and punishment, beating themselves and one another with heavy leather straps studded with sharp pieces of metal while the townspeople watched. They repeated this display three times a day for a month, and then would move on to the next town and begin the process again.[8]

Physicians, who had no idea the disease was both airborne and transmitted via fleas, relied on popular but crude techniques such as bloodletting and boil-lancing (practices that were dangerous as well as unsanitary) and superstitious rituals such as burning aromatic herbs and bathing in rosewater or vinegar, to no avail. "Dead bodies filled every corner," wrote Boccaccio. "Most of them were treated in the same manner by the survivors, who were more concerned to get rid of their rotting bodies than moved by charity towards the dead. With the aid of porters, if they could get them, they carried the bodies out of the houses and laid them at the door; where every morning quantities of the dead might be seen. They then were laid on biers or, as these were often lacking, on tables."[9]

Three hundred years after its initial devastating outbreak, the Black Death was still a pervasive threat in Europe. Two of Luther's brothers died of plague in 1505, around the time Luther entered the Augustinian monastery. Katharina and Luther lived through three outbreaks in Wittenberg—in 1527, 1535, and 1539—and Katharina cared for plague victims in their home after they were married. In Strasbourg alone, a city of about 25,000 inhabitants, 16,000 were killed by the plague in one year.[10]

Even when citizens weren't contending with outbreaks of the plague, death was a pervasive presence and threat. Life expectancy at birth during Luther's time was, by our twenty-first-century standards, shockingly low—twenty-eight to thirty years old for men and a bit higher for women.[11] The risk of death for childbearing women was extraordinarily high. In early modern England, for example, childbirth accounted for one-fifth of all deaths among women between the ages of twenty-five and thirty-four, an occurrence so common it didn't even warrant commentary at the time.[12] Low life expectancy was due in large part to the extremely high infant mortality rate. In general, approximately one-quarter of all babies born alive during the early modern period in Europe died in infancy, and another quarter died before reaching puberty, a rate that held steady even into the seventeenth and eighteenth centuries.[13] In Florence, Italy, at the height of the Renaissance, for instance, 61 percent of all infants were either stillborn or died within six months.[14] Nearly one child in two in early modern Europe failed to live to the age of ten, and two live births were required to produce one fully matured adult.[15] Luther's own family did not escape these ruthless statistics. At least one of his brothers was stillborn, a death his mother attributed to a female neighbor, whom she was convinced was a witch,[16] and Luther and Katharina lost two out of their six children. One daughter lived only a few months, and the other died as a young girl.

Even the cultural imagery popular at the time would have influenced Luther's views of life and death. Medieval Flemish artist Hieronymus Bosch's paintings such as *The Last Judgment*, *The Seven Deadly Sins*, and the third panel of *The Garden of Earthly Delights* triptych depict disturbing scenes of death, torture, demons, half-human–half-animal creatures, and menacing machines, all portrayed in ominous, brooding colors. In one scene, for instance, a monster with a catlike head and an ogre's muscled body swallows a naked man whole. In another, the gaping maw of a giant, melting face seems to inhale dozens of writhing, naked bodies.

Likewise, the series of fifteen woodcuts depicting the Apocalypse by Luther's contemporary, Albrecht Durer, offers unsettling scenes from the book of Revelation, complete with menacing demons, skeletal horsemen, and the writhing dragon with seven heads. Even the Gothic architecture of the churches and cathedrals—spiked spires, flying buttresses, pointed arches, soaring vaulted ceilings, stone facades, and brooding gargoyles hunched high over city streets—provoked a mix of fear and awe. While the gargoyles often served a practical purpose—they were part of the rain spout and gutter system of the building (rainwater typically exited away from the building out of the gargoyles' mouths)—their menacing demon, lion, and dragon faces also offered citizens a reminder and a warning: evil resided outside the church walls, salvation within.[17] Themes of evil, death, and damnation so pervaded the artwork and popular imagery of the time, it would have been difficult to escape their influence.

Fear of death prompted Luther to make his thunderstorm vow, and fear of sin and eternal damnation resulting from it prompted him to honor that vow. To make a vow to a saint was to make a promise to God, and to break such a vow was to commit a mortal sin, for "it was to admit that one did not truly believe in the God to whom the vow was made."[18] A person living in the late Middle Ages absolutely did not want to commit a mortal sin, the worst kind of sin imaginable, and risk plummeting to hell. Luther refused to pay an eternal price by breaking his vow to St. Anne and God. He entered the Augustinian monastery in Erfurt in July of 1505.

A Model Monk

Luther once remarked that the devil is quiet during a novice's first year in a monastery.[19] The new monk was relatively content during his early months behind the cloister walls. Much like Katharina in the Nimbschen convent, Luther performed the Daily Office, which began around 2:00 a.m. and concluded with the chanting by the cantor of the "Salve Regina," followed by the "Ave Maria" and the "Pater Noster" at the end of the day.[20] He led a largely silent and austere life, occupying a single cell that consisted of a bed with a straw mattress and one wool blanket. The cell was unheated, so when it was extremely cold, Luther and his fellow monks were allowed to gather in the heated common room. He did not speak with the other monks, save a few basic hand gestures, and his gaze was always directed downward, his hands hidden deep in the roomy sleeves of his robe.

Luther quickly took to the routines and rituals of monastic life, and as Richard Friedenthal points out, "Not a murmur of rebellion, or of the slightest disobedience, [has] ever been reported. The quiet and discipline did the intractable young man good."[21] From the start, Luther set out to become the model monk, and he did everything by the book. He even chose his

This portrait of Martin Luther as an Augustinian monk was painted by the workshop of Lucas Cranach the Elder after Luther died, circa 1546.

monastic order based on his desire to pursue the most righteous and holy life possible. From the dozens of monasteries in Erfurt, Luther chose the Augustinian monastery, set on the bank of the Gera River and surrounded by a high, thick wall. Only a few steps from his lodgings were the less rigid Benedictine,

Dominican, and Franciscan monasteries, as well as a number of other orders, but Luther chose the way of the Observant Augustinians. As James Kittelson acknowledges, "To be an Observant Augustinian was to engage in serious spiritual work."[22]

Even as a novice Luther fasted for days on end, drinking only the tiniest sips of water or beer and not allowing a crumb to pass his lips. He went above and beyond the Daily Office and prayed constantly. At night, he threw his wool blanket to the floor and exposed his flesh to the frigid air. When he was given his first Bible, he pored over the Latin text, memorizing the verses until he knew the book almost entirely by heart and was able to quote from it extensively with ease.

Luther even made a pilgrimage to Rome. He traveled more than nine hundred miles on foot, through the Swiss Alps, the path lined with crosses marking the spots where travelers had met their deaths; over the Italian Apennines in a treacherous snowstorm; and finally, two months later, into the Holy City. At his first glimpse of the city, Luther threw himself to the ground, crying, "Hail, holy city of Rome!" During the month he spent there, he toured all the most famous sites and viewed the most famous relics, including the rope with which the disciple Judas hanged himself after he had betrayed Jesus and a "stone with a furrow as broad as a man's fingers caused by Peter's tears after he had denied Christ."[23] Luther even purchased indulgences as remittance for his past sins and climbed the holy stairway at the Lateran Palace on his knees, reciting a "Pater Noster" on every step, as was the custom. When he reached the top he received a plenary indulgence, which he prayed would release the soul of his grandfather from purgatory.[24] "I believed everything," Luther later said.[25] Much later, however, in a sermon only months before his death, Luther said he stood at the top of the stairs and asked himself, "Who can know if it is so?"—suggesting that even then he had reservations about works-based faith.[26]

"I was a good monk," Luther said, "and I kept the rule of my order so strictly that I may say that if ever a monk got to heaven by his monkery it was I. All my brothers in the monastery who knew me will bear me out. If I had kept on any longer, I should have killed myself with vigils, prayers, reading and other work."[27] Try as he might, though, Luther could not live up to his expectations of being the most perfect, most holy, most sinless monk. He badgered his confessor, sometimes confessing his sins for as long as six hours in a single day.[28] Yet when he finally left the confessional, relieved to have been absolved of every last sin, the thought would strike him, "What a fine confession you just made," and, recognizing with dismay the sin of pride, he would head back to the confessional once again.[29] Luther didn't believe the doctrine of confession was flawed (as he would come to believe later), but only that he had not yet been able to achieve the perfect confession. It was torture, and as time went on and the frustrating cycle continued, Luther's fear of God's wrath intensified, and he began to succumb to depression and despair.

The Agony of Doubt

Fear of God's wrath was not a new experience for Luther. As a young boy he spent Mass paralyzed with fear as he gazed at the stained-glass window in his village church, the image depicting a stern Jesus gripping the sword of justice. He saw God as an angry, looming, threatening presence, always watching, always knowing, poised to punish the slightest transgression. Standing in front of the crucifix, Luther trembled, dizzy and faint with fear; the thought of the Eucharist filled him with nausea. There were times Luther felt that he hated God. He knew that "hating God was the ultimate blasphemy . . . he was hopelessly damned," yet he couldn't help himself.[30] Luther was terrified of his God.

The hours, weeks, and months Luther spent in his cell only exacerbated these inclinations toward despair. With so much time on his hands to brood over his sins and confess and re-confess, he spiraled into an obsessive cycle that led him deeper and deeper into depression. "When I saw Christ," he stated dramatically many years later, "it seemed to me as if I were seeing the devil."[31] Even as late as 1515, he stated in his lectures on the book of Romans that "he felt often that he must despair of God, and that whenever he thought of the test that lay before him at the end of life his heart trembled and shook. How could God be merciful to him?"[32]

Luther's spiritual director was remarkably patient with him, despite being forced to listen to hour after hour of confession and angst from the new monk. At one point he tried to explain the nature of God's love, declaring to Luther, "God is not angry with you; you are angry with Him."[33] Luther would often come away from these confessions and conversations with a sense of peace, but the consolation never lasted long. Although he believed in repentance and absolution in general, Luther couldn't bring himself to believe it was intended specifically for him.

"Despair—the horrifying thought that God's mercy is not for me or that I have fallen too far for it to help me—was the one unforgiveable sin," says Kittelson. "It was the sin against the Holy Spirit, and no one who died with it in their heart could escape the fires of hell."[34] People who lived in medieval and early modern Europe were terrified of dying with the feeling of despair in their hearts, so much so that depictions of angels and devils wrestling for the soul of a dying person were extremely popular images at the time, as was the prevalence of deathbed confessions and declarations. Loved ones often prodded a dying person to commend aloud their souls to God so that the declaration could be heard by those surrounding the deathbed and by God above. In fact, in Luther's time it was considered a grave sign of God's judgment and subsequent damnation to hell if a person died in his sleep or if he was suffering too greatly to utter any convicting last words.[35] That's why when Luther himself lay on his deathbed, his close friend Justus Jonas and the local preacher asked him, "Reverend father, are you ready to die trusting in your Lord Jesus Christ and to confess the doctrine which you have taught in his name?" They were able to report to his detractors that Luther had replied with a clearly audible yes, thereby ensuring his entrance into eternal life.[36]

Luther's struggles with depression and despair during his monastic years weren't uncommon, although it seems he suffered more than most monks. These were the occupational hazards of the monastic calling, specifically: *accidie* or *acedia* (sloth and torpor of the spirit) and *scruple* (a feeling of doubt or hesitance).[37] Monks all across Europe had slang terms for the kind of spiritual and mental wrestling that went on behind the cloister walls. They called the feeling of regret or frustration with spiritual shortcomings as being *in cloaca*, literally, "in the toilet" or "in the dumps."[38] Luther called his attacks of doubt and despair *Anfechtung*, an interesting word choice that can mean "temptation" or "doubt," but also "challenging," "contesting," or "disputing," implying that Luther felt, at times, like he was arguing with God or even that God was intentionally inhibiting his faith.[39]

Luther found himself at an impasse. He knew that for his sins to be forgiven, they needed to be confessed, and in order for them to be properly confessed, every last one needed not only to be accounted for but truly repented of. The body *and* the heart had to be expunged of every impurity. The problem for Luther was that true repentance and absolution seemed attainable for only a few minutes or, at most, a few hours at a time. Even when he could stop his body from sinning, he struggled to keep his mind and heart pure.

Ultimately it was his mentor and confessor, Johann von Staupitz, who finally put an end to Luther's torment. "If it had not been for Dr. Staupitz," Luther said himself, "I should have sunk in hell."[40] Aware that the traditional monastic life was doing the young monk more harm than good, von Staupitz ordered Luther out of the monastery in 1512—after seven years behind the cloister walls—and back into the world to teach at the nearby University of Wittenberg. Luther would still be a monk—in fact, upon arriving in Wittenberg, he moved into the Augustinian monastery known as the Black Cloister—but he would no longer live a contemplative, cloistered life.

A Critical Difference

Although Luther and Katharina shared a sense of isolation and abandonment in their march to the ascetic, they entered the monastic life under very different circumstances. Later in life, Luther claimed he became a monk with great reluctance; at times, he even implied that he had been forced toward the monastic life. Sometimes, as was mentioned earlier, he blamed his parents' severe disciplinary tactics for driving him to the monastery.

Other times he suggested his vow to St. Anne forced him to commit to the cloistered life. Yet Luther's demeanor in the early months of his enclosure indicates that he felt not resentment or bitterness but contentment and a sense of acceptance. Luther knew exactly what he was giving up to become a monk—a law degree, an illustrious career, a comfortable life—yet he did so anyway, in spite of his father's ire, and he remained committed to his vows, in spite of long periods of dark wrestling and despair.

Even in the midst of his deepest struggles, Luther never lost sight of his monastic vows and his commitment to obey God. He felt compelled by a sense of obedience to honor his vow, but beneath that ran a deep current of spirituality and faith and a powerful desire to live the most pure and holy life possible. Even his obsessive need to prove himself as the best, most dedicated monk points to his zeal for God and his deep spiritual convictions.

Katharina, on the other hand, didn't choose to become a nun out of a deep and abiding faith and a desire to commit her life to God. Rather, she entered the convent because she had to; her father made that decision for her. Katharina may well have been a deeply faithful person, but the fact is, she didn't commit her life to Christ in the same way and with the same intention that Luther did. This critical difference, as we will see, not only fueled Katharina's decision to flee the convent, it also informed her views on marriage in general and, more specifically, impacted her relationship with Martin Luther.

5

The Road to Damascus and a Nail in the Door

Little land, little land,
You are but a heap of sand.
If I dig you, the soil is light;
If I reap you, the yield is slight.[1]

This little ditty, written by Luther after his arrival in Wittenberg, tells you everything you need to know about his first impressions of the town. Compared to bustling Erfurt, Wittenberg was a quiet village of about 2,500 residents. The town took its name from the sand dune—*witten-berg*, "white hillock"—upon which it was built.[2] By the time Luther lived there, the dune had largely diminished, leaving the area flat, sandy, and nondescript, the Elbe River flowing along one side of the town,

Public domain

This 1536 drawing from the travel album of the Count Palatine Otto Heinrich would have been similar to the view Luther saw when he arrived in Wittenberg.

a moat surrounding the other side. Wittenberg's architectural highlights included a castle, the village church, a handful of small chapels, a Franciscan monastery, and the Augustinian monastery known as the Black Cloister, named after the black robes worn by the Augustinian monks.

When Luther moved in as a twenty-eight-year-old monk, the Black Cloister consisted of several large stone buildings: a monastery comprised of more than forty rooms (most were small monks' cells), stables and sheds for livestock, a brewing house, and an infirmary. In the middle of the complex was a courtyard bordered by a half-finished cloister church, the construction of which had been abandoned shortly after the foundation was laid in 1502.[3] There was also a tiny old church, barely thirty feet long and twenty feet wide and in such disrepair it was shored up with beams on all sides. Inside was a narrow, damaged choir loft barely large enough to hold twenty worshipers, and a "pulpit," which was actually a primitive chair constructed out of a few rough boards. Luther once remarked that the worship area "looked like the stall where Jesus had been born, above all in its 'lowliness.'"[4] Little did Luther know at the time, he would call this sprawling collection of dilapidated stone buildings home for the rest of his life.

A short distance from the Black Cloister was Wittenberg's claim to fame: its university. Founded by Elector[5] Frederick the Wise in an attempt to rival the prestigious University of Leipzig, which was located forty-four miles south in the territory ruled by his cousin (and rival) Duke George of Saxony, the new university struggled to gain recognition. In an effort to improve the school's reputation and the caliber of the academic staff, Frederick invited the Augustinians and Franciscans to supply three new professors. Luther arrived as a new hire in 1512, unaware that his time as a professor in the little town of Wittenberg, a mere "heap of sand," would be among the most pivotal periods not only in his own life but in the history of Western civilization.

As an Augustinian monk, Luther lived in the Black Cloister in Wittenberg, which is now the museum *Lutherhaus*.

Luther's Road to Damascus

By 1512 Luther had earned his doctorate along with the official title "Doctor of Biblia," translated as "teacher of the Bible."[6] In addition to his teaching duties, Luther was also required to publish on theological matters. His mentor, von Staupitz, also made him the official preacher to the Augustinian monks in Wittenberg, a task that required him to preach up to several times a week. Beginning with the Psalms and continuing with Romans, Galatians, and Hebrews, Luther dug into Scripture, and it was these years of study, exegesis, writing, teaching, and preaching that formed the foundation of his theology—a theology that not only informed the *Ninety-five Theses* and his belief in salvation through grace alone, but also saved Luther from his own spiritual despair. As Roland Bainton notes, "These studies proved to be for Luther the Damascus road."[7]

You might wonder how Luther's *Ninety-five Theses* is relevant to a discussion of his marriage to Katharina. After all, his primary concern in that famous treatise is the practice of selling indulgences, and more specifically, the power and authority of the pope and the Roman Catholic Church as a whole. Yet without the *Ninety-five Theses*, without that initial radical act of rebellion, Luther's theology of marriage, his own marriage to Katharina von Bora, and the entire movement of marriage reform during the Protestant Reformation likely would not have happened at all. Writing and then nailing the *Ninety-five Theses* to the doors of Castle Church in Wittenberg was the single act that set everything else in motion.

It all began with Luther's objection to the church's practice of selling indulgences. According to the 1471 Catechism of the Catholic Church, an indulgence was a remission of temporal punishment for sins that have been confessed to a priest and forgiven by God.[8] In other words, an indulgence didn't take the place of confession or absolution—the sinner was still required to confess his sins and be absolved of them by a priest—but it did take the place of penance: the prayers, fasting, pilgrimages, and other works a person offered to God as payment for his sins. Furthermore, an indulgence could be offered as remittance for temporal punishment only. Thus an indulgence could reduce time spent in purgatory. Hell, on the other hand, was not temporal but eternal and therefore subject only to the will of God.

Indulgences first became popular during the Crusades, when Pope Urban II, who needed an army to fight against the Turks, remitted all penance for soldiers who participated in the war.[9] The practice of selling and purchasing indulgences became extremely popular later in the Middle Ages and early modern period when pilgrims were offered indulgences for paying the fee to view collections of relics at shrine sites in Rome and elsewhere. Luther himself purchased indulgences on numerous occasions, most notably in Rome, when he bought an indulgence to decrease his grandfather's time in purgatory. The sale of indulgences was used by the Church to raise revenues and line the pockets of the clergy and political leaders, from the pope down to the local parish priests and from the Holy Roman Emperor to the electors, as well as to fund wars and the construction of churches, monasteries, hospitals, and even civic projects. Elector Frederick the Wise, for instance, used the profits from the sale of indulgences to finance the reconstruction of a bridge across the Elbe.[10]

The pope decreed churches across the Holy Roman Empire the privilege of dispensing indulgences, and Castle Church in Wittenberg was allowed an unusual concession: on one day each year—the first of November, known as All Saints' Day—penitents who visited Frederick the Wise's display of relics and paid the required admission fee would receive a highly unusual indulgence from the pope granting full remission of all sins, either for themselves or for a loved one who had died.[11] Frederick the Wise owned a massive collection of relics, more than 17,433 pieces, including nine thorns from Jesus's crown; thirty-five splinters from the cross; one wisp of straw from the manger; a bit of cloth from Christ's swaddling; one hair from Jesus's beard; one of his crucifixion nails; one piece of bread left over from the Last Supper; a few drops of the Virgin Mary's milk; four hairs from her head; four pieces of fabric from her girdle; one twig from the burning bush of Moses; and one tooth of St. Jerome.[12] These, among many others, were the treasures available to view on All Saints' Day—for a price—and citizens of Wittenberg and beyond stood in line for hours to do exactly that. Those who paid the appropriate fee and viewed the relics on the designated day received an indulgence from the pope for the reduction of purgatory up to 1,902,202 years and 270 days.[13]

A Hammer, a Nail, a Revolution

As Luther immersed himself in Scripture, he became increasingly uncomfortable with and angered by the idea of indulgences. The final straw for him came in 1517, when a Dominican friar by the name of Johann Tetzel began to hawk indulgences guaranteed by Pope Leo X to remit all sins and restore penitents to the state of purity and innocence they enjoyed at baptism. In addition, those who purchased Tetzel's indulgences, the proceeds from which would be used to complete construction of the new St. Peter's Basilica in Rome, were granted remission from purgatory, either for themselves or for a deceased loved one. No indulgence could offer a get-out-of-hell-free card, but Tetzel's deal proposed the next best thing.

Frederick the Wise actually didn't allow Tetzel to sell the indulgences in his part of Saxony—not because he was theologically opposed to the practice, but because he feared Tetzel's sales would decrease his own earnings from visitors to his relic collection. But the peddler traveled close enough to Wittenberg that Luther got wind of his wild claims. "As soon as the coin in the coffer rings the soul from purgatory springs," Tetzel shouted from the town square, where he displayed a cross bearing the papal arms and the pope's bull of indulgence presented on a gold-embroidered velvet cushion.[14] Among other claims, the friar reportedly stated, "Even if you have deflowered the Virgin Mary, an indulgence will free you from the punishment in purgatory!"[15]

Tetzel's bold promises infuriated Luther, who believed that the practice of buying and selling indulgences smacked of a works-based rather than a grace-based faith. He could not abide by a practice he considered not only corrupt but downright blasphemous. He had had enough.

On October 31, 1517, on the eve of All Saints' Day, the day Frederick the Wise would offer his own annual indulgence sale, Luther sent a letter to Archbishop Albrecht of Brandenburg, who had been using his own sale of indulgences to pay off the debt he'd incurred in obtaining the archbishopric.[16] In the letter Luther asked the archbishop to cease his sale of indulgences. He also included a list of ninety-five statements, written in Latin, which he titled "On the Power of Indulgences." This was a bold move. Luther was a no-name monk, Albrecht of Brandenburg a noble of the church; bishops could have monks thrown into prison for lesser transgressions. Treading cautiously at first, Luther's letter to Albrecht "heaped flattery on the archbishop's head and humility on his own."[17]

However, once Luther finished the opening formalities, he let loose; his list of ninety-five statements seared with a barely concealed rage. Not only did the treatise attack the sale of indulgences to support the construction of St. Peter's in Rome—"Why does not the pope, whose wealth is to-day greater than the riches of the richest, build just this one church of St. Peter with his own money, rather than with the money of poor believers?"[18]—Luther also questioned the notion of papal sovereignty again and again, declaring that God and God alone, not the pope nor anyone else, had the power to pardon man from sin:

> 6. The pope cannot remit any guilt, except by declaring that it has been remitted by God and by assenting to God's remission. . . .
>
> 26. The pope does well when he grants remission to souls [in purgatory], not by the power of the keys (which he does not possess), but by way of intercession. . . .
>
> 33. Men must be on their guard against those who say that the pope's pardons are that inestimable gift of God by which man is reconciled to Him. . . .
>
> 34. For these "graces of pardon" concern only the penalties of sacramental satisfaction, and these are appointed by man.[19]

These were serious statements, each written in Luther's signature no-nonsense style. There was no room for nuance or misinterpretation; even today, read five hundred years later, one can clearly see how Luther's document would have offended and enraged authorities. As Bainton points out, Luther's *Theses* differed from ordinary propositions for debate because they were "forged in anger," and therefore were "crisp, bold [and] unqualified."[20]

Luther's anger was fueled by his intimate understanding of a particular verse in the Bible, one he had obsessively reflected on day and night until he was finally brought to his knees in a moment of revelation. The verse was Romans 1:17: "For therein is the righteousness of God revealed from faith to faith: as it is written, The just shall live by faith." Luther admitted that ever since he was a child, he had hated the phrase "righteousness of God," because he had always assumed it referred to God's anger. For Luther, the word *righteousness* was associated with God's punishment.[21] After much contemplation, prayer, and study, however, Luther finally came to understand that this "righteousness" was not something God did *against* sinners as punishment but something God gave *to* sinners as a gift. Moreover, as Luther came to understand it, God's righteousness was not a gift earned or deserved, but given freely to the undeserving out of God's great mercy and compassion and made possible only by Christ's death on the cross. The key, Luther finally realized, was that God's love and grace were not merited, but freely given and freely received through faith alone.

This understanding of God's righteousness turned Luther's entire theology on its head, transforming his understanding of God from one full of anger and wrath, eager to punish the sinner's many transgressions, to an all-loving, all-merciful God. "I felt myself absolutely reborn," Luther wrote after his revelation, "as though I had entered into the open gates of paradise itself."[22] His understanding of grace-based faith versus works-based faith was more than a personal revelation; it informed his entire rebellion against the church. After all, if human beings couldn't possibly earn salvation by their good works, if human beings had no righteousness of their own and were entirely dependent on Christ for their salvation and hope, where, then, did that leave good works like pilgrimages and fasting? Where did that leave the notion of purgatory? Where did that leave the monastic vows of poverty, obedience, and chastity? Where did that leave the pope, with his sales of indulgences, and the priests, doling out penance in the confessionals? Luther came to believe that the church to which he had dedicated his life was built on sand, and each abuse, each indulgence, added an unsustainable weight to the structure. In his eyes, Romans 1:17 obliterated the very foundation of the Roman Catholic Church.

Interestingly, Reformation scholars today still debate whether or not Luther actually posted his *Ninety-five Theses* on the door of Castle Church. Martin Brecht notes that the posting of the *Theses* on the church doors was first mentioned well after Luther's death by his friend and fellow reformer Philip Melanchthon, who wasn't even living in Wittenberg in 1517, the time of the alleged posting.[23] In his thousands of *Table Talk* entries Luther never told the story of posting the *Theses*, nor did he mention it in any of his own writings that detail the beginnings of the reform movement. Brecht guesses that Luther probably did post the *Theses*, as nailing a notice on the church door was standard protocol for academics who wished to engage in a public debate, but the truth is, no one knows for sure if Luther stood before the doors of Castle Church with a hammer in his hand.

Regardless of whether the document was posted on the church doors or not, word got out. While no one showed up to the public academic disputation, when the document was printed and distributed not long after the alleged posting, the reaction was immediate and dramatic. Luther's *Ninety-five Theses* was a sensation, and news of it spread like wildfire, prompting printers to work feverishly to keep copies in circulation. Translated from Latin into German, printed and reprinted and carried from village to village across Germany and beyond, the *Ninety-five Theses* made Luther famous within a month. He had attacked the notion of papal sovereignty and, along with it, the pope and the Roman Catholic Church itself. In doing so, Luther had set a revolution in motion. There was no turning back now.

The Great Debate

Armed with scriptural authority and the support of much of the public, Luther began to question other aspects of papal and Church authority. He took issue, for instance, with the doctrine of papal primacy, which held that the pope was not only sovereign but infallible, an authority born out of Christ's proclamation that Peter was the rock upon which the Church would be built and passed down the line to each pope in succession.

Theologian Johann Eck, whom Luther referred to as "that little glory-hungry beast," was the first of many to accuse Luther of heresy.[24] In June of 1519, Luther traveled to Leipzig to debate the notion of papal primacy with Eck before a raucous audience of university students, professors, clergy, and theologians. The monk was in his element. He wore his doctor's silver ring and a black cowl over a white habit. Reporters described him as brilliant and genial, cool, almost casual in his demeanor, and above all, confident. One of his critics, the theologian Hieronymus Emser, called him "haughty, bold and presumptuous."[25] Luther clutched a bouquet of flowers at the podium (both men and women in the Middle Ages often carried a small nosegay of flowers and fragrant herbs as a defense against the rank smells of everyday life), and would pause from time to time in his argument to inhale their heady fragrance.[26] One wonders if burying his nose in the bouquet was Luther's not-so-subtle way of implying that Eck's arguments stunk.

The Leipzig debate raged for twenty-three days, which was somewhat unusual. Typically disputations—theological or academic debates—lasted anywhere from a few hours to a few days, although some lasted much longer (the Disputation of Tortosa, between the Christians and the Jews in fifteenth-century Spain, for example, continued off and on for more than a year).[27] At Leipzig, Luther argued for the authority of Scripture alone over doctrine, papal primacy, and even the Church itself. The Church required a leader, Luther agreed with Eck, but that leader was Christ, not the pope.[28] Luther insisted that his aim was not to overthrow or even to undermine the papacy, but simply to suggest that the pope was human—that he could, in fact, be wrong.

Then Luther took his argument one giant step forward: he stated that true doctrine was not that which the general council of the Roman Catholic Church deemed to be true (as had been the case up to this point in the history of the Church), but what the masses of Christians—the priesthood of all believers—deemed to be true. According to Luther, Scripture could, and did, contradict Church doctrine and well-established traditions, which made the Church wrong. Christ alone was the key to salvation.[29] In short, Luther argued, God speaks to *all* people through his Word; no mediator or intercessor is necessary between God and man except Christ himself, and Christ speaks "not to an institution but to the heart."[30]

At the end of the three weeks Eck declared himself the winner of the debate. As he gloated over his victory and boasted about the stag Duke George had sent him as a reward, Luther quietly retreated to strategize a fresh tactical approach.[31] Disappointed by the outcome of the debate and exhausted from the verbal jousting, Luther decided to turn his energy from speaking to writing. With the help of the printers, he aimed to broaden the reach of his reforms and address not just the stodgy theologians but the masses—the people he hoped would rally behind his convictions and help carry his message forward.[32]

One year later, Luther put the ideas he'd expressed during the Leipzig debate into three powerful treatises. In his *Address to the Christian Nobility of the German Nation Concerning the Reform of the Christian State*, *The Babylonian Captivity*, and *Freedom of a Christian*, all published in 1520, the Reformer not only declared war against the papacy and the Roman Catholic Church, he also began to formulate his views on clerical celibacy and marriage.[33] Up to this point, Luther had dealt mainly with lofty theological matters that riled church authorities but had little impact on ordinary citizens. His reforms concerning marriage and clerical celibacy, however, were about to change that. Little by little, as printers churned out copies of his treatises and Luther's words made their way into the hands of the common people, his radical ideas began to spread. Before long, they began to reach even those most removed from everyday society: the men and women living behind the cloister walls.

Hear This, O Pope!

On the morning of December 10, 1520, Luther gathered a small group of students and friends and proceeded to a location just outside Wittenberg's gates. Earlier, in a note he had posted on the door of the town church, he had invited "all friends of evangelical truth" to assist in the burning of "godless books of papal law and scholastic theology."[1] Outside the gate that cold morning, the group built a pyre, piled it with volumes of canon law and an assortment of books written by Luther's enemies, and then stood by to watch the tomes burn. As the fire raged, Luther stepped forward and, without fanfare, quietly dropped a document into the flames, reportedly pronouncing a few brief words in Latin as he did so: "May this fire destroy you, because you have obstructed God's truth."[2]

It was a quiet gathering; too quiet, in fact, to satisfy the university students, who, since the Leipzig debate, had come to be some of Luther's most fervent supporters. After breakfast that same morning, a larger group of students processed through town following a carriage decorated with antipapal placards, shouting and cheering and gathering more writings by Luther's foes as fuel for their own bonfire. The atmosphere sizzled with energy and anticipation. Trumpets blasted and the crowd roared as onlookers tossed a cloth effigy of Pope Leo X into the flames.

Luther was appalled by the carnivalesque display, and he told the students exactly that in a lecture the next day. This was a grave matter, he insisted, speaking in German rather than the academic Latin so as to be absolutely clear, and one that presented only two options: martyrdom or hell. Martyrdom, he informed the students, could be expected of all who joined the fight against the papacy. Hell, on the other hand, would be the fate of those who chose to side with the antichrist, the pope. Luther had made his choice. Which would they choose, Luther asked the now-somber group?

Racing against the Bull

The document Luther dropped into the bonfire on the morning of December 10 was an important one: an official copy of a papal bull, written principally by Johann Eck and threatening Luther's excommunication. The bull had been issued in Rome on June 15, 1520, and it listed and condemned as heretical forty-one points Luther had claimed during the Leipzig debate. Three copies of the bull, all inscribed on parchment with the papal seal, or "bull," attached at the bottom, were distributed:

one to Duke George of Saxony; one to Pope Leo X, who was on vacation, hunting wild boar outside of Rome; and the third to Frederick the Wise, who forwarded it to Luther.

The bull stated that Luther had sixty days to recant all forty-one articles or be excommunicated from the church.[3] Luther interpreted this to mean that he had sixty days to produce and disseminate as many of his views in writing as possible. Gone was the debonair, bouquet-sniffing monk who had appeared on the podium in Leipzig. Once he began to dismantle the notion of papal primacy and the Roman Catholic Church itself, Luther was relentlessly ruthless on the page, his words snapping with indignation and rage.

"Hear this, O pope," he fumed in the *Address to the Christian Nobility of the German Nation Concerning the Reform of the Christian State*, "not of all men the holiest but of all men the most sinful! O that God from heaven would soon destroy your throne and sink it in the abyss of hell!"[4] Luther was horrified by the rampant corruption he observed among the clergy in Rome, from excessive materialism—like the specially embroidered bishop's cape that cost 30,000 *Gulden* (*Gulden* is German for "gold coin"; to put it into context, Luther's annual salary at the time was about 100 *Gulden*) to the papal officials who traveled around Germany dissolving contracts, including marriages, for a fee. He condemned the funding of masses said for the living and the dead as good works and demanded that no dues be paid to Rome. "Cut down the creeping, crawling swarm of vermin at Rome, so that the pope's household can be supported out of the pope's own pocket,"[5] he raged.

He also criticized what he considered to be worship of the pope, advocating that Christians cease kissing the pope's feet and driving him about like an idol.[6] "What Christian heart can or ought to take pleasure in seeing that when the pope wishes to receive communion, he sits quietly like a gracious lord and has the sacrament brought to him on a golden rod by a bowing cardinal on bended knee," Luther scoffed. "As though the holy sacrament were not worthy enough for the pope, a poor, stinking sinner, to rise and show respect to his God."[7] The pope, Luther insisted, should be treated not like God but like a man, flawed and fallible like everyone else.

In the *Babylonian Captivity* Luther took on the sacraments, dismantling the ones that didn't originate with a direct command from Christ in the New Testament. Under his new rubric, only three of the original seven sacraments qualified—baptism, the Eucharist, and confession. (Luther emphasized personal, private confession between two laypeople or even between a person and God himself, rather than the more formal ritual of confessing to God through a priest. Later the reformers abandoned confession as a sacrament altogether, leaving only two.) Confirmation, ordination, marriage, and extreme unction (or last rites) went to the chopping block. He also reiterated his earlier claim that the pope was the antichrist, the ruler of Babylon, and restated his belief in the priesthood of all believers. All Christians were priests, he argued, differing only in the roles they held. Finally, in the *Babylonian Captivity*, as well as in an earlier essay titled *A Sermon on the Estate of Marriage* (published in 1519), Luther began to lay the groundwork for his views on marriage.

In *A Treatise on the Freedom of a Christian*, which appeared in November 1520 but was backdated to September to make it appear as though it had been written and published before the *Babylonian Captivity*, Luther's tone was more subtle. He had heard rumors that Pope Leo's attitude toward him was softening, and the thought, at least among Luther's confidants and advisors, was that perhaps he could retract the *Babylonian Captivity*, or even deny it had been written by him, should Pope Leo show signs of canceling the bull.[8] Pressured by Frederick the Wise to write an apology, Luther penned *Freedom of a Christian*, which on the surface seemed conciliatory but in actuality was simply a more savvy declaration against the pope and the Church. The tone of the letter was friendly and gracious—Luther reminded Pope Leo that he had never attacked him personally but, instead, had aimed his vitriol against the papacy in general—but the overall message was consistent with his earlier essays. He suggested that Pope Leo give up his title, retire to a parish, live on the income of a priest, and accept all the doctrinal changes Luther had outlined in his previous treatises. Then, Luther proposed, Leo could help him reform the church. In other words, Luther suggested that peace could be possible between them if Leo helped him destroy the papacy.[9] Not exactly the apology Frederick the Wise had in mind. Not surprisingly, Pope Leo was not swayed.

In addition to insulting the pope further, *Freedom of a Christian* also unpacked an important question, one consistently posed by Luther's detractors: If we can't earn salvation through doing our own good works, then why bother doing good works at all? Why not eat, drink, and be merry, living our lives contentedly and assuredly in God's good grace? Luther argued that freedom from sin through Christ's grace encouraged and inspired Christians to perform good works out of immense gratitude and love for Christ: "The works themselves do not justify him [man] before God, but he does the works out of spontaneous love in obedience to God."[10] Not only that, Luther argued, but the true Christian, inspired by his love for and gratitude toward

Christ, should take that love one step further and apply it to his relationship with his neighbor. "A man does not live for himself alone in this mortal body to work for it alone, but he lives also for all men on earth," Luther wrote. "Rather, he lives only for others and not for himself. To this end he brings his body into subjection that he may the more sincerely and freely serve others."[11]

Luther believed this selfless, sacrificial love for one's neighbor was the hallmark of a true Christian. Christians did good works because of the way Christ loved them and had transformed them by his love. "Although the Christian is thus free from all works," Luther wrote, "he ought in this liberty to empty himself, take upon himself the form of a servant and to serve, help and in every way deal with his neighbor as he sees that God through Christ has dealt and still deals with him."[12] As we will see, Luther will be challenged by his own words when, five years after the publication of *Freedom of a Christian*, he will begin to grapple with the question of whether or not to marry a destitute nun.

Here I Stand

Luther dropped the papal bull into the fire on December 10, 1520, for a reason. It was exactly sixty days after the bull had been served to him; his grace period—the two months he was given to recant—was over. Excommunication was imminent. Shortly after, he received his summons to testify in his own defense at a hearing before the Holy Roman Emperor, Charles V. The only small piece of good news was that the hearing would take place on German soil, at the Diet of Worms, rather than in Rome.

Luther was now officially living the perilous life of a heretic. Even traveling the three hundred miles from Wittenberg to Worms was to take his life in his hands. Although Luther had been guaranteed protection during the journey, he undoubtedly recalled the fate of reformer Jan Hus who, more than one hundred years earlier, had been arrested en route to his trial, imprisoned, and later burned at the stake as a heretic. "I would by all means come, if called, in so far as it would be up to me, even if I could not come by my own power and instead would have to be driven there as a sick man," Luther wrote to his friend George Spalatin on December 29, 1520. "For it would not be right to doubt that I am called by the Lord if the Emperor summons. No one's danger, no one's safety can be considered here. We must rather take care that we do not expose the gospel (which we have finally begun to promote) to the derision of the godless and thus give our enemies a reason for boasting over us because we do not dare confess what we have taught and are afraid to shed our blood for it."[13]

Luther survived the journey to Worms. He entered the city at ten o'clock on the morning of April 16. Led by eight knights on horseback, his arrival was announced with a triumphant fanfare of trumpets from the watchtower and steeples, a signal reserved for the most distinguished guests. More than two thousand fans mobbed Luther's small horse-drawn cart, and it took him more than an hour to travel from the city gates to the inn where he would stay during the hearing. Papal officials were disgusted by the fawning crowds. "When he alighted a priest threw his arms round him, touched his garments three times with his hand, and went away exulting as if he had handled a relic of the greatest of saints," complained Girolamo Aleandro, one of the pope's assistants. "I expect it will soon be said he works miracles!"[14]

For someone so critical of what he considered to be idolatry of the pope, Luther didn't seem to mind the attention when it was directed at him.

When he appeared in a meeting room in the bishop's palace the next morning, Luther came face-to-face with a towering stack of his books, pamphlets, and essays. The monk, who was dressed in his normal Augustinian habit, his tonsure recently shaven, was asked whether the books were authored by him and, if so, if he wished to retract any of them. Surprisingly, Luther did not offer an answer right away, but instead asked for time to consider, despite the fact that he had known about the hearing for weeks.

One wonders if the request for extra time was indicative of cold feet. Perhaps Luther had second thoughts about the immense decision he was about to make. Considering what a tormented monk he had been, always second-guessing himself, always fearing he was doing the wrong thing, one would assume there was something woven into his psychology that would have allowed for the shadow of a doubt, especially in the case of excommunication when the consequence—eternal damnation, according to the Church—was so high. On the other hand, perhaps Luther's request for more time was simply a tactical strategy aimed at heightening the drama and suspense of the moment. We can't know for sure what Luther's thoughts were that day or why he delayed answering the question he'd known was coming. What we do know is that twenty-four hours later, Luther entered the hearing room, stood before the crowd, and stated his answer with conviction.

The room that day was oppressively hot and packed so full only the emperor was allowed a seat. Luther later recalled that he and everyone else were sweating so profusely and were so uncomfortable that someone suggested he answer the questions in German only, to abbreviate the proceedings, but Luther insisted on replying in both Latin and German. Johann von der Ecken, who was leading the hearing, reiterated the question he had asked Luther the morning prior: Did he or did he not retract his writings, and please, he urged Luther, answer succinctly, "without horns or teeth."[15] Luther replied:

> Unless I am convinced by the testimony of the Scriptures or by clear reason (for I do not trust either in the pope or in councils alone since it is well known that they have often erred and contradicted themselves), I am bound by the Scriptures I have quoted and my conscience is captive to the Word of God. I cannot and I will not retract anything, since it is neither safe nor right to go against conscience. I cannot do otherwise, here I stand, may God help me, Amen.[16]

In a word, no, Luther would not retract a single sentence. Neither the pope nor the Church nor the threat of eternal damnation could convince him otherwise. Luther would stake both his earthly and his eternal life on *sola gratia*—on grace alone.

The crowd erupted in chaos. A member of the emperor's staff reported that as he left the room, Luther "turned to his friends [and] raised his two arms in the gesture of a victorious knight."[17] He also noted that a group of Spanish courtiers in the room jeered, "To the fire! To the fire!" as Luther exited.[18] The next morning Luther received written confirmation from Charles V. "It is certain that a single friar errs in his opinion which is against all of Christendom," the emperor wrote. "I regret having delayed so long to proceed against this Luther and his false doctrine. I am determined to proceed against him as a notorious heretic."[19]

The emperor made a valid point. Think, for a moment, about the monumental step Luther took in single-handedly attempting to subvert and overthrow one thousand years of Christian history. It was, literally, one man standing against all of Christendom. One can hardly begin to fathom the nerve required to stand firm behind those eight simple but radical words: "I cannot and I will not retract anything." Who was Martin Luther to think he could take on the institution of the Roman Catholic Church? Who was Martin Luther to think he was the one person, in the entire history of the Church, to interpret the Word of God correctly, to conclude that those before him had erred? Depending on how you look at it, it was either an act of astounding arrogance . . . or of great faith. Or perhaps a combination of both.

Officially excommunicated and branded a heretic, Martin Luther was "captured" in the forest near Eisenach by a band of horsemen sent by Frederick the Wise to usher Luther into safe hiding. Late on the evening of May 4, 1521, he stepped into a small room deep within Wartburg Castle, which stood high above the walled city of Eisenach. Over the following weeks, holed up in the castle, "drunk with leisure . . . reading the Bible in Greek and Hebrew,"[20] Luther grew a beard and long hair to cover his tonsure and began to refer to himself as "Junker George" (Knight George).

Luther's "sabbatical" lasted just ten months. He returned to Wittenberg against his protector Elector Frederick's wishes in March of 1522, still wearing a full, black beard and dressed in knight's clothing. Luther settled into his old residence—the Augustinian monastery known as the Black Cloister—and within three days was back preaching, dressed in black clerical robes, his hair shorn into the monk's tonsure. It was almost as if the Reformer had never left.

7

The Risks of Freedom

Historians are not certain how Katharina and her fellow nuns first heard about Martin Luther or how they gained access to his radical writings. After all, the nuns had little connection with the outside world. Two gatekeepers kept the keys to the main gate of the convent, and few people had permission to enter Marienthron. Even visitors who were allowed in had little to no contact with the nuns, and those who did speak to the nuns did so from the other side of a finely meshed grate, through which a book or even a pamphlet could not have easily been passed.

One visitor who might have smuggled in bits and pieces of Luther's writings was Wolfgang von Zeschau, the former prior of the Augustinian monastery at Grimma, less than two miles away.[1] After reading Luther's writings on monasticism, von Zeschau resigned as prior in 1522, withdrew from the order, and became a hospital chaplain in Grimma. He knew Luther from their days together at the Augustinian monastery in Erfurt. He also had two nieces, Veronika and Margarete von Zeschau, who lived at Marienthron. The fact that Veronika and Margarete were relatives would have given von Zeschau easier access into the convent, although there is no proof that it was he who made Luther's writings available to the nuns.

The other possible courier was Leonhard Koppe, a former city councilman in the town of Torgau, thirty-four miles away.[2] A merchant, and one of Luther's close friends, Koppe regularly delivered herring and other goods to the convent and could have smuggled in some of Luther's writings, or at least brief summaries of his seminal pieces, hidden amid the goods.

There is no proof that either man slipped Luther's words into the nuns' hands, nor do we know for sure which works they read, or if they read any at all. But it stands to reason that Luther's writings, particularly his statements about monastic vows, reached Katharina and her peers at some point and made a dramatic impact on them. "If some of the Marienthron nuns, including Katharina, came into possession of only one scrap of Luther's forceful condemnation of monasticism, his rousing battle cry against the orders and their vows," suggest Rudolf and Marilynn Markwald, "this would have set the stage for their next step: escape from Nimbschen."[3]

All That Glitters Is Not Gold

Luther's ten months in Wartburg Castle are often recalled as the period in which he launched his most prodigious literary achievement: the translation of the Bible into German. But he also wrote a lesser-known work in that small room perched high above Eisenach, a treatise that would radically impact Katharina, who was living her own cloistered existence less than 150 miles away. Luther's *Judgment on Monastic Vows*, published in Wittenberg in 1522, is not his most famous Reformation work, but perhaps it is the text that most profoundly influenced his future wife. In it Luther specifically attacked the vows of chastity, poverty, and obedience that nuns and monks made upon entry into the cloistered life. He argued that these vows were not based in Scripture and were opposed to grace-based salvation (in Luther's opinion the vows smacked of a works-based understanding of salvation), Christian freedom, God's commandments, and reason. "They teach that this kind of life, and all that goes to make it up, is the good life, and that by practicing it men become good and are saved," Luther wrote. "This is sacrilege, godlessness, and blasphemy. It is lies they have trumped up. It is delusion, hypocrisy, and satanic invention."[4]

The vow of chastity especially irritated Luther. He stated that only one in one thousand could truly and joyfully live a celibate life without any impure thoughts or actions (later he changed that estimate to one in one hundred thousand).[5] Women—including nuns, he argued—were not excluded from temptations of the flesh. "Unless she is in a high and unusual state of grace," he wrote, "a young woman can do without a man as little as she can do without eating, drinking, sleeping, or other natural requirements. Nor can a man do without a woman. The reason for this is that to conceive children is as deeply implanted in nature as eating and drinking are. The person who wants to prevent this and keep nature from doing what it wants to do and must do is simply preventing nature from being nature, fire from burning, water from wetting, and man from eating, drinking, or sleeping."[6] Luther believed that with the exception of rare cases, neither men nor women could keep a vow of chastity. They might succeed at honoring the vow in body, but they certainly couldn't succeed in thought.

We don't have a written account of Katharina's reaction to Luther in her own words, but the writings of her contemporaries offer insight into what she may have been thinking. For instance, in a 1528 letter to her cousins Lords George and Heinrich, Dukes of Saxony, Lady Ursula, Countess of Munsterberg (who actually lived with the Luthers for a few months after she fled monastic life), listed sixty-nine Christian reasons to explain why she abandoned the convent at Freiberg.

"Faith alone is our salvation," Ursula argued. "We have allowed ourselves to be glorified as brides of Christ and let ourselves even be lifted over other Christians who we have regarded unworthy."[7] Ursula considered the vows of chastity, poverty, and obedience to be idolatry—"the works of our hands"—and directly opposed to her baptismal vows in which she had promised to have no other gods.[8] In the convent, she argued, "We bind ourselves to obedience, but to people rather than God."[9] Like Luther, Ursula also suggested that true chastity was nearly impossible to achieve. "No one can deny that chastity is a quality that God alone can create in human hearts and bodies; how then, are we so arrogant as to pledge and sacrifice what is God's [to give] and not ours?" she wrote.[10] Ursula concluded her letter with a powerful appeal. "If we are put in such a place where we cannot serve anybody but are very vexed, is it not advisable to leave such a place?" she reasoned. "For who knows what crushes each heart? Even here, the saying comforts: All that glitters is not gold. Who would look for such a great danger under such a neat appearance of human holiness? We would not have believed it ourselves had we not been so deeply stuck in it."[11]

Ursula's words are a powerful example of the unrest many nuns and monks experienced as Luther's writings spread from convent to convent and monastery to monastery. Although we know Katharina didn't read Ursula's actual words before her own escape (the countess wrote her letter five years after Katharina left the monastic life), one can't help but wonder if Katharina experienced a similar "crushed heart" during her years in Marienthron. Might she have considered herself "deeply stuck" in the monastic life as well? Might some of the doubts and questions Ursula expressed in her letter to her cousins have occupied Katharina's mind too? At the very least she must have been intrigued by the hints trickling into the convent, rumors about a bold new voice.

The nuns were undoubtedly told Luther was scandalous and heretical, and as his teachings veered further from Rome, the convents must have restricted access to any news related to the Reformer. For women cut off from a world that was moving forward without them, snippets of news, particularly forbidden news, must have been tantalizing. Katharina, by now in her twelfth or thirteenth year in the cloister, must have initially viewed Luther's reforms as a curiosity, then as a danger, and ultimately as an opportunity to escape a life she hadn't chosen for herself. One can imagine both fantasies and fears would have preoccupied her during her many hours of quiet solitude, as she envisioned the dangers she would face in both escaping from the convent and in attempting to build a secular life beyond it. As bits and pieces of Luther's teachings turned her entire understanding of faith, God, and religion upside down, Katharina might have also wrestled with spiritual doubts and questions.

Yet despite what we don't know about Katharina's thoughts in the months and weeks leading up to her escape, her radical decision to flee the convent in the dark of night tells us one thing for sure: at some point Katharina realized she was living a sham, a "neat appearance of human holiness," as Ursula so succinctly put it. Like Ursula, Katharina began to understand that all that glittered was not gold. Perhaps she had understood it all along.

If Not a Nun, Then What?

As Luther's writings against monasticism spread like wildfire, convents and monasteries began to close across Germany. In general, there was a cultural shift in how monastic roles, and particularly those of nuns, were seen by laypeople. Prior to the Reformation, a significant part of a nun's daily responsibilities had revolved around praying for and remembering the dead. A nun typically recited the Office of the Dead (a litany of psalms, other Scripture readings, and formal prayers) and prayed for souls stranded in purgatory as part of her daily duties. At one point, the fees local townspeople paid for nuns to mark the death anniversaries of loved ones with prayers and songs comprised a significant portion of a convent's income.[12] As Luther's teachings on salvation through grace alone spread, however, laypeople began to view the monastics with skepticism. They accused the nuns of selfishness and saw them as following human rather than biblical dictates. This was a "fundamental shift in mentality from the Middle Ages, when the work of the nuns was seen as helping bring salvation for the entire community," and the nuns themselves were seen as intercessors for the souls of all. "Now their praying was seen as a selfish act that brought no benefit for society as a whole."[13]

Still, not every nun was as eager as Ursula of Munsterberg and Katharina von Bora to abandon the monastic life. In fact, many nuns openly resisted the upheaval, choosing instead to honor their vows and remain cloistered behind the convent walls. Nuns constituted a significant portion of the female population, as much as 5 to 10 percent of the total population in major German cities.[14] As Merry Wiesner notes, Reformation history books have long reported the closing of monastic houses, but until recently focused only on the monks who left the cloistered life to become pastors in the new Protestant churches. What these histories didn't explore was the effect of the closures on women "for whom there was no place in the Protestant clergy."[15]

Wiesner makes an important point. For women, especially the abbesses who oversaw the administration of the convents, the monastic life was one of the few realms of female independence and authority. The abbesses of the larger convents controlled vast amounts of property and were politically connected to the ruling nobility of the area. Although each convent was required to have a priest available to say Mass and hear confessions, all other administrative duties and much of the spiritual counseling of novices and others were carried out by women. Many of the cloistered nuns undoubtedly valued their positions in the convent and the work they did there and were not eager to relinquish it for a life of markedly less importance. "They realized, too, that as women they had no position in the Lutheran church outside the abbey," observes Wiesner. "Former monks could become pastors in the Protestant churches, but for former nuns the only role available was that of pastor's wife, an unthinkable decrease in status for a woman of noble or patrician birth."[16]

There were also the older nuns to consider. Matrimony may have been a viable solution for nuns of marriageable age, but who would want to marry an older former nun, one past child-bearing age? And what about the women who did feel a true inclination toward the celibate life? Where would such women live when the convents closed? Johannes Bugenhagen, the pastor who eventually married Luther and Katharina, devised what he considered an appropriate solution for such women: they could live in their parents' homes as servants. "If some parents or close relatives have a young girl who has been destined by God to remain a virgin, they should keep the girl by them (at home), so that she can help with the household and work, or help oversee the house, as she is bound by duty to do," Bugenhagen wrote. "And it is the duty of the parents or the relatives to teach her and to keep her for that."[17] Clearly he hadn't considered the fact that a nun's family might refuse to allow her to return home, even to live out the rest of her life as a spinster servant. Or that a young woman might not want to live out the rest of her life in servitude.

Ultimately the convents became some of the most vocal and resolute opponents of the Protestant Reformation. For example, when Duke Ernst of Brunswick (who was Elector Frederick the Wise's nephew, an ally of Luther, and a champion of the Protestant Reformation) began to encourage monasteries and convents to disband in the 1520s, almost all of the male monasteries agreed to hand over their property to the duke with very little resistance. The nuns, on the other hand, declined. In Walsrode and Medingen, Germany, the nuns even refused to listen to the Protestant preachers the duke sent to the convents. Instead, they locked the doors and took refuge in the chapel choir. Duke Ernst made a special trip to the convents to plead with the nuns personally, until, exasperated, he ordered the gates forced open and a hole blasted into the choir for the Protestant preacher to speak through.[18] In the town of Lune, the nuns burned old felt slippers in an attempt to drive out the preacher with smoke. They also sang loudly during his sermons and, when ordered to be quiet, demonstrated their rebellion by pointedly ignoring him and reciting the rosary under their breath instead.[19]

In 1525, when Nuremberg's city council ordered all the cloisters to close, four of the six male houses in the city immediately turned the monks onto the streets and shut their doors, but both female houses refused to follow the council's orders.[20] The more the nuns failed to heed the council's demands, the more pressure the council exerted, denying the nuns access to confession and Catholic communion and making it difficult for their servants to purchase food. The townspeople picketed outside the enclosure, singing profane songs, lobbing rocks over the convent walls, and threatening to burn the buildings to the ground.

Caritas Pirckheimer, abbess of the St. Clara convent in Nuremberg, vividly described in her memoir the ways in which three of her young nuns were violently dragged out of the convent by their parents. "The children cried that they did not want to leave the pious, holy convent, that they were absolutely not in hell, but if they broke out of it they would descend into the abyss of hell," she wrote. "The three children screamed in a single voice, 'We don't want to be freed of our vows, rather we want to keep our vows to God with his help.'"[21] The scene at the convent gate became violent, with four adults dragging each of the three young women, "two pulling in front and two pushing from behind."[22] One mother "threatened her daughter that if she did not walk before her she would push her down the stairs to the pulpit," Pirckheimer recounted. "She threatened to throw her on the floor so hard that she would bounce."[23] By the time the carriages pulled away from the convent with the weeping, screaming girls locked inside, a great crowd had gathered "in such numbers as if a poor soul were being led to his execution."[24] Pirckheimer said later she didn't know what had happened to the "poor children among the vicious wolves."[25]

In the end, the council failed to persuade Caritas Pirckheimer and the nuns of St. Clara to renounce their vows and abandon the convent. Three nuns were forced by their parents to leave the convent against their will, but only one nun left of her own accord; the rest remained. Although the convent no longer accepted novices, and the nuns who remained were not allowed to practice Catholic Mass and confession, St. Clara remained open until the last member died in 1596, more than sixty years after Pirckheimer's own death in 1532.[26]

Another nun, Katherine Rem, penned an angry letter in 1523 to her brother Bernhart, whose daughter Veronica was also in the same convent in Augsburg. "If you don't come in kinship, stay out," Rem wrote. "If you want to straighten us out, then we don't want your [message] at all. You may not send us such things any more. We will not accept them."[27] Bernhart had given one of his sister's earlier letters to the local printer and had it published, which had angered Katherine. "I see that you are angry," he responded. "Whoever has anger and envy is still in the world. . . . Your little human discoveries and trust in your own works, habits, convent, fasting, and such things will soon fall away. . . . For one does not presume to buy God's grace with spiritual simony. . . . And it is worthless straw, whatever one makes of it."[28] Katherine and Veronica ignored Bernhart's disdainful opinions and remained in the convent.

Caritas Pirckheimer, Katherine and Veronica Rem, and many other nuns like them refused to be swayed by the Protestant reforms sweeping across the land. Clearly many of these nuns truly felt called by God to the monastic life, while others were unwilling to relinquish the unexpected and rare autonomy they enjoyed behind the cloister walls. This is something Katharina surely considered as she weighed the benefits and challenges of abandoning the convent.

Obstacles to Freedom

The decision to abandon the monastic life was not a simple one, especially for women, who had far less opportunity outside the cloister walls than men and shockingly few rights in sixteenth-century Europe in general. As was noted earlier, single women were rarely granted city citizenship, which was based on one's ability to work, own property, and support the military. Citizenship fees increased as many towns experienced economic decline in the sixteenth century, making it even less likely for women, who were typically poorer than men, to afford citizenship.[29] In Nuremberg, for example, women made up 13 percent of the new citizens in the 1460s. That percentage dropped to 4.6 percent in the 1500s and to less than 1 percent by the 1550s.[30] Laws forbade unmarried women to move into cities, required widows to reside with one of their male children, and increasingly required unmarried women to be appointed a guardian to manage their financial and legal affairs. Once a nun left the convent, the city council either assigned her a guardian or transferred economic control to her new husband. Even if the nun left the convent with money, those funds were turned over to her guardian, new husband, or family members. A former nun would not have been allowed to sign her own name as a financially independent person.[31]

"The standard opinion was that women had to be taken care of by some male authority, whether a father, a husband, a son or the church," explains Protestant Reformation historian Amy Leonard. "If none of these were available, the council [in Strasbourg] decided in the late fifteenth century, a guardian must be assigned to handle all of a woman's public business. In particular, she could not carry out any financial transactions herself, but rather had to defer to her male custodian."[32] This was a significant issue for Katharina, who, having been virtually abandoned by her family, did not have a male relative or guardian she could turn to for support.

In short, virtually the only way a nun could become a citizen (and thus have any social, financial, or legal power) was to marry, which meant, of course, that she was no longer a nun. "A priest could be both a citizen AND a priest, but a nun could not be a citizen and a nun."[33] The legal status of a woman depended on whether she was unmarried, married, or widowed, whereas adult males were generally treated as a single legal category.[34] As she considered the possibility of fleeing the convent, Katharina undoubtedly played out these scenarios in her head. Her father had abdicated his responsibility for her the day he transferred her to Marienthron. Aside from her confessor, she hadn't spoken to a man in years, so marriage prospects were slim to none. And she didn't know anyone who could serve as her male guardian. Katharina's options were limited, at best.

Employment was yet another area fraught with difficulty for women during this time. While it was recognized and accepted by society that some women had to work for wages (for example, women of the middle or lower classes), this work was often viewed as a temporary measure until the women could attain, or return to, a married state.[35] The kinds of paid employment available to women were also highly regulated by city and state laws, which often detailed exactly which professions were considered acceptable for women. For example, a sixteenth-century Nuremberg ordinance listed female tailors, shopkeepers, money changers, innkeepers, wine handlers, and market women as appropriate positions for middle-class women.[36] Still, even a married woman who pursued these acceptable employment opportunities couldn't sign a business contract without the agreement of her husband (although married women often gained the right to conduct business on a regular basis by appealing to the appropriate governing body).[37]

Of course, mulling over possible employment options would have been an exercise in futility for Katharina. As a noblewoman, she would not have been allowed to consider even temporary paid employment as, say, a shopkeeper or innkeeper. Women of noble birth like Katharina didn't work for pay, even if they didn't have a cent to their names.

Marriage was increasingly the best means of survival for most women, as unmarried women during the late Middle Ages and early modern period were treated with outright hostility and suspicion. Women in general were viewed as intellectually and emotionally inferior to men, and unmarried women in particular were seen as a menacing threat. "Sweeping generalities about women's nature were made not only by moralists and preachers, but also humanists and writers of popular satire," observes Wiesner. "Many of these expressed or reinforced the notion that women suffered from uncontrollable sexuality and lacked the ability to reason."[38] Because it was believed that a woman's libido increased with age, older unmarried women were considered particularly threatening. Seen as potential seductresses who were willing to go to any lengths to satisfy their sexual desires, they were frequently accused as witches (the devil was believed to promise sexual satisfaction) and almost always viewed with suspicion.[39]

Women were seen as threatening in part because relatively little was known about their physiology and sexuality; what was unknown was considered mysterious and therefore frightening. For example, according to popular beliefs of the time, a menstruating woman could rust iron, sour wine, spoil meat, and dull a knife with her touch, a glance, or even her mere presence.[40] On the other hand, menopause, and even the cessation of menstruation during pregnancy, was considered dangerous for women because it was thought to leave impure blood within a woman's body, which could harden into a tumor, or compel excess blood to run into her brain, which would lead to overheating.[41]

Not only was the health of postmenopausal women considered at risk, the women themselves, particularly those who were unmarried, were considered dangerous to others. Often depicted as witches with an insatiable sex drive that drove them to seek demon lovers, postmenopausal women were thought to emit invisible vapors from their mouths which could cause a nursing mother's milk to dry up and children and animals to become ill.[42] Luther himself believed the common folklore about witches, and once recounted a story about his mother, who blamed a female neighbor for cursing her young son and causing his death. Luther remembers his mother wailing, "That wicked witch, our neighbor, has murdered my poor child."[43]

The foundation for understanding female sexuality and human sexuality in general was always male sexuality. For example, female reproductive organs were often thought of simply as the male genitals pushed inside the body—the sixteenth-century anatomist Vesalius depicted the uterus as an inverted penis—and several female anatomical parts didn't even have their own unique names. Since they were thought to be congruent with a corresponding male organ, they were simply called by that same name.[44]

The fact that female reproductive organs were contained inside the body was considered a sign of female inferiority, a result of a woman's colder, damper nature, which hadn't generated the heat necessary to push the organs out.[45] Sex manuals from the early modern period depicted female sexuality negatively, and this negative view was supported by contemporary religion, which saw sexuality as base and corrupt, originating from Adam and Eve's fall rather than as part of God's original plan for creation. Women were seen as more sexual than men because they were associated with Eve, who was the first to succumb to the serpent's temptations and eat from the Tree of the Knowledge of Good and Evil.

As open as he was about human sexuality, Luther subscribed to popular beliefs about female sexuality and its dangerous lure. "For girls, too, are aware of this evil [lust] and if they spend time in the company of young men, they turn the hearts of these young men in various directions to entice them to love, especially if the youths are outstanding because of their good looks and strength of body," he wrote in his *Lectures on Genesis*. "There it is often more difficult for the latter to withstand such enticement than to resist their own lusts."[46] It was one thing for men to wrestle with their own lust, Luther suggested, but to be confronted with the enticement of female sexuality was a worse and far more threatening situation. In short, a woman, simply by being in a man's company, was to blame for his lust.

The Church even regarded sex within marriage as a sin and considered the best possible marriage an unconsummated one. (This belief led to the popular medieval idea that Jesus was birthed out of Mary's ear, so as not to defile himself with passage through the birth canal like a common man.[47]) Initially Luther's thoughts about sexual intercourse within marriage for reproduction purposes only aligned with those of the Church. However, he began to shift his perspective in 1519 with his *Sermon on the Estate of Marriage*, in which he concluded that God allows desire within marriage—even desire not intended for the purpose of procreation—as long as "one seriously tries to moderate that desire and does not make a manure-heap and a sow-bath out of it."[48] By the time he published his 1520 treatise *To the Christian Nobility of the German Nation*, he was firm in his convictions, stating that the pope should "not have the power to prohibit [sex], just as he does not have the power to prohibit eating, drinking, natural secretion or becoming fat."[49]

This understanding and perception of female sexuality and society's view of women in general meant that as an unmarried woman approaching middle age, Katharina von Bora would have been considered a threat to the accepted social structure of the time. As a convent escapee and a former nun, she also would have been viewed by conservative Church authorities and others as an overly sexual woman, someone who had likely fled her cloistered existence and abandoned her vows of chastity in order to satisfy irrepressible sexual desires. She might have even been suspected a witch, an accusation that, as we'll see in the next chapter, would have posed a grave threat to her life.

Katharina knew she would face serious obstacles in her bid for freedom. Despite the fact that she had lived a sheltered existence behind cloister walls for nearly her entire life, she was well aware of the challenges she would face as an unmarried woman outside the convent. As a member of the landed gentry, she knew paid employment would not be an option. Yet with no dowry, she also understood that finding a suitable husband would be challenging, if not impossible. Katharina knew that her family would not provide for her, yet she also realized that as a single woman, she would be viewed with suspicion and perhaps even ostracized by society.

Still, something drove her to take the risk. One can imagine how Luther's words would have impacted Katharina, whose life up to this point had been entirely determined by others. As a woman forced into the convent against her will, Katharina would have been rocked to the core by Luther's treatises against monasticism. "They lose this life and the next," he wrote, "they are forced into hell on earth and hell in the other world. . . . You bring them to this point for the sake of your accursed property."[50] From the day of her birth, events and circumstances over which she'd had no say and no control had determined her life's path. Born female to noble but poor parents, she had endured the early death of her mother and the loss of all familial connections when she was placed in the convent school far from home. From there she'd been forced into the nunnery and required to take the vows of chastity, poverty, and obedience; after that, marriage and motherhood were out of the question.

In Luther's impassioned words, Katharina saw herself. Her identity—her past, present, and future—was defined by the vows she'd proclaimed at the altar at age sixteen. These vows were the foundation upon which Katharina's entire life and self-identity revolved, and now one man, a renegade monk, had questioned their validity. In doing so Martin Luther undoubtedly prompted Katharina to question not only her identity and calling as a nun but also perhaps her life and faith as a whole.

Until now, Katharina hadn't had any options; her life had been laid out, determined for her by others. Luther's powerful words cracked open a door, allowing the possibility of another path—a path Katharina might discover and travel herself.

8

Escape

Each of the dozen or so nuns waited alone in her cell, nervous, perhaps even terrified as she sat poised on the edge of her bed in the dark. Escaping from a convent was a punishable offense, and it was a particularly egregious crime in Duke George's Saxony, the territory where Marienthron was located. Though the women had weighed the pros and cons of their decision carefully, the tension and anticipation must have held them rigid with fear as they waited, knowing one tiny mistake could destroy their carefully orchestrated plan.

Initially the nuns had taken a conservative approach in their bid for freedom. Most of them had penned letters to their families, requesting to be released from Marienthron and allowed to return home. Encouraged by Luther's writings, they declared that they were done with the cloistered life, which they now believed to be unnecessary for, and perhaps even a hindrance to, their salvation.

As was expected, the women's families were unwilling to offer any assistance or support. After all, they'd already paid a one-time fee to have their daughters placed in the convent for life; it didn't make financial sense to encourage their release, especially when their dowries had likely been used to support other family members.[1] Many were also afraid of Duke George. A person caught facilitating the abduction of a cloistered nun faced stiff fines and exclusion from court appointments, which were highly sought positions.[2] Nuns were very occasionally allowed to leave the convent, but the official release process was complicated and required a papal dispensation, which was expensive and typically available to only the highest nobility.[3] There is no evidence that Katharina attempted to contact her family. She likely knew her father's answer without even asking.

Ignored by their families, the discontented nuns made a bold move: they turned to Martin Luther himself. Leonhard Koppe, the Torgau merchant who delivered herring and other goods to the convent, carried their letter from Nimbschen to Wittenberg. Moved by their plea, Luther vowed to aid their escape. "For God is not pleased with any worship, unless it comes freely from the heart," he wrote, "and consequently no vow is valid unless it has been made willingly and with love."[4]

It's not known how the escape plan was formulated and communicated to the nuns. In an environment in which silence was rigorously enforced, we can only imagine how stealthily the women collaborated on the details of such a complicated plan. Perhaps notes were passed from nun to nun and kept hidden in the folds of their habits. Maybe they snatched quick bits of conversation while weeding the garden or washing dishes. Perhaps they had a clandestine meeting place, shielded by the trees on the outskirts of the convent grounds. Historians surmise that an older nun by the name of Magdalene von Staupitz, a teacher in the convent (and the sister of Luther's former mentor, Johann von Staupitz), served as the lead contact.[5] Because she often received school supplies from Koppe, she would have known him personally and had regular contact with him. But we don't know how she conveyed the plan to the other nuns or how they worked out the intricate details Koppe couldn't orchestrate. All we know is they succeeded; the plan went off without a hitch.

On the evening of April 4, 1523, the cloistered nuns at Marienthron celebrated Easter eve much like they did every year. They gathered in the church for the Easter vigil service, a time of quiet reflection, meditation, prayer, and Holy Communion, and then made their way outside to the courtyard, where they participated in the consecration of the Easter fire. The Paschal candle, representing the light of Christ, was lit and the flame was passed from woman to woman.

The nuns chose to flee on Easter eve for a reason: it was the one night of the year in which their worship practice diverged from the regular routine. Instead of performing Compline and retiring early as they normally did, the nuns stayed up much later for the lighting of the Paschal fire. Katharina and her peers hoped the abbess and the other nuns would be too distracted by the disruption in their routine to notice any late-night stirring or noise once everyone had retired to bed.

The ritual lighting and passing of the Paschal candle was performed the same way it always was, but for a handful of the nuns gathered in the courtyard that night, an undercurrent of tension and anticipation sparked just below the surface. As the candlelight flickered, bathing the women's faces in a warm glow, the Easter fire they passed from hand to hand symbolized a personal resurrection of sorts—hope for a new beginning and a new life.

Late that night, while the rest of the convent slept soundly after the evening's festivities, a single sharp sound like the crack of a whip pierced the air. It was the signal the nuns had been waiting for all night. Dressed in their white habits and black veils, they fled their cells with just the clothes on their backs and ran silently down the dark halls and outside to where the wagon waited. Details about their escape are so scant, we don't even know for sure how many nuns fled with Katharina that night. In a letter to a friend four days following their escape, Luther mentioned that nine nuns left the Nimbschen cloister.[6] In their biography of Katharina von Bora, the Markwalds cite twelve nuns, nine of whom are mentioned by name.[7] Luther biographer Edith Simon lists eleven nuns by name, noting that two were placed immediately with their families.[8]

The nuns and Koppe evidently kept the details of the escape to themselves and refused to boast about their feat, even after they'd made it to safety. Years later, rumors about the nuns' infamous escape continued to circulate. Long after the convent had fallen into disrepair, some suggested the small window covered in wild grapevines and still visible in the rubble was the window from which Katharina escaped. Others claimed that a silk slipper which was displayed for years at an inn on the convent grounds belonged to Katharina, who had lost it as she fled (modern historians dismiss this story; as a Cistercian nun, Katharina wouldn't have been wearing such a fancy silk slipper).[9] Some speculated the nuns climbed over the garden wall, others insisted they chiseled a hole through the stone, and still others assumed the guard colluded with the nuns and simply unlocked the gate for them to leave. As Katharina von Bora's biographer Ernst Kroker notes, each of these stories is purely speculative.[10] The truth is, there were many ways for the fugitives to escape, and no one knows for sure how the nuns reached the wagon that waited outside the convent walls. That part of Katharina's story is and will probably always remain a mystery.

It was cold that early April night. The nuns huddled together under a tarp on the hard planks as the wagon jolted over the bumpy roads. Rumor has it the women hid in herring barrels, but the more likely scenario is that Koppe simply used his merchant wagon, in which he often carried herring and other goods, to transport the nuns under cover. The women held their breath as the wagon lurched beyond the boundaries of the convent's land and skirted along the borders of Duke George's territory.

Even without the fabled herring barrels, the escape was nothing short of miraculous, says Kroker. No one had revealed their secret; there'd been no traitor among them; none of the many letters that had passed back and forth between the nuns and Koppe had been intercepted; and anywhere between nine and twelve nuns had managed to sneak out of their cells undetected on Easter eve and escape from the convent unimpeded.[11] As dawn's first light began to streak the sky, the wagon made its way into Torgau to the sound of church bells ringing in Easter morning. The nuns had made it; they were free.

Jilted

In Torgau, the women had a bite to eat, rested a bit, and exchanged their habits and veils for secular clothes provided by the local pastor. Imagine for a moment how odd it must have felt for Katharina to don the dress and head covering of a typical sixteenth-century German woman after almost twenty years of wearing only the plain habit and veil. One wonders: Did she feel vulnerable and exposed, or was there a sense of liberation and excitement in the air as the women dressed in the borrowed clothes, the fabric smooth and unfamiliar against their skin, their waistlines and bodices accentuated, free of the bulky, shapeless robes? We don't have a description of the hand-me-down dresses the nuns wore that first day of freedom, but regardless of the quality or the detailing of the cloth, the clothes must have been more elaborate than anything they had worn in a long time.

On Monday, the day after Easter, the nuns traveled the thirty-one miles to Wittenberg. With a population of 2,500 people, the town would have seemed like a booming metropolis to Katharina. As the horse-drawn wagon jostled over the city's cobblestone streets, she took in the sights: the Elbe River on one side of the city and the moat on the other; the marketplace, noisy and bustling with merchants and shoppers; the Castle Church, where Martin Luther had presumably nailed his *Ninety-five Theses* six years before; and the Church of St. Mary, where, little could she have imagined at the time, Katharina would recite her marriage vows just over two years from that very day.

A short distance from the church the wagon stopped in front of a formidable stone building. The complex was known as the Black Cloister, the driver informed the nuns, and at one time had housed Wittenberg's Augustinian monks. In the wake of Luther's reforms, however, most of the monks had moved on, leaving only two remaining in residence: an elderly monk and Martin Luther himself. As the wagon drew to a halt, Luther stepped from the Black Cloister to greet the nuns whom he had helped escape.

On April 8 Luther had casually mentioned to a friend, "I heard yesterday that nine nuns have left cloister Nimpschau, their prison, among whom are the two Sessatzers, and the Staupitz."[12] He reported this tidbit of information as if it was a piece of unfamiliar news or gossip (along with misspelling Nimbschen), which we know it was not, as Luther helped to orchestrate the nuns' escape. Perhaps this was Luther's attempt to distance himself from the crime, at least with those outside his inner circle. Maybe he intentionally played ignorant to throw those suspicious of his involvement off his trail. When Koppe and the nuns arrived on his doorstep, however, Luther graciously welcomed them, praised them for their courage, and set about finding temporary quarters for the refugees. A few days after the nuns' arrival in Wittenberg, however, the reality of the situation set in.

Clearly the women did not have the skills to support themselves, and most were rejected by their families, who refused to accommodate them. Luther expressed frustration and resentment over the fact that he had been burdened with the nuns' care. "I ask that you, too, would do a work of love and beg for some money from among the rich courtiers for me, and perhaps give some yourself," he pleaded with his friend, George Spalatin, "so I can get food for the refugees for at least eight or fourteen days and also some dresses, since they have no shoes or clothing."[13] Luther learned the hard way that advocating on paper for the closing of monasteries and cloisters was one thing; the reality of dealing with it personally was a much different story.

Immediately after helping Katharina and her fellow nuns escape from Marienthron, Luther continued to call for the widespread closing of convents. His introduction to a memoir written by Florentina von Oberweimar, who escaped from a

Cistercian convent in Eisleben in 1524, for instance, was filled with passionate rhetoric against both the monastic life and the families who forced that existence upon their daughters. "Behold, dear people, what poisonous, evil, bitter, false, and lying folk the nuns are, whereas they want to be the holy and tender brides of Christ," Luther wrote in 1524. "Woe unto you now and forever, lords and princes, parents and relatives, who push your children, your relatives, or your neighbors, body and soul, into such murderous graves or allow them to remain therein."[14] For a long time Luther considered himself a liberator of cloistered women. Once, when accused of being a thief of women because he'd helped to plan the Nimbschen nuns' stealthy midnight escape, he responded, "I freely answer, yes, a blessed robber am I." But, he was quick to explain, he believed he had freed the poor souls from jail and human tyranny and set them on the right path.[15]

As time went on, however, Luther's rhetoric softened, and his approach to the widespread closing of convents became much more conservative, most likely as a result of the hardships he had witnessed among the nuns who had fled Marienthron without a backup plan. "I'm pleased to hear that the remaining nuns at Nimbschen have put aside their cloister habits. But first they have to decide what they want to do when they leave the nunnery so they do not regret their withdrawal," he cautioned Spalatin in 1534, upon hearing that the remaining Marienthron nuns had decided to leave the cloister. "Unless they are assured of having a future spouse or of a place where they are permanently taken care of, I would not advise their leaving."[16] Luther hadn't fully realized the burden of responsibility that came with the closing of convents when he'd so cavalierly advocated for the release of all cloistered nuns in his earlier writings. Now that he'd personally lived through the reality of finding support for the Nimbschen nuns, he suggested a more cautious plan.

Wittenberg's Matchmaker

Despite the fact that Luther and Koppe endeavored to be discreet about the nuns' escape, the women quickly became the talk of Wittenberg. "A wagon load of vestal virgins has just come to town all more eager for marriage than for life. May God give them husbands lest worse befall," one young man wrote to a friend.[17] Luther's friends Nikolaus von Amsdorf, a theology professor at the University of Wittenberg, and George Spalatin joked between themselves: "They're beautiful, dignified, and all from the aristocracy," wrote von Amsdorf. "The oldest among them . . . I have appointed for you, my dear brother, to be her husband. If you want a younger one, however, then you are to have the choice among the most beautiful."[18] All joking aside, marriage was the best and most viable option for the former nuns, and for a time, Luther took on the role of Wittenberg's matchmaker, writing letters to potential suitors and helping to arrange engagements for the nuns who hadn't been taken in by their families.

Certainly not an old maid by early modern standards (compared to the High Middle Ages, when girls were legally allowed to be married at age twelve and boys at age fourteen[19]), at age twenty-four, Katharina was considered to be at her prime marriageable age, and it wasn't long before she had a suitor. Hieronymus Baumgartner of Nuremberg was an alumnus of the University of Wittenberg and a friend of both Luther and Melanchthon. Baumgartner visited Wittenberg often and became acquainted with Katharina, who at the time was staying with Philipp and Elsa Reichenbach, who were friends with the Baumgartner family. Rumors swirled around town as Katharina and Hieronymus were seen together more and more frequently. Katharina adored Baumgartner, but it was not one-sided; he reciprocated her affection.[20] When he traveled back to Nuremberg, everyone, including Katharina, assumed Baumgartner would return to Wittenberg with his parents' blessing and a promise of marriage.

Katharina's hopes were dashed when weeks and then months passed with no word from her suitor. Even Luther intervened on her behalf, advising Baumgartner in an October 1524 letter: "If you intend marrying Katherine von Bora, make haste before she is given to some one else. She has not yet got over her love for you. I wish that you two were married."[21] Still, there was no reply until the spring of 1525, when Baumgartner announced his engagement to fourteen-year-old Sibylle Dichtel von Tutzing, who brought a sizable dowry to the marriage.[22] Clearly Baumgartner's parents, themselves nobility, had considered a runaway nun with no dowry an unacceptable bride for their son.

The breakup was a huge blow to Katharina. Not only was she heartbroken, she was also nearly out of options. Katharina had moved in with Lucas and Barbara Cranach, who lived in a huge, three-story house on the corner of Market and Schlossstrasse streets in Wittenberg. The fifty-year-old Lucas Cranach the Elder was an influential man and one of the wealthiest in the city: a city councilor, a good friend of Luther, and, most importantly, the court painter to Elector Frederick the Wise. He also operated a pharmacy, a wineshop, and a print shop; as Luther's publisher, he made a great deal of money from the sale of Luther's German New Testament and other writings.

Lucas and his wife, Barbara, had been very kind to Katharina—taking her in, providing clothing, food, and housing for her, standing in as her family when Katharina had no family to claim as her own. Yet the truth was, Katharina was penniless, and worse, she could not stay with the Cranachs forever. They had been exceedingly gracious and generous, but they were not Katharina's blood relatives and could not be expected to provide for her for the rest of her life.

Nearly two years had passed since Katharina had escaped from the convent. All of the nuns who had fled Marienthron with her had either returned to their families or married. Katharina was the only one who had not found a sustainable living situation, and her options grew more limited by the day.

A Bold Proposal

Luther had one last idea—one more eligible bachelor he hoped would make a suitable match for Katharina. Kaspar Glatz was a doctor of theology and pastor of a parish in nearby Orlamünde. Intelligent, resourceful, a man of faith, and, most importantly, available, Glatz seemed to be the perfect suitor for Katharina . . . with one glaring exception: she didn't like him. Katharina had heard Glatz was stubborn, opinionated, argumentative, and miserly. (These accusations largely proved to be true; Glatz later had to be removed from his congregation in Orlamünde because he argued so much with his parishioners.)[23] She refused to have anything to do with Glatz and wouldn't be swayed from her decision. Instead, she asked Nikolaus von Amsdorf to persuade Luther to abandon his plan. When von Amsdorf asked Katharina why a man of Glatz's standing—a doctor, professor, and pastor—was not good enough for her, Katharina responded with a bold declaration: she would not refuse either von Amsdorf or even Luther himself, should either seek her hand in marriage, but Glatz she absolutely would not accept.[24]

Katharina must have realized the huge risk she took in refusing to accept Glatz as her husband. She was essentially out of options, and she knew it. She did not have the means to support herself. She could not continue to stay with the Cranachs indefinitely. She could not, or would not, return to the convent. Yet Katharina not only refused to settle for a husband she didn't like, she did something virtually unheard of at the time: she essentially asked Luther (and von Amsdorf as well—it apparently didn't matter which of them said yes) to marry her. "How much considered effort did it take in those days to do that?" wonders German biographer Eva Zeller. "How much excessive daring [*Ubermut*]—more than courage! And how much self-assurance!"[25] Katharina's bold move was daring indeed. Even more than self-assurance, her proposal illustrates the gravity of her plight.

Katharina von Bora had laid every last one of her cards on the table. She had risked it all because she had nothing and everything to lose. The ball was now firmly in Luther's court. Would the renegade monk, the leader of the Protestant Reformation, the man who had single-handedly transformed the ways in which marriage was viewed in sixteenth-century Europe, accept this most unlikely proposal? We know Luther's answer. The question is, why did he say yes?

9

Marriage Makeover

Today, Western Christian weddings generally follow a standard protocol. A couple becomes engaged; the engagement is announced, followed by a period of wedding planning; the couple is married by a priest or minister in a church before a gathering of friends and family; and the union is celebrated at a reception following the church ceremony. We have Luther to thank for this tradition. Prior to his reforms, marriage was not regulated in any way, which, as we will see, led to a matrimonial mess of confusion and chaos.

Defining Matrimony

Marriage during Luther's time was considered part of the Church's jurisdiction and thus was not managed by the state.

However, while the Roman Catholic Church officially claimed it as one of the seven sacraments (which was decided at the Council of Verona in 1184), marriage was not administered within the framework of the Church's liturgy.[1] In other words, it was not required that the marriage ceremony take place in a church or be officiated by a priest. Because marriage was viewed by the Church as a gift from God and an act of consent between a man and a woman, canon (church) law failed to regulate the act of marriage in any substantive way.[2]

In the early Middle Ages, a father's transferal of legal authority over his daughter to the groom comprised the essential "marriage act." The exchange of promises and property was accomplished entirely within the family, with little outside intervention by either the Church or the state. The ceremonial handing over of the bride from her father to her new husband was then followed by consummation, which often entailed a ceremonial bedding of the couple in the presence of their family and friends.[3]

Later in the Middle Ages, however, it became increasingly common for boys as young as fourteen and girls as young as twelve to betroth themselves to one another without any parental involvement. A couple who said "I do" to one another were considered by the Church to be married, regardless of whether they had announced their engagement publicly, exchanged their vows in a church, or even obtained the consent of their parents. They essentially performed the sacrament of marriage themselves.[4] In the eyes of the Church, because marriage was made by God, and a priest could only bless what God had already decreed, a couple who promised to love one another and live together until death was considered officially married, especially if the couple had consummated their vows by sexual intercourse.[5] It was also common for young couples to make a secret commitment to one another by promising to marry in the future and then validating that promise with consummation.[6]

The Marriage Mess

These rogue marriages and promises of marriage between minors resulted in thousands of "he said/she said" arguments. The ecclesiastical courts were overrun with cases of contested betrothal: "girls seduced on alleged promises of marriage, parents challenging the secret unions of their children, bigamous 'Casanovas' accused of secretly promising marriage to two or more women, and possibly, most embarrassing of all, men and women sincerely attempting to make public their private vows, only to be challenged by someone claiming to have been secretly promised marriage by one of the partners."[7] In Augsburg, for example, almost half of all the marriage cases brought before the ecclesiastical court were for contested vows, while nearly two-thirds of the marriage cases in the Regensburg episcopal court were for contested marriages.[8] The courts simply could not keep up with the thousands of cases brought before them.

The state of marriage was a mess. The pope and church officials had made marriage a sacrament, yet ironically, a wedding in a church, if it happened at all, was still an optional extra. Adolescents pledged lifelong commitment to one another, engaged in sexual intercourse to make the marriage official, and *then* informed their parents and their church that they had wed. Young men pledged marriage, consummated the "marriage," and then denied having done so, leaving the woman no longer a virgin and, in some cases, pregnant.

Even more frustrating to Luther was the fact that the Church, which charged fees to dissolve marriages (as well as for dispensations in cases of third- or fourth-degree consanguinity, which mandated that a person could not marry his or her third or fourth cousin), made money off the marriage mess they had created. In short, people paid the Church to marry or separate from whomever they wanted. "The Romanists of our day have become merchants," Luther wrote in *The Babylonian Captivity of the Church*. "What is it that they sell? Vulvas and genitals—merchandise indeed most worthy of such merchants, grown altogether filthy and obscene through greed and godlessness. For there is no impediment nowadays that may not be legalized through the intercession of mammon."[9]

The bottom line: canon law as it related to the sacrament of marriage was confusing, easily abused, and impossible to uphold. Luther set out to transform the institution of marriage across Germany and beyond, and over a very short period did exactly that. In the wake of published works including his *Sermon on the Estate of Marriage* (1519), *The Babylonian Captivity* (1520), *On Monastic Vows* (1521), and *On Marriage Matters* (1530), society's understanding of marriage underwent a radical shift. When Luther was finished with it, marriage in Reformation Germany simply did not resemble the institution of marriage from centuries past.

Away from Sacrament, into the Church

One of Luther's first reforms was to "desacramentize" marriage—that is, he declared marriage should not be a sacrament. (Luther originally defined the sacraments as those rituals commanded by Christ: baptism, holy communion, and confession. Later he narrowed his definition by declaring only those experiences in which Christ himself participated to be sacramental, thus eliminating confession and keeping only baptism and holy communion as sacraments.) Interestingly, although reforms desacramentized marriage, they also gave the new Protestant church a greater role in the marriage ceremony itself. Luther and his peers emphasized the couple's presence in a church and the minister's benediction as critical parts of the marriage ceremony. Prospective couples were first required to meet with their pastor before announcing their marriage intentions. Then, if no impediment surfaced after the public announcement of the engagement—called the *banns*—at the couple's parish, the two were allowed to marry.

The *kirchgang*—literally "church going"—became a prominent part of the marriage ceremony.[10] Initially this ritual took place outside the front door of the church, and many late medieval churches were even adorned with elaborately decorated entrances specifically for this purpose.[11] As the Protestant Reformation progressed, the ceremony moved inside the church, and couples were expected to recite their vows before the altar in the presence of the pastor and their family and friends. Often two wedding ceremonies took place; private ceremonies at home were still popular, but it was the church wedding that validated the marriage.[12]

Family and friends chaperoned the bride and groom around the clock in the weeks between the official engagement and the *kirchgang*. If premarital sexual relations were known to have occurred between the engaged couple prior to the ceremony, there was often a shaming element to the wedding ceremony. In the second half of the sixteenth century, a known nonvirginal bride wore a veil or a straw wreath, instead of a wreath of flowers, and her groom wore a straw crown to the church ceremony.[13] They were also only permitted a single table of guests and were not allowed to dance or demonstrate any physical affection at the post-wedding celebration.[14] In the most severe instances, the groom might be forced to spend two weeks sequestered in a tower and the bride two weeks in the stockade, depending on the magnitude of the scandal.[15]

Luther also insisted that marriages of minors that took place without parental approval were considered "invalid in the eyes of God and all legal tradition."[16] "Who would approve my action if after I had reared my daughter with so much expense and effort, care and danger, zeal and toil, and had risked my whole life with body and goods for so many years, she should receive no better care than if she were a cow of mine that had strayed into the forest where any wolf might devour it?" Luther wrote in 1530 in *On Marriage Matters*. "Every reasonable person must concede, I say, that this is violence and injustice which could be easily avoided if one prohibited secret engagements."[17] Luther's emphatic statements on the necessity of parental consent make one point very clear: for him, marriage was not only an issue of filial duty, but of familial property and power as well.[18]

Luther's reforms were effective. Couples who were required to meet with a priest, publicly announce their engagement in advance, receive their parents' blessing, avoid engaging in premarital sex, and be married in the presence of family and friends in an official church ceremony were much more likely to take their vows seriously and keep them. Within ten years of Luther's reforms, the number of contested marriages was dramatically reduced.

Be Fruitful and Multiply

Luther's second major contention with marriage was related to what he considered the spiritual dangers of celibacy. Time and time again he argued that because human beings are innately lustful as a result of Adam and Eve's fall, forced celibacy could only lead to eventual sexual sin (except in the rarest of cases in which God had actually blessed a person with the gift of celibacy).

Luther attacked clerical vows of celibacy on two grounds, both biblical. First, he argued, God ordained marriage when he created Eve out of Adam's rib and brought her to him to assuage his loneliness. This, Luther concluded, constituted the first wedding (although it was not enough to qualify marriage as a sacrament). "For it was not by accident that Almighty God instituted the estate of matrimony only for man and above all animals," he wrote in his 1519 *Sermon on the Estate of Marriage*. "To the other animals God says quite simply, 'Be fruitful and multiply.' But in the case of Adam, God creates for him a unique, special kind of wife out of his own flesh. He brings her to him, he gives her to him, and Adam agrees to accept her. Therefore, that is what marriage is."[19] In Luther's view, God intentionally differentiated between the general command he gave animals to be fruitful and multiply, and his act of creating a specific partner for Adam with whom Adam could share his life.

Second, in order to ensure the continuation of the human race, God gave Adam and Eve, and their progeny down through the ages, a desire that found no other release than through sexual intimacy. "For this word which God speaks, 'Be fruitful and multiply,' is more than a command, namely, a divine ordinance which it is not our prerogative to hinder or ignore," wrote Luther in 1522. "Rather, it is just as necessary as the fact that I am a man, and more necessary than sleeping and waking, eating and drinking, and emptying the bowels and bladder. It is a nature and disposition just as innate as the organs involved in it. And wherever men try to resist this, it remains irresistible nonetheless and goes its way through fornication, adultery, and secret sins, for this is a matter of nature and not of choice."[20]

Sex was absolutely necessary and unavoidable, Luther argued—a fact of nature and a gift given to human beings by God himself. He found scriptural support for this view in Genesis 2:18, and because this passage was so critical to his theology, he made multiple attempts to translate it into the clearest, most comprehensible German possible. He ultimately settled on this translation: "It is not good that the man should be alone; I will make an help meet for him."[21] In 1525 he wrote, "This is the Word of God, by virtue of which the passionate, natural inclination toward woman is created and maintained. It may not be prevented by vow and law. For it is God's work and Word."[22]

Sexuality as Divinely Ordained

Celibacy had long been esteemed by the Roman Catholic Church as the highest, most pure state. The next best option for those who couldn't achieve a celibate state was marriage, but the Church maintained that sexual intercourse even within marriage was permissible only for the purpose of procreation. Sex for the purpose of pleasure was a sin, though only a minor one if procreation had not been intentionally prevented.[23]

According to fourth-century theologian Augustine, marriage was not equally sanctified by God like complete sexual abstinence was. Although Augustine considered marriage a satisfactory cure for lust, he couldn't quite bring himself to view sex within marriage as entirely sinless and suggested that it could be atoned for by almsgiving and other good works.[24] Theologians Jerome and Ambrose took Augustine's views even further, exalting "the celibate state over the necessary, worldly compromise of marriage."[25] "Any man who loves his wife excessively is an adulterer," warned Jerome. "Marriages fill the earth; virginity [fills] heaven."[26] Married men and women occupied the second tier, far below the holier, more pure status of celibates. "Let married women take their pride in coming next after virgins," wrote Jerome.[27]

Luther was raised on this theology. "When I was a boy, the wicked and impure practice of celibacy had made marriage so disreputable that I believed I could not even think about the life of married people without sinning," he wrote in his *Lectures on Genesis*. "Everybody was fully persuaded that anyone who intended to lead a holy life acceptable to God could not get married but had to live as a celibate and take the vow of celibacy."[28] But as he dug into Scripture, he grew more and more appalled by this theology. "Whoever is ashamed of marriage is also ashamed of being and being called human and tries to improve on what God has made," he claimed.[29] For Luther, human sexuality was divinely ordained. God created the body to function in specific ways, Luther argued, and to interrupt or prohibit that process was wrong.

"What made Luther's theology so vivid and intelligible was not the outer rhetoric, but the connection of the Word of God with corporeality," says biographer Heiko Oberman.[30] Nature will persevere, in spite of man's efforts to intervene, Luther argued. "Nature does not cease to do its work when there is involuntary chastity. The flesh goes on creating seed just as God created it to do," Luther wrote with his characteristic candor in 1522. "To put it bluntly for the sake of those who suffer miserably: if it does not flow into flesh it will flow into the shirt."[31]

Without an outlet, natural human sexual urges become lust, Luther insisted, which is dangerous for the body. Luther agreed with the common medical theories at the time, which purported that restraining the natural sexual drive caused the body to become poisoned and thus "unhealthy, enervated, sweaty, and foul-smelling. . . . Unless there is terrific hunger or immense labor or the supreme grace," Luther wrote, "the body cannot take it; it necessarily becomes unhealthy and sickly."[32] This is why barren women are sick and weak, Luther reasoned, while those who are fruitful are "healthier, cleaner, and happier."[33]

Furthermore, he argued, lust was dangerous for the spirit and the soul. As historian David M. Whitford notes, when Luther used the word *lust*, he connected it with the German word *Anfechtung*, which connoted "more than temptation: it is a powerful, even existential force that can overwhelm a person. It is satanic in origin and destructive to the soul."[34] In fact, Luther considered lust so dangerous, he proposed some shockingly radical solutions to address it. For instance, he advocated divorce in cases of impotence, adultery, desertion, absolute incompatibility, or the refusal of a spouse to engage in sex. Reconciliation was always preferable, but if it wasn't possible, Luther insisted the innocent party should be granted a divorce with the right to remarry.[35]

In extreme instances he even advocated bigamy, as in the infamous case of Philip of Hesse. Philip was married to Christina, the daughter of Duke George of Saxony, but he didn't care for her. He didn't like her breath, the look of her face, the smell of her body, or anything else about her (except for the fact that she bore him several children).[36] Luther suggested to the womanizing Philip that instead of engaging in multiple adulterous relationships, he should marry his seventeen-year-old girlfriend Margarethe and be content with two wives. Luther reasoned that because bigamy was notorious in the Old Testament and not outright prohibited in the New Testament, it was therefore acceptable in rare cases, although he advised Philip to keep his second marriage a secret. When the scandal broke, people were shocked to discover that Luther had condoned the second marriage, but he maintained his radical view, insisting that in rare and extreme cases, necessity demanded an unorthodox solution.

No Intention of Marrying

Luther's views were crystal clear. Marriage should not be seen as less sacred than celibacy, and married couples should not be considered less holy or less spiritually pure than monks, nuns, priests, and other celibate clerics. Furthermore, marriage and sexual relations within marriage were not only imperative against the sin of lust, but also divinely ordained, a gift from God to be honored and esteemed.

Yet for all his verbosity on the subject of marriage, Luther was obviously reluctant to take the plunge into matrimony himself. While in exile in Wartburg Castle, when he learned that several former monks and nuns were marrying, he reportedly exclaimed, "Will our Wittenbergs give wives even to monks? They wouldn't give one to me."[37] Later, in a letter written to Spalatin in November 1524, he claimed, "According to my present frame of mind I have no intention of marrying, not that I am insensible to the emotions of the flesh, being neither wood nor stone, but because I have no desire to, and daily expect to die a heretic's death."[38] It wasn't that he didn't experience physical desire—"emotions of the flesh"—he assured his friend, but more that he was simply not interested in marrying. Plus, he reasoned, marriage for a wanted man in danger of being burned at the stake for heresy was far too risky; the woman who married him would likely end up a widow.

Five months later Luther penned another letter to Spalatin, convincing his friend to marry, while at the same time still attempting to explain why he himself hadn't married. "I do not want you to wonder that a famous lover like me does not marry," he wrote, tongue-in-cheek. "It is rather strange that I, who so often write about matrimony and get mixed up with women, have not yet turned into a woman, to say nothing of not having married one."[39] In that same letter Luther joked about having "three wives simultaneously, and loved them so much I have lost two that are taking other husbands; the third I can hardly keep with my left arm, and she, too, will probably be snatched away from me."[40] Historians surmise that Luther was referring to three nuns who had caught his attention, the third of which was Katharina, but his joking tone leads one to question whether he had ever seriously considered marrying any of them at all.

Luther was not amused when he heard about Katharina's refusal to marry Kaspar Glatz. In fact, her pickiness downright infuriated him, especially in light of her limited opportunities. He accused Katharina of being influenced by her aristocratic pride and snobbery.[41] Von Amsdorf, on the other hand, sided with Katharina: "What the devil are you doing, trying to coax and force the good Kate to marry that old cheapskate whom she neither desires nor considers with all her heart as husband?" he challenged his friend.[42] Luther responded with exasperation: "What devil would want to have her, then? If she does not like him, she may have to wait a good while for another one!"[43]

Clearly Luther did not seriously consider himself a viable candidate for Katharina's hand, regardless of the fact that von Amsdorf had undoubtedly told him about her bold marriage proposition. In fact, it's likely Luther had not seriously considered marrying at all up to this point, in spite of the marriage reforms he had so passionately endorsed, as well as his vocal opinions about clerical celibacy and his treatises on the purpose and benefits of marriage in general. Luther, it seems, was in favor of marriage generally, but much less enchanted with the prospect of marrying himself.

10

Tying the Knot

Luther wasn't exaggerating when he claimed that at any moment he could be hunted down, captured, and burned at the stake. Branded a heretic and known across the land as a dissenter, execution was a very real threat and had been the unfortunate fate of many reformers before him.

Yet one wonders if this was truly the reason behind Luther's reluctance to marry. Perhaps, after forty-two years as a bachelor, he was simply accustomed to and comfortable with living alone. Maybe he considered how marriage might compromise his authority or even distract him from his primary work. Luther was used to being on his own and answering only to himself, and while sixteenth-century marriages certainly were not equitable by modern-day standards, at the very least, as a married man, Luther would have to consider another's opinions, thoughts, and will in addition to his own. Part of him might also have secretly seen himself—or at least wanted to see himself—as one of those unique men who could transcend the carnal, a man in whom God had bestowed the rare gift of true chastity. Or perhaps Katharina von Bora herself was the real stumbling stone. After all, Luther had already tried to marry her off to two other men, first to Hieronymus Baumgartner, who had jilted her, and most recently to Kaspar Glatz, whom Katharina had emphatically refused. Clearly his preference was for Katharina to marry someone else.

It Pleased God

A number of factors ultimately impacted Luther's decision to marry Katharina, the first of which was his desire to please his father. Luther had carried his father's disappointment with him for years. Offering Hans a grandchild was a way to make amends. During a visit to Mansfeld in the spring of 1525, Luther confided his thoughts about marriage to his father, and Hans urged his son to marry so that he could eventually provide him with a grandchild.[1]

A second factor was Luther's regret over the Peasants' War, for which he felt at least partially responsible. Sparked by Luther's reforms, more than 100,000 of the 300,000 peasant insurgents involved in the revolt were killed during the spring and summer of 1525, right around the time Luther was considering marriage.[2] In a letter to John Rühel, a councilor to Count Albrecht of Mansfeld, on May 4, 1525, Luther declared that he would marry Katharina when he returned home to "spite the devil," whom he blamed for provoking the peasants to revolt.[3] Later Luther claimed his marriage would "please his father, rile the pope, cause the angels to laugh and the devils to weep."[4]

Politics were a factor in his decision as well. In a June 1525 letter Luther encouraged the archbishop, Albrecht von Mainz, to marry and later declared, "If my marrying will strengthen him, I am ready. I believe in marriage."[5] Luther knew his reforms would take hold much more quickly if church officials like von Mainz married. He was willing to serve as an example to others in order that they might be encouraged to follow in his radical footsteps.

"[I did this] to silence the evil mouths which are so used to complaining about me. For I still hope to live for a little while," Luther wrote in a letter to von Amsdorf, inviting him to the wedding banquet. "In addition, I also did not want to reject this unique [opportunity to obey] my father's wish for progeny, which he so often expressed."[6] At the same time, he added, he wanted to make a statement, to practice what he preached and to serve as an example to others who might feel intimidated or afraid to take such a bold step, despite the fact that God willed it.[7] In the same letter Luther admitted that he was neither romantically nor physically attracted to Katharina, though he cared about her. "For I feel neither passionate love nor burning for my spouse," he confessed, "but I cherish her."[8] His reasoning sounds rational and his explanation makes sense, yet at the same time one senses a deeper reason behind his decision to marry Katharina—a reason Luther himself may not have realized until much later.

A Dutiful Servant

Perhaps the most telling explanation for marrying Katharina was the one Luther offered years later to the friends and students gathered around his dining room table, when he admitted that he'd initially had his eye on another of the escaped nuns, one of

Katharina's closest friends. "If I had wanted to get married thirteen years ago, I would have chosen Eva Schonfeld," he said. "I didn't love my Kathe at the time, for I regarded her with mistrust as someone proud and arrogant. But it pleased God, who wanted me to take pity on her."[9] It seems the real reason Luther married Katharina was not for love, politics, or theology, but out of obedience to Christ. Luther's decision to marry sprang directly from his new vision of the redeemed Christian's relationship to God.

The foundation for both Luther's theology and his personal faith was found in Romans 1:17: "For therein is the righteousness of God revealed from faith to faith; as it is written, The just shall live by faith." In other words, Luther believed God's grace, rather than his own merit, was the key to salvation, and he came to realize that, seen through the lens of God's mercy, righteousness meant the justification that a merciful God bestowed through faith.[10] "The theological consequences of this turn were immense," says historian Martin Brecht, "for it undermined the traditional medieval piety based on good works."[11]

Yet Luther didn't entirely disregard the purpose of good works in faith either. As was mentioned earlier, he believed good works were still an integral part of faith, and were, in fact, a result of one's faith. In his famous treatise *The Freedom of a Christian*, Luther wrote that in order to truly comprehend the freedom Christ won for us, we must first wrap our minds around a paradox: "A Christian is free and independent in every respect, a bondservant to none. A Christian is a dutiful servant in every respect, owing a duty to everyone."[12] Christians, Luther wrote, are bound by love. They want to obey Christ and perform good works because of their deep and abiding love for Christ, and they love Christ because he loved them first from the cross. Good works, Luther argued, were a natural outgrowth of Christ's love for us.

For Luther, faith was, at its essence, a matter of the heart. Human beings have the gift of faith because God gives them that gift through Christ. And because of the gift of Christ and the presence of Christ in the Christian's heart, Luther expected the Christian to have the same selfless attitude of love, discipline, and service toward the world that Christ possessed.[13] And he expected it most of himself.

"To my neighbor, I will be, as a Christian, what Christ has become to me, and do just what I see is needful, helpful, or acceptable to him, for I have enough of all things in Christ through my faith," Luther wrote. "Lo, that is how love and joy in God flow out of faith. For just as our neighbor is needy, and requires our excess, so we were needy in God's eyes, and required His grace."[14] It's tempting to romanticize Luther and Katharina's relationship, but the truth is, romantic love wasn't part of the picture, at least at the outset. Katharina married Luther because he was the most promising out of a very limited number of options. Luther married Katharina out of his love for Christ, a love that flowed naturally out of his faith toward the person in his midst who was most in need of compassion. Katharina was Luther's "good work." Marrying her was an act of Luther's discipline, love, and service born in the name of Christ. What he couldn't possibly see at the time, however, was that his obedience would produce fruit beyond his wildest expectations.

To Bed, to Church, to Feast

Once Luther made up his mind, wedding plans quickly fell into place. He proposed, presumably at the Cranach residence, where

Katharina was living at the time, and she, not surprisingly, accepted. Unlike Luther, Katharina had much less freedom in her decision of whether to marry or not. For her, marriage was an issue of survival. She was still single, living under the Cranachs' roof, and unwelcome in her childhood home. When Hans von Bora placed his daughter in the convent, he certainly hadn't expected her to flee eighteen years later. He had relinquished responsibility for Katharina in 1505. Though he was still alive when she left Marienthron, Hans von Bora was as good as dead to Katharina, and she to him.

We don't know for sure how Katharina felt about Luther at the time of their engagement and wedding. It's obvious from both his letters and his later statements around the table that Luther didn't marry Katharina for romantic love, and we can safely assume the same was true for her. Katharina undoubtedly crossed paths with Luther when he visited Lucas Cranach, but the two likely spent very little time together. However, we also know from her refusal to marry Kaspar Glatz that Katharina was not willing to marry just any man. Clearly, the frequent threats on his life, his unstable income, his reputation as a radical reformer, and the fact that he was not a member of the nobility (as she was) were not enough to dissuade Katharina from tying the knot with Martin Luther.

What might very well be considered the most famous wedding in Christian history took place on an ordinary Tuesday in Wittenberg. It was a modest affair, as far as sixteenth-century weddings go. On the evening of June 13, 1525, a small bridal party—just five guests, plus the bride and groom—walked briskly down Wittenberg's main lane in their wedding finery and made their way to the door of Luther's home, the Black Cloister, on the southeast edge of town.

A wedding portrait of Luther and Katharina does not exist, so we don't know for sure what the bride and groom wore on their special day. It's likely Katharina's hair, now grown long in the two years since she'd fled the convent, was worn loose and flowing to her shoulders. She also probably wore a wreath of woven fresh flowers on her head. In late medieval German wedding ceremonies, the bride often presented the groom with this wreath, which symbolized an offering of her virginity. Likewise, at the wedding festivities that followed, the bride's young maiden friends often distributed similar wreaths to the guests.[15] As historian Lyndal Roper points out, "It's hard to determine whether the wreath had always symbolized the offering of the bride's virginity to the groom, or whether this was a later development

Lucas Cranach the Elder [Public domain], via Wikimedia Commons

As far as we know, a wedding portrait of Katharina and Luther does not exist. Lucas Cranach the Elder painted these portraits of Luther and Katharina in 1526, a year after they were married.

as the Church, continuing its pre-Reformation campaigns, tried to prevent the couple from celebrating their sexual union until after the wedding."[16]

Katharina, Luther, and their guests—Lucas and Barbara Cranach, friend Justus Jonas, jurist Johann Apel, and local pastor Johannes Bugenhagen—gathered in the living room of the Black Cloister. The couple recited their simple vows, slipped ruby and diamond rings upon one another's fingers, and were pronounced husband and wife by Bugenhagen.[17]

In late medieval unions the bride typically brought her own bed—often handed down from mother to daughter—to the marriage, along with feather quilts, pillows, and embroidered linens as part of her trousseau, but Katharina owned nothing of her own and thus came to her marriage virtually empty-handed. Instead, she and Luther retired to his bed, which, Luther later admitted, was basically a pile of dirty straw that hadn't been changed out in a year.[18] That said, rancid straw was probably the least of Katharina's concerns that night. Although Protestant reforms had altered the format of weddings, consummation was still considered an important and required part of the matrimonial ritual. And so, as was the German tradition of the time, the newlyweds consummated their marriage while Justus Jonas witnessed the event from the doorway of the bedchamber.[19]

One can only imagine the awkwardness of this first intimate encounter between the former nun and monk, she aged twenty-six, he aged forty-two, a witness lurking in the background to keep a watchful eye. Nonetheless, Katharina and Luther managed to survive this most uncomfortable of wedding rituals. "Yesterday I was present and saw the bridegroom on the bridal bed—I could not suppress my tears at the sight," wrote

Justus Jonas. "Now that it has happened and God has desired it, I implore God to grant the excellent honest man all the happiness."[20]

Biographer Heiko Oberman suggests Jonas's tears were prompted by disappointment over Luther's marriage to Katharina (Jonas and Melanchthon were not in favor of Luther's marriage and were concerned it would distract him from his reform work).[21] Ernst Kroker, on the other hand, implies Jonas's reaction to the consummation were tears of joy and affection for the couple.[22] Regardless of his personal feelings, Jonas confirmed that Luther and Katharina could officially claim the distinction of husband and wife.

The wedding festivities didn't end with the witnessed consummation. In accordance with Protestant reforms, two weeks later Luther and Katharina publicly celebrated their marriage with the *kirchgang* ceremony. On Tuesday, June 27, 1525—Tuesday was considered a lucky day for weddings—church bells rang out over Wittenberg as the bridal party followed a pair of pipers from the Black Cloister to the city church. Crowds lined the street along the way and packed around the entrance of the church as Bugenhagen performed the public consecration of marriage. Then, with all the requirements of an official marriage met, Luther and Katharina and their guests returned to the old monastery for a traditional wedding feast.

After the banquet, the bride and groom, their guests, and the musicians walked to the town hall, where the sounds of dancing, drinking, and revelry echoed throughout Wittenberg until the party was shut down by order of the magistrate an hour before midnight.[23] Luther's parents attended the festivities, as did dozens of his friends and professional colleagues. Noticeably absent at the celebration were any members of Katharina's family. Though she kept in sporadic touch with one of her brothers, Katharina's father, who historians surmise was still living at the time of her wedding, had essentially disowned his firstborn daughter.

Weddings were as significant in sixteenth-century Germany as they are today and were considered a statement of a couple's social prestige. Among the nobility and even the merchant class, weddings were the most expensive celebrations an individual was likely to host, usually far exceeding the amounts spent on burials or even for the festivities honoring the births and baptisms of children.[24] A proper wedding offered an overabundance of food—enough for leftovers to be sent to those who had been unable to attend, and even to offer as charity for poor people in need.[25] The more lavish and festive the wedding, the more powerful and prestigious the couple. "Such visible consumption of wealth was of course in pointed contradiction to the civic authority's policy of careful housekeeping and preventing the wastage of city and individual resources," observes Lyndal Roper.[26]

As a result, German cities often regulated weddings, limiting the number of guests and restricting festivities so as to control social order and create a more somber atmosphere. City council members interviewed wedding guests to ensure that a reasonable sum had been spent on gifts, that guest limits had not been exceeded, and no extra parties had been hosted. City ordinances even dictated how much money a groom could spend on wedding rings for his bride, as well as the order in which people walked to the church and were seated at the dinner table. "Weddings [became] pageants of the town's social structure, where each individual might read off his or her place in that society," says Roper.[27]

In comparison, Luther and Katharina's wedding feast was fairly modest, primarily because Luther, though famous, was poor. Despite the fact that he had written hundreds of pages of published material, preached far and wide, and still taught at the university, he had little steady income. And Katharina, of course, came to the marriage penniless. When Luther sent out his wedding invitations prior to the June 27 celebration, he requested that several of his guests bring venison and barrels of beer to be served at the banquet. Their guests rose to the challenge and supplied Luther and Katharina with ample provisions for the wedding feast, as well as a number of generous monetary gifts to help establish their household as husband and wife. Elector Johann of Saxony (brother of the late Frederick the Wise, Luther's protector, who had died in May), Archbishop Albrecht of Mainz, and the city of Wittenberg gave the couple sizable cash gifts, while other guests brought valuable coins and silver cups (many of which the Luthers would later sell to make ends meet).

Snared with the Yoke of Marriage

Along with the request for wedding banquet provisions, Luther's invitations also alluded to the fact that even a week or more into marriage, he was still reeling from the shock. "Doubtless the outcry has reached your ears that I have actually ventured to enter the married state," Luther wrote to Electoral Chancellor Johann von Doltzig on June 21, 1525, eight days after his wedding ceremony at the Black Cloister. "Although my change in condition seems very strange to myself, being as yet scarcely able to believe it, still the fact is attested by so many honoured witnesses that I must believe it to be true."[28] The tone of the letter, though lighthearted, clearly indicates that Luther was hardly able to wrap his mind around the fact that he was now married.

To another friend, Luther wrote, "Suddenly, unexpectedly, and while my mind was on other matters, the Lord snared me with the yoke of marriage."[29] One of Luther's closest friends, Philip Melanchthon, sought to reassure his friend, as Luther clearly seemed "somewhat troubled and perplexed over this change in his life."[30] Later Luther himself admitted that marriage required significant adjustments: "I was alone, and now there's someone else here. In bed, you wake up in the morning and see a couple of pigtails on the pillow."[31] One can only imagine Katharina's thoughts. Considering the fact that Luther hadn't freshened his bed straw in a year (the sixteenth-century equivalent of not laundering the sheets), the transition to life as a wife couldn't have been easy for her either.

The truth was, the odds were against Luther and Katharina living happily ever after. For starters, marriage between a twenty-six-year-old former nun and a forty-two-year-old former monk, each of them independent, stubborn, and accustomed to living a quiet, cloistered life, would have been challenging even under the best circumstances. Moreover, their precarious financial situation, Luther's reluctance to marry in general and his hesitance to marry Katharina in particular, and the daily threats against his life inevitably added to the instability of the match. And finally, aside from his parents and a few close friends, much of the world, from the Holy Roman Emperor to the peasants in the fields, opposed their union. According to canon law, the Luthers' marriage was a capital offense—a scandal, a blasphemy, and the work of the devil. According to Protestant reformers, the union would be nothing but a distraction, with the potential to derail the entire movement.

The deck was stacked against them. As husband and wife, Martin and Katharina Luther faced a long road ahead, with myriad obstacles along the way.

11

Backlash

With most weddings, it's reasonable to assume that the majority, if not all, of those who hear about the union will have an optimistic view of the couple's future together. In the sixteenth century—much like today—the days leading up to and following a wedding were typically filled with joy, celebration, and positive wishes for the bride and groom.

Not so for the Luthers.

Most of Luther's friends feared marriage would set the Reformation back and cautioned him against it. In fact, his closest confidant, Reformation collaborator Philip Melanchthon, was so adamantly opposed to the union, Luther refused to invite him and his wife to the ceremony at the Black Cloister or to the church ceremony and the reception that followed two weeks later. This social and personal slight angered Melanchthon, provoking him to lash out at his longtime friend. "Luther has married the woman Bora, without letting one who is his friend know of his intention," he griped. "You may perhaps wonder that at a time like this, when the good are suffering at every hand, he does not suffer with them, but rather, it seems, devotes himself to revelry and compromises his good name, at the very moment when Germany is in special need of all his mind and authority."[1]

The outset of the Peasants' War was not, Melanchthon fumed, the time for amorous frolicking and celebratory revelry. He had a point. Celebrating at a time when thousands of peasants were dying in the revolt sparked by Luther's reforms would have been viewed as insensitive, if not downright offensive. On the other hand, his accusation that Luther married Katharina as an act of self-indulgence, rather than compassion or obligation, suggests that Melanchthon misperceived Luther's intentions altogether.

Those who didn't oppose Luther's marriage generally or on the basis of political reasons objected to Luther's choice of Katharina, whom they considered far beneath him. As a poor former nun with no dowry, they deemed her unfit for a man of Luther's prominence. "All my friends screamed when hearing that I had my eye on Kate. 'No, not that one, but another,'" Luther admitted later.[2] Ironically, Katharina was the one with noble lineage, so it was she, in fact, who technically married beneath her social status.

Shunned

Martin Luther wasn't the first monk to marry, nor was Katharina the first nun. Augustinian monk Bartholomew Bernhardi married in 1521, and in 1522 the former monk Martin Bucer married a nun, Elisabeth Silbereisen.[3] By 1524 more than seventy-five priests, forty-six monks, and thirty-three nuns had married in Germany.[4] Nevertheless, laypeople distinguished between priests marrying and monks and nuns marrying. By the 1520s the former was somewhat acceptable; the latter was not.

Laypeople generally supported the idea of clerical marriage because they saw it as the best solution to the problem of concubinage among priests. *Concubinage* was defined as "unmarriage"—that is, unmarried couples living together as husband and wife—and it was a trend that had reached epic proportions among priests by the late Middle Ages. In some places, clerics appeared in public with their wives and children with hardly anyone batting an eye. Everyone knew concubinage among priests was morally wrong, but until Martin Luther came along with his marriage reforms, no one knew quite how to stop it.

As historian Wolfgang Breul observes, the "desacralization of priesthood and Luther's desire to normalize the priestly estate formed the central social tenets of early Reformation propaganda. But what drove the change was the widespread criticism of the immoral practice of concubinage and the popular demand that priests marry."[5] In other words, ordinary citizens were fed up with priests living in sin, and they saw Luther's reforms as the only way to halt the practice once and for all. The general population decided to support Luther's reforms, and in doing so they ensured that those reforms would be upheld. It was an idea whose time had come.

In 1523, for example, Hersfeld's town council issued a mandate threatening those who lived in "unmarriage" with physical punishment and banishment unless they married within fourteen days. Two of the priests in town married, which infuriated the local abbot. Up to this point, Abbot Krafft Myle von Hungen had been largely tolerant of the Reformation movement, but he saw the council's mandate as a direct challenge to his ecclesiastical jurisdiction. As a result, he exiled the two married priests from Hersfeld, an action that enraged the townspeople, who stormed and destroyed both the office of the chancellor of the imperial monastery and the homes of the priests in town who were still living in concubinage. The laypeople took matters into their own hands, overthrowing the abbot's authority and carrying out the council's mandate.[6]

While laypeople generally condoned the marriages of priests, monastic marriages were another story. These marriages were considered transgressive, and the former monks and nuns who married were viewed as deviant. Many argued that monastic marriages would damage the institution of marriage, and by extension, society as a whole.

"While celibacy was expected of all clergy, and they made a clear vow of chastity, the vows made by the monastics, male and female, were held as more binding because of the separation of the monks and nuns from the rest of society," says historian Marjorie Plummer. "It became a more complicated argument to explain why they should leave the convent and even more so why they should marry."[7] Monastic marriages were even viewed by many as incestuous. Theologically, a monk and a nun were already married to God—a nun was often called a "bride of Christ"—which made them spiritual siblings and thus violated prohibitions against incestuous unions.[8]

Laypeople struggled to accept former nuns and monks as regular members of society, and thus, they applied different societal rules to them, particularly to the women. Former nuns were criticized and publicly shamed for participating in any social event that involved frivolity or revelry, even wedding celebrations. In 1525, Leipzig authorities questioned Georg Crucinger about the presence of his daughter-in-law, a former nun, at his daughter's wedding. Crucinger tried to defend her, claiming his daughter-in-law had not danced at the wedding, "because it was not allowed her as a former nun," although he admitted that she had participated in the wedding festivities at the inn.[9]

In a similar incident, a former Dominican nun by the name of Anna Grab was arrested in 1528 and forced to swear that she would "live as a nun should and not forget the vow she made when she entered the convent." Grab was informed that she would be banished from the village if she did not adhere to the demands. Her father, in a separate agreement with officials, agreed that neither he nor other family members would interfere with his daughter's punishment.[10] In short, former nuns were held to different standards than other young, single women. They were expected to live like nuns, even when they no longer lived behind the cloister walls.

To be married in sixteenth-century Europe was to be automatically invited to and included in society . . . unless, that is, you were a married monk or especially a married nun, in which case the opposite was true. Married former monastics were, for the most part, considered outsiders and excluded from society. As Marjorie Plummer notes, "Their marriages [were] a significant contrast to the usual social inclusion that marriage signaled."[11] We can see evidence of how this played out in Luther and Katharina's marriage as well. While Luther took some heat from his friends and colleagues, Katharina bore the brunt of the public slander that only escalated and intensified after the couple exchanged their vows. While her peers who married after their escape from the convent were undoubtedly the center of harmless town gossip, Katharina was ruthlessly slandered, ostracized, and even threatened. She was a lightning rod for scandal, not just because she married, but because of *who* she married.

Scandalized

Instead of good wishes and words of encouragement, malicious rumors swirled around the couple during the weeks leading up to the wedding and in the days, months, and even years following their nuptials. Melanchthon accused Luther of succumbing to feminine wiles, suggesting that the Marienthron nuns were responsible for Luther's actions. "I think the explanation is this: the man is extraordinarily easily influenced, and so the nuns, who chased him in every way, ensnared him," he wrote to his student, Joachim Camerarius, on June 16. "Perhaps having so much to do with the nuns softened him up, although he is a noble and upright man, and caused the fire to flare up in him."[12]

Melanchthon ultimately regretted this letter and actually didn't send it (he sent a more delicately worded revised version in July), but Luther's detractors got ahold of the original letter and circulated it around Wittenberg and beyond.[13] Even though Melanchthon eventually made peace with Luther's marriage, he still didn't give his friend much credit for his ability to resist what he claimed were the nun's desperate advances.

Melanchthon wasn't alone in his opinions. Many of Luther's detractors accused him of being overly lustful, and some, like the Dominican historian Heinrich Denifle, whose 860-page *Luther and Lutherdom* was published in 1904, saw Luther's lust as one of the main causes of the entire Reformation.[14]

The slander only escalated after the couple's nuptials. In December 1525, Duke George of Saxony claimed that insanity, wild ambition, and lusts of the flesh had enticed Luther. A year later the duke accused the Luthers of running the other monks out of the Black Cloister—the former monastery where they had been married and where they made their home afterward—so Martin and Katharina could have the place to themselves to feast in "carnal lust."[15] In reality, only a single elderly monk still lived in the abandoned monastery when Katharina moved in as Luther's wife, and the monk stayed on the premises and shared the residence with the Luthers. Even King Henry VIII of England added his own condemnation to the litany of complaints against the Luthers. In 1526 the king, who ten years later would have his second wife, Anne Boleyn, beheaded simply because the Catholic Church would not grant him a divorce, accused Luther of "disgraceful lust in violating a nun who was consecrated to God."[16]

It was Katharina, however, who was the main target of the malicious slander. In the weeks and months following the wedding she was accused in pamphlets and letters that circulated far beyond Wittenberg's city walls of being a whore, a "dancing girl," and a traitor of Christ.[17] Many of Luther's detractors viewed Katharina as a sex-crazed seductress—a former nun who had broken her lifelong vow of chastity to seduce not just any man, but a monk, and a famous one at that. Even the theologian and Dutch humanist Erasmus of Rotterdam took a turn at the backstabbing, claiming in his letters that Katharina had borne a child a few days after the wedding. This was a grave accusation—recall the punishment of the tower and stockade for the bride and groom who were discovered to have engaged in premarital sex. When he realized his error—the Luthers' first son arrived a proper twelve months after the nuptials—Erasmus was forced to retract his accusation, yet he couldn't help but ponder a popular legend of the time: that the "Antichrist"[18] in the form of a two-headed monster would be born to a monk and a nun.[19]

Melanchthon defended Luther on this count, insisting, "The talk that he had already slept with the woman Bora is a lie," but the rumor persisted for years, despite the fact that it was obviously false.[20] Even a seemingly innocuous copper engraving was used by the rumor mongers against the Luthers. The engraving depicts Luther and Katharina along with their six children, but a seventh child lurking in the background (Andreas, actually Luther's nephew, who lived at the Black Cloister) was said to be Katharina's oldest child, "proof" that she'd come to the marriage pregnant.[21]

This vilification of Katharina continued long into her marriage and even long after her death. As Luther biographer Richard Friedenthal points out, as late as the seventeenth and eighteenth centuries, writers were still producing "fat, fictitiously elaborated biographies in the most colorful baroque style," including one titled *Lucifer Wittenbergensis*—the "*Morning Star of Wittenberg*" (one of Luther's many nicknames for Katharina)—in which Katharina was depicted as a "nymphomaniac virago who jumped into bed with all [of Luther's] students."[22] "The fact that the moral indignation continued so long shows how violently this step of Luther's roused people's feelings, more so indeed than other steps of his which were far more significant," says Friedenthal.[23] It also illustrates the deep-seated suspicion with which women, particularly single women, of that time were viewed by much of society.

A "Domestic Danger and a Delectable Detriment"

Since only eight of her letters have survived, none of which address the early months and years of her marriage, we don't know for sure how Katharina responded to these vicious attacks on her character. We can only assume she was mortified and perhaps even afraid for her life. This was, after all, the late Middle Ages—a time when women were accused as witches and heretics and burned at the stake for far lesser "wrongs" than marrying a monk.

It's impossible to know exactly how many witches were hanged or burned between 1400 and 1800, but conservative estimates usually cite between 40,000 and 50,000, with some estimates as high as 100,000 or more.[24] The vast majority of those executed on charges of sorcery were either unmarried single women or widows. Katharina was born only a few years after the publication of the *Malleus Maleficarum*—known in English as the *Hammer of Witches*—which instantly became the go-to source for information about witches and witchcraft. Although there had been witch treatises written before, the *Malleus* was different, both because it was so readily available—it was reprinted dozens of times after its initial publication in 1487—and because it pointed to witchcraft as one of the primary reasons for the world's ever-increasing ills.[25]

The authors, Dominican inquisitors Jacob Sprenger and Heinrich Kramer, aimed to answer two main questions in the *Malleus*—What is witchcraft? And who is a witch?—as well as offer advice to priests and assistance to judges, both of whom were combating sorcery in the trenches. They dedicated a significant portion of the book to the question of why witchcraft was chiefly practiced by women. Women, the authors concluded, were much more prone to engage in sorcery because they were more impressionable, more apt to doubt in their faith, feebler in mind and body, and defective in form, having been created from a "rib of the breast, which is bent as it were in a contrary direction to a man."[26]

Furthermore, Sprenger and Kramer continued, a woman was a "liar by nature"; vain in gait, posture, and habit; and insatiable in carnal lust, as well as wicked: "a foe to friendship, an unescapable punishment, a necessary evil, a natural temptation, a desirable calamity, a domestic danger, a delectable detriment, an evil of nature, painted with fair colours!" "A woman either loves or hates; there is no third grade," wrote the authors, quoting Seneca. "When a woman thinks alone, she thinks evil."[27]

The *Malleus* is a lengthy document, but much of the authors' argument regarding the origins of witchcraft is summarized in one succinct statement: "All [witchcraft] comes from carnal lust, which is in women insatiable."[28] As historian Hans Peter Broedel notes, "Witchcraft in the *Malleus* thus emerged as a phenomenon that is explicitly gendered and sexual. It arises from the insatiable sexual appetites of women."[29] Witches, for example, were blamed for infertility, miscarriages, male lust, and even impotence and sexual dysfunction in men, including the disappearance of a man's penis, so that he could "see and feel nothing except his smooth body, uninterrupted by any member."[30] If something went awry with a man's sexuality or in his marriage, a witch was undoubtedly to blame, and that witch was usually found to be a spinster or a widow.

Katharina was surely familiar with the *Malleus Maleficarum*, and she would have been keenly aware, too, of the "witch hunt" that was exploding across Europe, the primary target of which were single women very much like herself (before she married). In fact, while she was still living, four witches were executed in Wittenberg, an event that would have garnered significant attention.[31] The Catholic Church would likely have viewed her as a witch, and even Protestant reformers would have considered Katharina a "witchly" seductress. There was danger in every direction, and all anyone needed back then to incite the cries of "Witch!" was a motive. We can't know for sure if Katharina was afraid of being accused as a witch, but we do know that the threat of such an accusation was real.

The So-Called Wife

While we don't know Katharina's reaction to the rumors and gossip that dogged her, we can look to one of her contemporaries for insights. Katharina Schütz Zell was the first woman in the city of Strasbourg to marry a priest. After she wed Matthew Zell in 1523, she crafted a letter to the bishop, later printed publicly, in which she defended her husband, calling the letter an "apologia for Master Matthew Zell . . . because of the great lies invented about him."[32] Zell systematically invalidated each of the rumors and accusations aimed at her husband, and in doing so, cleverly succeeded not only in defending her husband but also herself and her own motives for marriage as well.

"He began such a marriage because he wanted very much to raise up God's honor, his own salvation, and that of all his brothers," Zell wrote. "For I can perceive in him no dishonorableness, no inclination toward lust or other such thing—for I am not gifted with either overwhelming beauty or riches or other virtue that might move one to seek me in marriage!"[33] Zell dismissed the rumors that her husband had seduced another woman before their marriage and the family maid after, and insisted that she was not physically abused, nor had she run away to her father's house to escape her husband's wrath. In short, Zell concluded, "I know nothing else in this hour than that we would want to satisfy each other in all our intentions insofar as they are godly, and we do that. I attest that such liars forcibly struggle against him without any reason and lie about him. These lies are also against me and all people."[34]

Simmering with anger and indignation, Zell's words offer us a glimpse into some of the emotions Katharina Luther may have experienced as the slanderous rumors swirled around her. As far as we know, she chose not to respond to her detractors, either verbally or in writing. Or perhaps, given her status as the wife of someone so famous, Katharina felt she could not respond. Luther, on the other hand, obstinate, rebellious, and sharp-tongued as always, vocalized his reaction loud and clear for all to hear. Clearly spurred on by the resistance to his marriage and the malicious gossip it provoked, he rarely missed an opportunity to respond with vigor, and often a bit of fun, to those who slandered him.

A year after they were married, Katharina and Luther received two letters, one from Johann Hasenberg and the other from Joachim von der Heyden, both protégés of Duke George. Hasenberg addressed his letter in Latin, the language of the clergy, to "M. Luder and his unmarried wife, Katharina von Bora," and called for them to repent and "return remorsefully to their cloisters."[35] At the very least, Hasenberg insisted, Luther should "send his nun back to her bridegroom Christ and to her Mother Church."[36] If he refused, he should "suffer the torments of hell."[37] Von der Heyden, on the other hand, addressed his letter in German specifically to Katharina, calling her Luther's "so-called wife," blaming her for leading other nuns astray, and accusing her of abusing evangelic freedom through her lustful sin.[38]

Luther simply couldn't resist. He penned an anonymous satirical reply, noting that the two letters had been bound into a "beautiful little book" and entrusted to his household servants, who took it to the privy and then sent it back to Luther after using it (implying that their letters had been used as toilet paper). The servants, the anonymous response read, had also enclosed a reply, bluntly informing the two men that they were asses and concluding with a stinging attack aimed specifically at von der Heyden: "How dare you preempt the power of a common judge and condemn publicly, and before all the world, a godly woman as though she were a perfidious, perjuring, gone astray whore. Where have you, impudent young brat, learned to defame the virtue of other people?"[39]

As a man, and a man of power and prestige, Luther could get away with such a vehement response. Katharina's role, on the other hand, was to stay as quiet and unobtrusive as possible and hope that her husband's word would be enough to restore her honor and secure her future. She was in a uniquely terrible position at this point. After fleeing the secure, albeit confining, life of the convent for the unknown, Katharina had leapt from the precarious life of single womanhood into the security of marriage, only to discover that she was a lightning rod for controversy and anger, a threat to the reform movement, and completely powerless to defend or save herself.

12

Hausfrau Extraordinaire

As dawn lit the interior of her new home on her first morning as Luther's wife, Katharina likely looked around at her surroundings in dismay. The Black Cloister was in shambles. Most of the rooms in the cavernous building were empty, and aside from a handful of kitchen utensils and a few pewter pieces, the majority of household items had disappeared or been stolen. The place was also filthy. "I was tired," the longtime bachelor said, explaining why he hadn't changed his bed, "and wore myself out during the day and then fell into bed, and didn't notice it."[1] A marriage bed rank with smelly, disintegrating straw was undoubtedly *not* what Katharina had pictured as a new bride.

As the Cranachs' houseguest for the last two years, Katharina had grown accustomed to the leisurely lifestyle of a noblewoman. Barbara Cranach had taught her protégé some important and necessary household skills, but as a guest rather than the mistress of the house, Katharina would have had far fewer burdens and responsibilities during her time there. Prior to that, Katharina was only responsible for caring for her own basic needs and participating in the communal chores. Now, however, she suddenly found herself faced with a sprawling property that was, quite literally, falling down around her. As mistress of the Black Cloister, it was Katharina's job to wrestle it into order.

Home Sweet Home

Katharina and Luther lived in four main rooms on the second floor of the former monastery: an ante room (or foyer), a living room, a bedroom, and a smaller room that served as a space for reading and devotions. As was typical during the late Middle Ages, there was no formal dining room. The Luthers ate at a table in the living room, which was also where Luther met with his students and guests, and where Katharina did her sewing and other work. Artwork adorned the ceiling and walls of the living room, including paintings of the Virgin Mary with the Christ child and Christ on the cross. Later a portrait of Katharina by Lucas Cranach was displayed in this room as well.

The kitchen was located on the first floor, accessible through a trap door and a narrow staircase leading down from the living room. Luther's tiny study, "the poor little room,"[2] as he called it, was situated up a spiral staircase in the tower on the third floor. There was no modern-day bathroom, of course, as indoor plumbing didn't exist at the time. However, in 2004 archaeologists discovered what they surmised were the remains of the Luthers' lavatory, a stone niche in an annex off the main

The Luthers' living room in the Black Cloister as it looks today in the *Lutherhaus* museum.

building.[3] The 450-year-old "toilet," which was very advanced for its time, was made out of stone blocks and, unusually, had a thirty-square-centimeter seat over the hole, underneath which was a cesspit attached to a primitive drain.[4]

One of Katharina's first chores as mistress of the Black Cloister was to whitewash all the walls with a solution of lime and water. This was a monumental task; records indicate that she had two and a half wagonloads of lime, plus two additional barrels, delivered to the Black Cloister during her first year of marriage.[5] Whitewashing brightened the dingy walls and was often undertaken as a health precaution, as lime was thought to deter vermin and insects.

Another of Katharina's immediate concerns was the garden, which was an unkempt mess of weeds, plants, and flowers when she arrived. Luther had always enjoyed flowers, but Katharina was much more practical. She focused on planting and tending vegetables—peas, beans, carrots, cabbage, lettuce, and other greens—and herbs, which were critically important for both cooking and medicinal remedies. By 1526, a year after Katharina moved into the Black Cloister, the once-overrun garden was flourishing. Even Luther was known to putter around there, at one point planting seeds to grow "Erfurt radishes," which were purportedly famous for their size.[6]

"She plants our fields, pastures and sells our cows, et cetera,"[7] said Luther about his wife, whom he nicknamed "the Morning Star of Wittenberg," due to the fact that she rose daily at 4:00 a.m. in order to complete her day's work by 9:00 p.m.[8] The "et cetera" Luther tossed out so casually encompassed an enormous amount of work. Although Katharina had at least one or two servants to assist her (especially later on, after the Luthers had children), in addition to her Aunt Magdalena (who lived with the Luthers after leaving Marienthron), she oversaw the labor and tackled much of it herself. While Luther gardened for pleasure and relaxation, Katharina gardened for the same reasons she bred and slaughtered livestock and poultry; caught pike, loach, trout, perch, and carp in the local streams and ponds; planted and tended the fruit and nut orchards and the vineyard; raised bees; preserved meats, fruits, and vegetables; and brewed beer. She did all this at least in part to sustain the household and Luther's continuous stream of visitors and houseguests.

Beginning on their wedding night, when Luther's rival Andreas Karlstadt, fleeing the Peasants' War and seeking shelter, banged on the door of the Black Cloister just before midnight, it wasn't long before every one of the forty cells in the monastery was occupied by an out-of-town guest.[9] Students, professors, theologians, political and religious refugees, and nuns and monks who had escaped the cloistered life were all fed, entertained, boarded, and welcomed with gracious hospitality by Katharina. With ongoing renovations (the Luthers built a basement, added a small room for Katharina's aunt, repaired the roof, and added the aforementioned lavatory) and a house constantly full of guests, Luther and Katharina didn't exactly enjoy a quiet honeymoon period in the early months of their marriage.

A Day in the Life of a Sixteenth-Century Housewife

With every twenty-first-century amenity at our disposal, it's almost impossible for us to fathom a sixteenth-century housewife's daily domestic workload. Sixteenth-century housekeeping handbooks such as *The Boke of Husbandry* offer us at least a glimpse of what everyday life was like for Katharina.

> When thou art up and ready, then first sweep thy house, dress up thy dishboard and set all things in good order within thy house; milk thy kine, feed thy calves, sile (strain) up thy milk, take up thy children and array them, and provide for thy husband's breakfast, dinner, supper, and for thy children and servants, and take thy part with them. And to ordain corn and malt to the mill, to bake and brew withal when need is. Thous must make butter and cheese when thou may; serve thy swine, both morning and evening, and give thy pullen (fowl) meat in the morning, and when time of year cometh, thous must take heed how thy hen, ducks and geese do lay, and to gather up their eggs; and when they wax broody to set them thereas no beasts, swine or other vermin hurt them. And in the beginning March is time to sow flax and hemp . . . and thereof may they make sheets, board-clothes (table cloths), towels, shirts, smocks, and

> such other necessaries; and therefore let thy distaff be always reading for a pastime, that thou be not idle.[10]

Water wasn't accessible with the twist of a faucet handle, of course, but had to be hauled in from the well. The woman of the house also chopped and carried in wood for the fire, which was used for both cooking and heating and had to be maintained constantly, especially in the winter. Likewise, laundry wasn't simply tossed into an electric washer and dryer but rather was lugged down the stairs, out of the building, and across several yards of fields to the banks of the Elbe River, where it was manually scrubbed piece by piece, laid on the shore to dry, and then gathered and lugged back home again at the end of the day. Though she probably didn't do laundry every week, when she did, it was a chore that would have taken a significant amount of Katharina's time and energy.

Keeping the Black Cloister's myriad guests fed also required constant work. When Katharina wasn't milking cows and goats, churning butter, making cheese, tending the garden, or butchering a cow, she visited the market in the center of Wittenberg to purchase anything she couldn't or didn't make herself, including bread (most people who lived in the city bought bread from a baker rather than baking it themselves), spices, and fish, beef, or fowl, depending on what gaps she needed to fill in her weekly menu.

Meals were cooked entirely from scratch, from slaughtering and butchering the meat—including chickens, pigs, cows, sheep and lamb, and game birds such as pheasant and quail and even the occasional peacock—to growing and harvesting the vegetables and herbs, grinding spices and herbs with a mortar and pestle, and preparing the food over an open fire. If the meat was not consumed immediately, it was smoked, salted, or pickled to preserve it and stored in the cool cellar (there was no refrigeration). Meat was almost always served generously spiced, which was both a way to preserve it as well as mask the taste if it had gone slightly bad. Germans also often served their meat with a generous dollop of mustard, and as was typical in the Middle Ages, medieval and early modern cooks made good use of the whole animal, including parts many of us would balk at today, like the brains, tongue, gizzard (throat), sweetbreads (pancreas and thymus glands), lungs, digestive organs, liver, udder, testicles, feet, and even the tail.[11]

Germans had a particular fondness for pastry deep-fried in lard, as well as fruit dishes, and what medieval culinary historian Terrence Scully calls "animal viscera," especially intestines and lungs.[12] For the noonday meal, for instance, Katharina may have prepared something called morels, which entailed boiling a calf's lung, then dicing the lung into smaller chunks and deep-frying the pieces in lard until browned. She would have then sliced open the deep-fried morels, stuffed them with herbs and grapes, and roasted them on a small spit over the fire before finally serving the morels still on the spits and arranged in a bowl on the table. Katharina might have opted to serve the morels with a dish called "heathen peas," which she would have mixed with almonds finely ground with a mortar and pestle, honey, herbs, and spices, and served either warm or cold. Finally, she may have rounded out the meal with *Conkavelit*—a fruit compote comprised of boiled sour cherries, wine, "a good milk out of almonds," rice flour, lard, and spices and garnished with sugar.[13]

People in the sixteenth century generally ate two meals a day—the main dinner around midday, and a simpler "supper" (based on the tradition of serving soup, or sops) at dusk.

Breakfast was not typically consumed, or, at most, consisted of a hunk of bread and a mug of beer or diluted wine.[14] Not only were two meals a day practical from a preparation standpoint (because it took so long to prepare the food), the practice was also recommended by physicians of the time, who considered eating before the previous meal had been completely digested (or at least made its way out of the stomach) unhealthy and even dangerous.

What Katharina cooked was also based on the medieval belief in the four humors, which posited that all living things were composed of a combination of two pairs of elements: warmth and cold, and dryness and moistness. In humans, the humoral agents were blood, yellow bile, black bile, and phlegm, on which the temperaments sanguine (warm and moist), choleric (warm and dry), melancholic (cold and dry), and phlegmatic (cold and moist) were based. "If all things have their own peculiar temperament, then all foodstuffs certainly must have, too," observes Scully. Therefore "everything he or she consumes is logically bound to influence his or her own personal temperament."[15] As Luther was prone to a melancholic disposition and frequently suffered from bouts of depression and anxiety, Katharina would have likely focused on warm, moist food to counter his dry, cold temperament: ripe grapes; figs sweetened in wine; plump mutton, chicken, or game birds prepared in a ginger or saffron sauce.[16] Likewise, it was thought a fever could be cured with ice water and herbs considered to be cold (like hemlock), while someone who was suffering from the chills or listlessness might be offered a dish prepared with peppers.[17]

Even when her husband wasn't struggling with a bout of melancholy, Katharina likely prepared foods to balance the warmth and dryness or coolness and wetness of a particular season. So, for instance, during the temperate spring, the Luthers might have dined on foods like quail and partridge, eggs, goat's milk, and lettuce. Summer demanded foods that would counter the season's heat and dryness: acidic apples, cucumbers, veal or kid dressed in vinegar, and any type of meat or fish dressed in verjuice—the sour juice of crab apples, unripe grapes, and other fruit. Autumn's combination of coolness and dryness suggested foods beneficial to the melancholic temperament, such as those listed above. And finally, to help the body resist the cold, damp winter weather, Katharina likely served roasted game animals and hens and rich meat pies generously seasoned with pepper and other spices and served with spiced wine (although Luther preferred beer).[18]

Katharina was also the brewmaster of the house, and on more than one occasion Luther commented on the fact that he preferred his wife's home brew over anyone else's. Because water was largely considered unsafe to drink, beer was the beverage of choice for early modern Germans, and it was even offered to children as young as four months old as a supplement to breast milk.[19]

Brewing was a complicated, time-consuming process that involved germinating grain into malt, mashing various types of malt (depending on how light or dark you wanted your beer) with hot water, allowing the grain to soften, and then boiling the mixture in order to convert the starch in the grain to fermentable sugars. Precise temperatures were required at this point in the process (which, as you might imagine, was difficult with a wood-burning fire)—low heat inhibited conversion; on the other hand, heat too high could kill the enzymes. Once all the starch was converted to sugar, the mixture—called *wort*—was transferred to a special tub with a false bottom, which allowed the wort to filter through the grains that had settled. The wort was then boiled for two hours, after which hops were added, which helped to preserve the beverage and gave it the classic bitter taste of German beer.[20]

The introduction of simple instruments like thermometers and hydrometers and the development of the pasteurization process in the nineteenth century greatly improved quality control, but until that point, brewing was more art than science. Quality varied widely from batch to batch, a fact that greatly frustrated Katharina. "There is a German saying that goes, 'Hops and malt are lost,' meaning it is hopeless," Luther said in *Table Talk*. "As my Kate is now struggling with her beer, this sentence takes on a new meaning."[21] Brewing was hot, laborious, time-consuming work, and Katharina was vexed to no end when all her labor resulted in a batch that had, in Luther's words, "turned to 'convent'"—that is, a weak, thin beer like that served in the monastery.[22] Beer was Luther's beverage of choice, and like most Germans of the time, he drank a generous amount of it daily. A bad batch was bad news because it meant a cranky husband and more work for Katharina.

House Calls

Katharina was also a skilled nurse and prepared her own medicinal remedies from the plants and herbs she grew in her garden. Historians are unsure how she learned these skills. She may have served in the infirmary at Marienthron, but it's just as likely she gleaned her knowledge here and there: from Barbara Cranach and other acquaintances, through trial and error, and via popular cookbooks. Katharina may have even owned a "book of secrets," which were popular vernacular works containing prescriptions, recipes, and advice concerning medicine and other practical arts, including alchemy, cosmetics, perfumery, veterinary science, and more.[23] For instance, a book of secrets might offer instructions on everything from how to remove unwanted body hair or ease menstrual cramps to how to make soap and glue to how to determine if your husband is impotent.

In short, most women during the late Middle Ages and early modern period had at least some knowledge of medicinal remedies, although it seems from Luther's and others' comments that Katharina had more skills than most. Many years later, her grown son Paul, a medical doctor, complimented his mother's nursing skills and praised her for being half a doctor herself.[24] The German reformer Wolfgang Capito also noticed Katharina's medical aptitude, writing to Luther after he had visited the Black Cloister: "[Your wife] was created to maintain your health so you will be able to serve for many years that church that was born under you."[25]

In fact, as many of her critics began to observe her positive impact on Luther's physical and mental health, their opinions of Katharina began to soften. Eventually she earned the begrudging respect of several of Luther's allies and advisors, who came to see Katharina not as the impediment they had feared, but as an integral part of his success.

Luther's health struggles kept Katharina busy, especially later in their marriage, and since he didn't have much confidence in the physicians of the time, he relied on Katharina's skills and home remedies for his ailments. People in medieval and early modern times didn't typically see a physician (unless it was a life-or-death situation, and often not even then), both because physicians weren't readily available (there were far fewer doctors during medieval and early modern times than there are today) and because people either couldn't afford a visit from a doctor, or because they trusted their own home remedies more. If they did see a medical practitioner, surgeons, barber-surgeons, and apothecaries, rather than physicians, provided most of the care.

Surgery as we understand it today—heart surgery, for example—didn't exist during Luther's day. Radical surgery, which mainly consisted of amputations during wartime, was rare; most surgical procedures were restricted to lancing boils, setting broken bones, treating contusions, stitching lacerations, and the like.[26] Barber-surgeons, on the other hand, in addition to cutting hair, also specialized in leeching, bloodletting, lancing boils, cauterizing, and pulling teeth (one cure for toothache was to rub urine on the gums; if that failed to alleviate the problem, the tooth was often knocked out using a hammer and chisel).[27] When they weren't taking care of humans, barber-surgeons often cared for sick animals.[28]

Apothecaries were responsible for the sale and distribution of medicines, including simple herbs and other single-ingredient medicines as well as compounded varieties, which were specially mixed and oftentimes exceedingly complex formulas.[29] For example, one sixteenth-century English recipe for "a most precious and excellent balm" called for sixty-eight herbs, twenty types of gum, six laxatives, and twenty-four different roots.[30] Every city and most towns and villages had apothecaries, and Katharina likely visited one in Wittenberg for the medicines that were too complicated to make herself or for which she didn't have the proper ingredients.

Luther suffered from an array of maladies and symptoms, including kidney stones, asthma, dizziness, shortness of breath, alternating bouts of diarrhea and constipation, and chronic ear infections, in addition to his struggles with melancholia. He considered many of these ailments the result of the devil's work or a spiritual imbalance, and thus believed they could be cured only with God's help through prayer and faith.[31] Yet he let Katharina doctor him, and he often sent for her home remedies when he was on the road.

The treatments weren't always successful, nor were they very appealing. "Your skill doesn't help me, even with the dung," Luther complained in 1537, when he was suffering from kidney stones while in Smalcald. Excrement and urine—both human and animal—were frequently used to treat common, chronic conditions during the medieval and early modern period.[32] For example, an ointment made of honey and pigeon dung and applied warm to the inflamed or painful area was commonly thought to be helpful in alleviating kidney stones, while gout was treated with a poultice of rosemary, honey, and a generous sprinkling of goat droppings.[33]

Luther wasn't Katharina's only patient, nor was he the only Wittenberger who appreciated her nursing skills. She also cared for her children, as well as guests who fell ill while visiting the Luthers. At one point illness swept through the Black Cloister, leaving Katharina with forty ill guests under her care.[34] When the plague hit Wittenberg and most of the residents fled, Luther and Katharina stayed and turned the Black Cloister into a hospital. "We did not flee," Luther said about the plague in 1539. "I am your preacher and visitor of the sick, and Kate is the nurse, doctor, pharmacist, counselor, etc."[35] As to why they didn't flee, Luther explained, "We have been blessed in this city in good days, why should we leave when suffering strikes?"[36]

Katharina even gave birth to her daughter Elizabeth during the plague outbreak of 1527 while Luther was out of town. She doesn't seem to have feared the plague or other dire illnesses like many of her contemporaries did, perhaps because Katharina had a remarkably strong constitution and rarely became ill herself.

Mistress of Finances

Money was tight in the Luther household from the beginning. For a long time Luther didn't own the Black Cloister; he simply lived there as one of the last two monks left in the house. When Katharina moved in, Elector Johann Frederick—who succeeded his brother, Frederick the Wise—allowed them both to live there tax free until his death in 1532, when he left the former monastery, along with all the rights to brew, malt, sell beer, keep cattle, and conduct all other civil matters, to Luther in his will, with one stipulation: that the elector's successors would retain the right to buy it if Luther ever decided to sell the property.[37]

Despite the fact that they inherited their home and all the property that went along with it, the Luthers still struggled to pay their bills and frequently owed money to various merchants around town. The problem stemmed from the fact that, although by the time he married Katharina he was paid a respectable annual salary of 100 *Gulden* for his work as a professor and frequently received gifts of grain, meat, lumber, bricks, hay, and lime from the elector and the town of Wittenberg, Luther gave away or spent nearly all his earnings. What remained wasn't nearly enough to cover the expenses of such a large household. Furthermore, Luther refused payment for his published writings, he wouldn't accept honoraria for his lectures, and he often tried to give back gifts, including some of the gifts he and Katharina received for their wedding. When Luther couldn't afford to hand out cash to those in need, he would often donate silver cups and tankards from his own cupboards.

Eventually, however, after he'd pawned his last silver cup to pay off a debt, Luther realized his spending and charity were out of control, even when, later in their marriage, he was earning significantly more than 100 *Gulden* a year. "I have a peculiar budget: I consume more than I take in," he admitted. "Every year we need 500 *gulden* for the kitchen alone, but my annual pay is only 300 *gulden*. . . . What am I to do?"[38] Luther's solution? To hand the household finances over to Katharina. This was not altogether unusual for the time period—wives often managed the household finances during medieval and early modern times—but it's clear that Luther trusted Katharina completely, and he outright admitted that she was a far better financial manager than he. "In domestic affairs I defer to Katie," Luther acknowledged, "otherwise I am led by the Holy Ghost."[39]

With complete control over the finances, Katharina made two important decisions: she purchased additional land in nearby Zülsdorf in order to expand her farming operations and produce more income, and she began to charge many of the Black Cloister's visitors room and board, a decision that irritated the men who had always stayed at Luther's house for free. Reformer and theologian Veit Dietrich called Katharina a "tightwad and a miser," and Gregor Brück, the elector's chancellor, accused her of being a "stingy householder."[40] As Ernst Kroker points out, even contemporary critics tend to portray Katharina as miserly, stingy, and greedy.

The more likely truth is that Katharina was simply a good businesswoman and a frugal housewife who upset the applecart and bruised some male egos when she crossed the threshold of the Black Cloister as Luther's wife. Kroker notes, "Not a single time do we hear that she seriously opposed her husband's lavish charity."[41] At the same time, Luther never spoke "of her alleged greed, but instead praised her thriftiness."[42] "What she has now, she got without me," he admitted with obvious admiration in 1542.[43] In his letters to her, Luther often addressed Katharina as "Lord," "Sir," and "Doctor," not sarcastically, but with obvious respect, admiration, and love. Luther had the good sense to appreciate his wife's intellect and her savvy business finesse.

Although Katharina has often been criticized by biographers for her supposed arrogance and aloofness, one wonders if she was simply too busy running what was essentially a midsize business, complete with brewery, vineyard, farm, and a forty-room hotel (in addition to raising six of her own children and four adopted children, which we'll cover in a subsequent chapter) to spend time making small talk with the neighbor ladies.

Luther biographer Edith Simon, for instance, states that Katharina was "generally regarded as stuck up,"[44] while another Luther biographer, Richard Marius, paints her as a shrew: unattractive, controlling, miserly, and disliked. "She often seems grasping and even petty in her quest for money, and we have many hints that the Wittenbergers did not like her," he writes. "She was apparently crotchety—not an advantage in a day when husbands expected wives to be submissive or at least pretend to be so until the time of marriage."[45] Yet as historian Elsie McKee points out, "The sheer physical effort of living [in early modern Europe] consumed a great deal of energy," something we who live in modern times can hardly begin to comprehend.[46]

For the twenty-one years she was married to Martin Luther, Katharina worked seventeen hours a day, from well before dawn until far past dusk. Add to that the fact that Katharina's responsibilities went far above and beyond that of a typical sixteenth-century housewife, and the result is not someone who was merely aloof or crotchety but simply busier than most of us could ever possibly imagine. The Wittenbergers and Luther's colleagues and peers may not have appreciated Katharina's industriousness, but Luther clearly did. And as we will see, Luther came to rely on his Morning Star of Wittenberg in more than just domestic affairs.

13

Two Pigtails on the Pillow

Although Luther's quip about awaking and being startled to glimpse two pigtails on the pillow beside him was intended to be humorous, one hears the truth loud and clear in his seemingly lighthearted admission: marriage was hard, especially for two people accustomed to living unattached to anyone else for so long.

The truth is, Luther and Katharina were virtual strangers on their wedding day. The two might have had cursory contact or exchanged a passing word or two while Katharina was living with the Cranachs, but it's doubtful Luther and Katharina ever engaged in a meaningful conversation before their nuptials. They certainly didn't spend much, if any, time alone together, nor did they enjoy the kind of lengthy engagement that most couples do today. Within a week or two of the proposal, Luther and Katharina found themselves husband and wife, two strangers sharing a bed, a home, and a life.

Idealism Meets Reality

For Luther, the reality of marriage as it played out day to day departed significantly from his preconceived notions of it. His early writings convey a surprisingly idealistic, romantic vision of marriage and the relationship between husband and wife.

"God makes distinctions between the different kinds of love, and shows that the love of a man and woman is (or should be) the greatest and purest of all loves," Luther wrote in 1519, six years before wedding Katharina. "Over and above all these [kinds of love] is married love, that is, a bride's love, which glows like a fire and desires nothing but the husband. She says, 'It is you I want, not what is yours: I want neither your silver nor your gold; I want neither. I want only you. I want you in your entirety, or not at all.' All other kinds of love seek something other than the loved one: this kind wants only to have the beloved's own self completely."[1] Marriage was intended to be an intimate, emotionally fruitful bond, Luther believed. Nothing was as sweet as what he called "bridal love," the deepest, most gratifying and selfless kind of love possible between human beings.

"There are many kinds of love," Luther declared three years later in 1522, "but none is as fiery and hot as the bridal love that a bride has for her groom; again, the love is not looking for pleasure or presents, not wealth nor golden rings, but rather looks at him alone. Even if he were to give her everything there was, she would disregard it all and say, 'I want to have you alone.' And if he had absolutely nothing, she still would pay no attention to that but would want him anyway. That is the proper bridal love."[2] Although Luther was comparing the love between a man and a woman to the love Christ has for his church, it's also clear from these words and others that he had certain expectations of what ideal marital love should look and feel like. He believed the love between a married couple was passionate and selfless, truer and purer than all other kinds of love.

Fast-forward to 1525. As is often the case, the reality of marriage in day-to-day experience didn't perfectly reflect Luther's premarriage expectations. For starters, Luther didn't experience the deeply intimate "bridal love" he had written about years earlier. Luther married Katharina not because he was in love with her, nor because he felt a romantic attraction toward her, nor even because he considered her an ideal mate. Rather, Luther proposed to Katharina out of compassion and a sense of Christian duty. As he later said himself, he had initially considered proposing to Eva Schonfeld, another of the escaped nuns who was younger and had a gentler, more amenable disposition than Katharina, but Schonfeld married a local pharmacist before Luther could make up his mind.[3]

In contrast, Luther felt obligated to marry Katharina, a sentiment clearly conveyed in his personal correspondence. "I feel neither passionate love nor burning for my spouse, but I cherish her,"[4] Luther wrote to Nikolaus von Amsdorf about his new wife on June 21, 1525, just a few days after the private wedding ceremony at the Black Cloister. Biographer Heiko Oberman translates this same line to read, "I do not love my wife, but I appreciate her."[5] Richard Marius's translation reads, "I neither love nor lust for my wife, but I esteem her."[6] Regardless of the translation, the message is clear: Luther was not in love with Katharina, nor was he especially attracted to her. He respected her, and even more importantly, he believed God led him to marry her. "God has willed it and brought about this step," he declared to von Amsdorf.[7]

Katharina's strong-willed nature didn't align with Luther's definition of the ideal woman, nor did it complement Luther's own obstinate, opinionated personality. "If I were to court a girl again, I would chisel myself an obedient wife from rock," Luther once quipped to friends and students gathered around his table.[8]

Although Katharina spoke respectfully to her husband—she always used the more formal "*Herr Doktor*," rather than the familiar "*Du*,"[9] when speaking to him—she also didn't hesitate to challenge him, and it's clear from some of his comments and hers that she stood her ground and refused to let Luther boss her around. "If I can bear the wrath of the devil, of sin, and of conscience, then I can also stand Kate von Bora's anger," Luther once said, implying that he may have borne the brunt of that anger once or twice himself.[10]

On another occasion, when Luther tried to get Katharina to read the Bible from start to finish in a year (he even promised her 50 *Gulden* if she succeeded), she argued, "I've read enough, I've heard enough. I know enough. Would to God I lived it."[11] One wonders, in light of her daily domestic workload, when Katharina would have found time for Bible study, which is perhaps why Luther didn't insist on a structured reading and study plan, in spite of his belief in *sola scriptura*. At any rate, Katharina made her point clear: she refused to read the Bible from start to finish under a deadline, and her husband didn't dare press the issue further.

Katharina also engaged Luther in complex theological discussions. She asked him to explain why God had demanded that Abraham kill his son Isaac;[12] she questioned how David could ask to be judged according to his righteousness when he was a sinner;[13] she wondered how she could be both a saint and sinner at the same time;[14] and she expressed her curiosity about prayer, at one point asking Luther why it seemed like they prayed less frequently and with less fervor since leaving the Roman Catholic Church.[15] In spite of her refusal to read the Bible through in a year, Luther also acknowledged that Katharina knew the Psalms "better than ever the papists had done."[16] In other words, Katharina didn't relegate herself to the domestic realm and leave intellectual, theological talk to the men; she participated in the discussions around the table and engaged Luther privately in conversation about such topics herself. She was both spiritually inquisitive and a critical thinker, two qualities Luther admired and respected in her, and, as time went on, grew to find quite attractive.

As Reformation scholars Susan Karant-Nunn and Merry Wiesner-Hanks note, Luther's view of women and their role in marriage and in society was compatible with the opinions of many other sixteenth-century theologians.[17] That is to say, Luther was very much in line with the times when it came to his views on women—at least on paper. His statements on women and marriage in everything from his lectures and sermons on Genesis to many of his informal statements compiled in *Table Talk* all clearly point to his belief in separate and distinct roles for a husband and wife within marriage, with the man as the natural leader and the woman his subordinate.

"In the household the wife is a partner in the management and has a common interest in the children and the property, and yet there is a great difference between the sexes," Luther stated in his *Lectures on Genesis*. "The male is like the sun in heaven, the female like the moon, the animals like the stars, over which sun and moon have dominion. It was written that this sex [female] may not be excluded from any glory of the human creature, although it is inferior to the male sex."[18] He expounded on the topic of male and female roles when he gathered with his students and friends around the table: "[Women] have been made by God to bear children, to delight men, to be merciful," and "God created male and female—the female for reproduction, the male for nourishing and defending," Luther said in *Table Talk*.[19]

He made dozens of formal and informal statements on the proper role of women in society, in the home, and in marriage, some of them extreme. "Women are created for no other purpose than to serve men and be their helpers," he wrote. "If women grow weary or even die while bearing children, that doesn't harm anything. Let them bear children to death; they are created for that."[20] In his writing, Luther's views were crystal clear: man was the head of the household and made superior by God; woman, as the inferior sex, was made to serve her husband and bear his children. Women were adjuncts to men, just as Eve had been intended for Adam.

Yet it's clear from Luther's personal letters to Katharina and others that his marriage was, in reality, a much more equitable one than he ever condoned in his lectures or treatises and even in the statements he made among his students and peers around the table. As Karant-Nunn and Wiesner-Hanks point out, "In the abstract, Luther envisioned each woman's and girl's confinement to the home, where, in pious mood, she labored efficiently and frugally. When we shift our gaze to Luther's own experience, we see him closely bound to, and dependent upon, his Kate." Therefore, they conclude, "We ought to assess Luther from the dual perspective of theory and practice."[21] In other words, Luther said and wrote one thing about the roles of man and woman within marriage; how he lived with Katharina in their day-to-day life as husband and wife was another thing entirely.

Around the Table

Imagine, for a moment, the scene around Luther's dinner table most evenings. At the head of the table sat Luther, surrounded by men, his fan club, if you will—the university students, colleagues, and theological and political leaders who gathered to exchange ideas and hear Luther's thoughts on everything from town gossip to the Holy Roman Emperor. The talk was loud, boisterous, and brash as the men refilled their beer mugs and passed plate after plate prepared and served by Katharina.

Luther's faithful students and friends sat transfixed by his every word and dutifully transcribed the conversations that transpired around the table (as well as in the garden and even snippets of conversation overheard between Luther and Katharina around the house). These seven-thousand-plus statements comprise what's known as Luther's *Table Talk*, a compilation of informal thoughts, ideas, and opinions on everything from religion and politics to marriage and child rearing. The language and tone of these conversations was often earthy, sometimes outright crude—the kind of talk you might hear from men enjoying a beer together at the local tavern. Outspoken to begin with and emboldened by drink and the attentions of his audience, Luther's tongue was often loosened in this casual setting. One has the distinct impression that many of Luther's statements around the table were uttered with more than a little boasting, bravado, and jest.

"Men have broad chests and narrow hips; therefore they have wisdom. Women have narrow chests and broad hips. Women ought to be domestic; the creation reveals it, for they have broad backsides and hips, so that they should sit still," he declared.[22] "There is no dress that suits a woman or maiden so badly as wanting to be clever," he stated during another dinner.[23] "Female government has never done any good," he announced on still another occasion. "God made Adam master over all creatures, to rule over all living things, but when Eve persuaded him that he was lord even over God she spoiled everything. We have you women to thank for that! With tricks and cunning women deceive men, as I, too, have experienced."[24] "When God installed Adam as lord over all creatures, everything was still in good order and proper, and everything was governed in the best way," he claimed. "But when the wife came along and wanted to put her hand too in the simmering broth [*Sode*] and be clever, everything fell apart and became wildly disordered."[25]

Around his table Luther had the rapt attention of his fandom and he made the most of it. Holding court as head of his own personal boys' club, Luther tended to make exaggerated, emphatic declarations for effect. Not only did he bluster about women generally, he also joked and postured about his own wife, usually in her presence. He accused her of being chatty and disobedient, chided her for interrupting his work with silly questions,[26] suggested she pray the Lord's Prayer instead of talking so much, and called her his "*Kette*" (German for "chain," as in "ball and chain"), a play on her nickname, Kethe.[27]

At the same time, however, Luther did not tolerate the misogynist comments of his peers. In his introduction to Johannes Freder's 1545 *Ein Dialogus dem Ehestand zu ehren geschrieben* (*A Dialogue Written to Honor the Matrimony* of

Queen Dorothea of Denmark), Luther devoted most of his attention not to Freder but to another contemporary theologian, Sebastian Franck, who had authored a collection of misogynist aphorisms that Luther found highly offensive.[28] When Luther called Franck a "great arse-bumble bee" he was not joking or trying to be funny.[29] Instead, he was issuing a scathing reprimand to Franck and all others who passed "such a stink and devil's filth under our nose" and "daubed such a great dirt-heap in our face."[30]

Such seemingly contradictory statements in Luther's own writing and conversation might lead one to conclude he was a hypocrite, or at the very least, inconsistent in what he said and wrote about women. However, to do so would be to neglect the significance of the context in which Luther's comments about women were written and uttered. As Susan Karant-Nunn points out, "Luther deliberately cultivated humor in the household setting where he was surrounded by his closest family members and also by guests and boarders."[31] There was a time and place for serious commentary, as well as a time and place for humor, pun, and innuendo.

The truth was, Luther deeply respected women, especially his Katharina. "One has to have women," he declared in a rare moment of solemnity at the table. "If one did not have this sex, womankind, housekeeping and everything that pertains to it would fall apart; and after it all worldly governance, cities, and order. In sum, the world cannot dispense with women even if men by themselves could bear children."[32] The world and its governance depended on women, Luther asserted—quite a provocative statement from an early modern man.

It's clear from the statements and conversations recorded in *Table Talk*, many of which also include Katharina's responses in her own words (or at least as her words were transcribed by Luther's guests), that Luther's quips and jabs were largely a game—and a game in which he was not the only player. Unlike most early modern households, Katharina didn't disappear into the background once her expected duties as wife and lady of the house were fulfilled. Rather, she was an active participant in the male-dominated world of the Black Cloister. She didn't hesitate to express her opinions among Luther's peers and was quick to rebuke her husband, albeit gently, in the presence of their guests for remarks she found crude or rude. At one point, for example, she chided him, "Ah, dear Sir, that's much too coarse!" when he lashed out against theologian and reformer Caspar Schwenckfeld, with whom he disagreed theologically over the sacrament of the Eucharist.[33]

Katharina may have prepared the food and served the men gathered around the table, but she didn't remain on the fringe of these male-dominated social interactions. Katharina had a seat at the table and participated in the conversation, voicing her own opinions, asking questions, and contributing to the discussion. Many of the *Table Talk* recorders referred to the gathering as "Katy's table," and one scribe in particular, Konrad Cordatus, complained about Katharina's long speeches and the fact that she, as a housewife, didn't refrain from interrupting her husband. When Luther once joked to a guest, "Indulge a meek host, for he is obedient to the lady," Cordatus wrote irritably, "This is most certainly true!"[34] Not only did Cordatus not appreciate the fact that Katharina was allowed a voice, he clearly considered Luther weak because of it. Luther, on the other hand, didn't seem to care whether his friends and guests approved of the nontraditional social etiquette around his dinner table.

Luther behind the Scenes

Luther may have blustered and complained about his "*Kette*" in the presence of his male students and guests, but behind the scenes, his personal letters both to his closest friends and to Katharina herself paint a much more intimate picture of their marriage. Luther's most personal correspondence reveals a surprising tenderness and a man who not only had compassion and respect for his wife but deeply loved her and valued her as his partner as well.

This softer and arguably more authentic representation of Luther's feelings for Katharina began to surface in his letters as early as one year into their marriage. "Katie, my rib, sends her greetings and her appreciation that you honored her with such a kind letter," Luther wrote in 1526 to his good friend, the Augustinian friar Michael Stifel, announcing the birth of his first child, Hans. "She is well, by God's grace, compliant, and in every way is obedient and obliging to me, more than I had ever dared to hope (thank God), so that I would not want to exchange my poverty for the riches of Croesus."[35] On one hand, Luther referred to his wife as his "rib"—an allusion to Eve having been created from Adam's rib, and a traditional, albeit lighthearted, reference to Katharina's role as her husband's subordinate. On the other hand, it's clear from his gushing praise that Luther had already developed a deep respect and admiration for Katharina and had begun to see her not as arrogant and proud, as he had first assumed, but "obedient and obliging." Not only that, but marriage agreed with him, it seemed, so much so that he wouldn't trade it even for "the riches of Croesus." Just one year into marriage, Luther's feelings for his wife had already transformed from dutiful compassion to genuine admiration and affection.

Luther participated in the popular rhetoric of the time, and while he used this language as a way to fit into his peer group as "one of the boys," there was obvious affection beneath his bravado. For example, in calling Katharina his "rib," he reminded her and others of the hierarchy of Adam over Eve and placed the blame for sin on Eve's (and Katharina's) shoulders. Yet his pet name for his wife also expressed a tender sentiment. He was reminding her and others that she was a part of him by alluding to the "one flesh" definition of marriage. Similarly, Luther referred to Katharina as his "*Kette*" in the same way a husband today sometimes jokes about his wife as his "ball and chain." There was admiration and intimacy in Luther's words. He may have felt the need to maintain a certain superiority and dominance, but his words also clearly expressed how integral Katharina was to his life as well.

This deepening respect and affection was also reflected in Luther's letters to Katharina herself. "To my kind, dear Lord, Catherine Luther, a doctor and preacher in Wittenberg, Grace and peace in Christ, Dear Sir Katie!" he wrote from a conference in Marburg in 1529[36] (see the appendix to read the full letter). After updating Katharina on business and political developments at the conference, asking her to pray for him, and instructing her to give the children kisses from him, Luther signed his letter, "Your obedient servant, Martin Luther." Helmut Lehmann, general editor of the American Edition of *Luther's Works*, notes that addressing Katharina as "Lord" or "Sir" might sound strange to the modern reader, especially since Katharina was neither a doctor nor a preacher and certainly not a "sir." But, Lehmann notes, these phrases should not be simply interpreted as jokes or as a reference to his wife's nobility. Luther considered Katharina not only his wife and the mother of his children, but "above all, a spiritual companion."[37]

The fact that Luther signed his letter "Your obedient servant" is no joke either, but a "major comment on the relationship between husband and wife as Luther understood it—the same Luther who took literally St. Paul's statement that wives should be subordinate to their husbands," says Lehmann.[38] In short, what looks like teasing or joking on the surface was actually an admission of Luther's profound admiration of and respect for Katharina not only as his wife and the mother of his children but also as "lord" of the household and his true partner in every sense of the word.

A Trusted Confidante

In the early months and years of their marriage, Katharina proved herself more than capable, whipping the dilapidated household into shape, managing the finances, reining in Luther's spending, and planning for the future. Impressed by his wife's savvy business skills and industriousness, Luther gave Katharina more and more responsibility and authority. Not only did he release full control of the household and the finances into her hands, Luther also trusted Katharina to make business decisions for the Black Cloister and for the livelihood of their family and their future—even when he didn't entirely agree with those decisions. For example, as noted earlier, she expanded the estate with the purchase of additional property in Zülsdorf and began to charge visitors room and board as a way to help support the household. Luther did not favor either of these decisions; nonetheless he supported Katharina and encouraged her to do what she thought would benefit the household and her future security.

In private, Luther spoke to Katharina as an equal, confiding in her as he did his closest friends about politics and theology, trusting her with his work, and encouraging her to make business and even political decisions on her own. Luther considered Katharina a confidante, advisor, and business partner. It was she, for example, who persuaded Luther to respond to Erasmus's attacks.[39] Luther had intended to stay silent, but at Katharina's urging, he took up his pen in 1525 to wage an argument against Erasmus's theology of free will. He also listened to his wife and, more often than not, heeded her counsel. When just five months into their marriage Katharina asked Luther not to attend his good friend George Spalatin's wedding because she had dreamed about him being murdered en route and worried about him traveling through dangerous territory, Luther complied: "I cannot come viz. the tears of my wife, who believes you would be deeply grieved were my life imperilled. I am full of pity for my dear Kathie, who would be half-dead with anxiety before I returned."[40] Luther was not mocking his wife's fears; he was respecting them.

He also indicated in several letters that he relied on Katharina to convey critical pieces of information and news to key people, and he trusted her to ensure his writing was printed and distributed properly. In August of 1530, for instance, Luther conveyed his frustration over the delayed printing of a manuscript and instructed Katharina to retrieve the sermon from one printer and give the job to another. "If this has not yet happened," he wrote, "then see that it is done soon, and that the sermon is completed as quickly as possible."[41] Luther had dozens of students at his beck and call, yet he entrusted Katharina with the important job of getting his writing published as expeditiously as possible. Furthermore, Luther readily confided the details of his political and theological negotiations to Katharina. While staying at Coburg Castle during the Diet of Augsburg in 1530, Luther reiterated his anxiety about the Diet time and time again in his letters to his wife, implying not only that he trusted her with this confidential information but also that she was well informed about the political climate of the time.

Finally, Luther trusted Katharina to oversee a ministerial search committee to fill a pastor position at a church in nearby Greussen (see second letter in the appendix). As Rudolf and Marilynn Markwald note, this request, which would have been extremely rare during the sixteenth century, a time in which women were not typically consulted in such matters, demonstrates Luther's respect for his wife.[42] It also illustrates the complexity of their relationship, which was based on mutual trust and respect. In print Luther was firm on what he believed to be the God-ordained roles for men and women, husbands and wives. In reality, those distinct lines of demarcation were significantly blurred.

The Empress Katie

Luther may have married Katharina out of a sense of Christian duty, but he grew to care about her and love her in every sense of the word. A close look at some of his informal comments around the table as well as his personal letters to Katharina reveal a progressive deepening of his feelings for her, feelings that began pragmatically and progressed over time to genuine love.

"I wouldn't give up Katy for France or for Venice—first, because God gave her to me and gave me to her; second, because I have often observed that other women have more shortcomings than my Katy (although she, too, has some shortcomings, they are outweighed by many great virtues); and third, because she keeps faith in marriage, that is, fidelity and respect," Luther said early in their marriage (this comment, by the way, was recorded in *Table Talk*; Luther was nothing if not contradictory).[43] While this statement still speaks to Luther's belief that he is fulfilling his God-given duty, and it isn't exactly effusive praise, it does allude to Luther's deepening feelings for his wife, especially when we compare it to this comment, made by Luther just two years later. "To have grace and peace in marriage is a gift second only to the knowledge of the Gospel," Luther said in 1533. "Kate, you have a god-fearing man who loves you. You are an empress; realize it and thank God for it."[44] Still later he declared, "If I should lose my Katie I would not take another wife though I were offered a queen."[45] When Katharina became gravely ill in 1540, Luther was beside himself, fretting by her bedside and pleading, "Dear Kate, don't die and leave me."[46] By 1540 he was also signing his letters, "Martin Luther—who loves you from his heart"[47] (see second letter in the appendix).

Luther's later letters to Katharina also reveal a sweet side rarely seen in the outspoken, boisterous Reformer:

> "To my dearly beloved . . ."
> "To my most beloved Lady of the House . . ."
> "My sweetheart Kate . . ."
> "To my dearly beloved Katie . . ."

The couple also enjoyed a good-natured repartee, and their teasing banter reveals how comfortable they were in each other's company, as well as how much they simply enjoyed one another. "The time will come when a man will take more than one wife,"

Luther once quipped to Katharina, who was quick to respond, "Let the devil believe that!" The two volleyed back and forth before Katharina triumphed with a quick-witted response. Rather than put up with polygamy, she retorted, "I'd rather go back to the convent and leave you and all our children."[48] Katharina and Luther's exchange sounds like the typical repartee of two playful people in love.

Then there's the story of the study door. Katharina reportedly called a locksmith to open the heavy wooden door to the tower when Luther failed to emerge, despite her pounding and shouting, after three days. She knew he was writing about Psalm 22 and had locked himself on the third floor with only a bit of bread, some salt, and water, but she grew anxious when he didn't respond to her calls. When she finally burst into the study, Katharina found her husband deep in thought, his Bible open on the desk. Amused by her dramatic action, Luther teased Katharina, asking if she had thought he was up to no good,[49] a comment that undoubtedly exasperated the already frazzled wife. Despite Katharina's frustration in the moment, it's clear the couple could joke with and tease one another because they had reached a place of security and comfort in their relationship. As Susan Karant-Nunn observes, "Humor provided a mechanism for preventing or diminishing tension among those who lived (and ate) in close proximity to one another, so that they might discuss sober matters and yet endure their closeness."[50]

In short, Luther came to be quite taken with his wife, a fact that undoubtedly surprised him. What's more, he clearly liked her as a person and partner and missed her when he was away. One can hear the disappointment in Luther's voice, for example, in a 1540 letter when he mentions she has not written in a while: "I have received letters from the children, but from Your

Grace I have received nothing. If it please God, then you might now, at least once, answer this, the fourth letter, with your gracious hand"[51] (see the appendix for the complete letter). Luther sounds a bit like a petulant child or a disappointed lover as he not-so-subtly points out that he has written Katharina four letters yet received not even one in response from her.

Not only was she the mother of his children, his nurse, his business manager, and the manager of his household, Katharina was Luther's confidante, a person whose companionship he truly enjoyed. It's obvious the two respected and trusted one another and delighted in each other's company. It may not have been head-over-heels love from the start, but it didn't take long for Luther to become quite smitten indeed.

A "Dear and Precious Man"

As we've noted all along, we don't definitively know how Katharina felt about Luther because we don't have her perspective on their marriage. We must make do with the bits and pieces we can glean from the observations of others and from the few words we do have from Katharina herself.

For example, the number of letters written by Luther in reply to Katharina hint at how frequently she wrote to her husband when he was traveling. We also know that she fretted about his health and worried about his overall safety. As was noted earlier, after having a premonition that danger would befall him, Katharina begged Luther not to travel to his dear friend Spalatin's wedding—a request Luther heeded. When Luther became gravely ill with an attack of kidney stones while traveling in Smalcald and it was thought he might die, Katharina left

Wittenberg immediately in order to be by his side (he recovered before Katharina arrived and subsequently wrote to her that he was happily on his way home to her).[52] Luther also frequently consoled Katharina in his letters and tried to ease her anxieties about him. When he was in Eisleben, for instance, just before his death in 1546, he urged her to read John and the *Small Catechism* and gently reminded her that rather than worrying herself, she should hand her fears and anxiety over to God[53] (see the third letter in the appendix). Just a handful of Katharina's own words about her husband exist today, and they are all contained in a single letter, written to her sister-in-law, Christina von Bora, two months after Luther's death. In this brief but moving correspondence we glimpse the depths of Katharina's grief.

> I can easily believe that you have heartfelt sympathy for my poor children and me. For who would not easily be troubled and saddened over such a precious man as my dear husband was? He served not just one city or a single country, but the entire world. For that reason I really am so sad that I can't tell anyone how full of sorrow my heart is. And I don't know what I'm thinking and how I'm feeling. I can't eat or drink, nor even sleep. And if I had had a princedom or empire and lost it, I wouldn't have been as sad as now when our dear Lord God has taken this dear and precious man from me, and not just from me, but from the whole world. If I think about it, then I can't speak nor even have someone write because of the pain and crying (God surely knows that).[54]

One can hear in her words Katharina's attempt to be strong, to put on a brave face in the midst of such a devastating loss. She begins her letter resolutely, declaring the impact Luther's death has had on the world, but her resolve quickly dissolves into an expression of personal grief. She can't eat, she can't drink, she can't sleep. Grief has so muddled her thoughts and emotions, she admits that she can't even think straight. Ernst Kroker notes that Katharina had dictated this letter, but even that task was nearly impossible, given her incessant weeping and unrelenting pain. This is the heartbreaking letter of a grief-stricken wife. As Philip Melanchthon and Reformation leader Paul Eber later reported, Katharina especially lamented that she had been unable to tend to Luther during his last days and hours and that he had died without her at his bedside.[55]

The Perfect Match

A 1530s portrait of the Luther family (which biographers Rudolph and Marilynn Markwald suggest was likely painted by Lucas Cranach) depicts Katharina sitting in a chair in the garden, their daughter Magdalene sliding from her lap and beginning to toddle away from her. Their oldest child, Hans, stands next to his mother, while Luther sits across from Katharina, seated comfortably in a large chair with an open book on his lap. Standing behind Luther is a man, possibly Philip Melanchthon, and sitting behind Katharina is an elderly woman, presumably her aunt, Magdalena, bent over her needlework.[56]

As the Markwalds note, at first glance the painting seems to portray a typical family gathering, but a closer look reveals something interesting. Katharina is not depicted in the background, sewing or knitting, but is seated front and center in the foreground. And while her maternal qualities are highlighted, with one child on her lap and another standing nearby, she also appears to be discussing or perhaps even arguing a point with her husband. Katharina is speaking, and Luther is listening.[57] The message is clear: Katharina was not a mere bystander; she was an engaged and devoted partner to Luther and an active participant in the Reformation.

Stubborn, opinionated, blunt, and often crass, sickly, prone to melancholy, and a classic workaholic, Luther was not an easy man to live with. As biographer Edith Simon so aptly noted, Luther may have claimed he wanted a more obedient spouse, but "how would he have fared with a meek wife?"[58] Luther found the best possible partner in Katharina, a woman who deeply loved and respected him, yet also managed his volatile moods and his difficult personality and offered him intellectual stimulation and companionship. Luther undoubtedly understood how challenging and difficult he was. Feisty and strong, courageous and smart, industrious and utterly devoted, Katharina was, in fact, the perfect match for Martin Luther, and he knew it.

14

A Family Affair

"Katie is fulfilling Genesis 3:8 where the Lord God said to the woman, 'in pain shall you bring forth children,'" Luther wrote to a friend on October 21, 1525—his way of announcing that Katharina was expecting their first child.[1] The news spawned a revival of the malicious rumors and gossip that had plagued the couple leading up to and following their wedding. Some speculated that Katharina would give birth to the antichrist or a two-headed monster. Others suggested that the pregnancy smacked of blasphemy and sacrilege, "a double breach of monastic vows."[2] Luther and Katharina ignored the rumors, delighted that God had blessed them so quickly and easily with a pregnancy.

As marriage was essentially a sixteenth-century noblewoman's only viable option outside the convent, bearing and rearing children was the natural expectation of such a union. In fact, marriage was so closely equated with pregnancy, motherhood, and family, standard wedding gifts of the time often included swaddling (diapers), cradles, and infant bathing tubs.[3] Motherhood was by far a woman's most important role during medieval and early modern times, and childlessness was viewed as a curse of the devil.

Augsburgian Bernhard Rem described the ideal Christian woman as "a wife who washes her children's nappies each day, who feeds them pap, gives her husband food to eat, and nourishes her children in the sweat of her brow," a definition that inextricably linked marriage with motherhood.[4] Likewise, Luther also had plenty to say about the role of women as mothers. He praised the biblical Rachel as "an example of very beautiful and motherly affection and chastity," noting, "the only thing she seeks is offspring from her flesh."[5] "The saintly women desire nothing else than the natural fruit of their bodies," he said, speaking of both Rachel and Leah in his *Lectures on Genesis*. "For by nature woman has been created for the purpose of bearing children. Therefore she has breasts; she has arms for the purpose of nourishing, cherishing, and carrying her offspring. It was the intention of the Creator that women should bear children and that men should beget them—with the exception of those men whom God Himself has excepted."[6]

Katharina fulfilled her expected wifely duty quickly. On June 7, 1526, just a few days short of their first wedding anniversary, she gave birth to their first child, a son, Johannes, whom they called Hans. The baby was named after Luther's father, Hans, and Johannes Bugenhagen, the Wittenberg pastor who had married Luther and Katharina one year before. Luther wrote to his good friend, John Rühel, the following day: "Yesterday

. . . at two o'clock, my dear Katie, by God's great grace, gave to me a Hansen [one of the variations on his nickname] Luther."[7] Two months later Luther was still eagerly spreading the good news: "God in his great goodness has blessed me with a healthy and vigorous son, John, a little Luther,"[8] he wrote to his friend, Michael Stifel.

Luther was obviously overjoyed as well as undoubtedly relieved that both his son and wife had survived the rigors of labor and delivery. Childbirth was a dangerous endeavor for both mother and child in the Middle Ages and early modern period, although maternal mortality, at between 1 and 2 percent, was lower than one might assume for the time. While major complications like eclampsia or hemorrhaging were rare, when they did occur they were almost always fatal, as were instances in which the infant was breech or otherwise not positioned correctly and had to be turned in utero.[9] The widespread introduction of forceps in the eighteenth century helped with delivery challenges, but during Katharina's time such tools were not yet available. Thankfully, none of Katharina's six pregnancies and deliveries presented any extraordinary challenges.

Luther celebrated his son's arrival, but as was the custom of the time, he wasn't present during the labor or delivery. Instead, Katharina was attended by a midwife, perhaps a close friend or two, and probably at least one servant, all of whom would have assisted with the delivery. Whom she invited to attend the birth was an important decision; as historian Merry Wiesner points out, accusations of witchcraft had been known to result from the curses and anger of a neighbor excluded from the event.[10] Katharina gave birth at home, in her own bedroom and in her own bed, as hospitals were not nearly as prevalent during the Middle Ages and the early modern period as they are today.

Even if there had been an official hospital in Wittenberg at the time, labor and delivery was always relegated to the private realm of the home. A male physician was only called if either the mother or the infant, or both, had died or were dying, so his appearance was dreaded.[11]

To prepare for her delivery, Katharina's midwife, and perhaps Katharina herself, likely referred to Eucharius Rösslin's *Rosengarten*, a popular manual first printed in 1513 and considered to be the foremost guide to gynecology, obstetrics, and infant and child care across much of northern Europe.[12] Although the *Rosengarten* was a scholarly manual and drew on classical and medieval authorities, including Hippocrates, Galen, and Albertus Magnus, Rösslin himself was a practicing physician and thus offered practical and detailed instructions for prenatal care, labor, and delivery, as well as information about the possible complications that could occur in childbirth.[13] The most harrowing section of the manual, for example, included eight pages of instruction for how to remove a dead child from the womb, a situation which, because of the primitive surgical skills of the time, posed the gravest threat to the mother's life. Rösslin also devoted a section to the reverse situation: how to deliver a baby when the mother had died in childbirth.[14] If Katharina had studied the *Rosengarten* in preparation for the birth of her first child, parts of it would have been sobering—if not downright terrifying—to read.

When labor commenced, Katharina most likely followed the twofold regimen suggested by Rösslin. The first part aimed to speed the baby through the birth canal, and the second part was designed to lessen the mother's pain. To hasten birth and encourage dilation, Katharina probably alternately stood and sat upright during labor and quite possibly used a special birthing chair that was popular in Germany and Italy during the time. The midwife also would have instructed Katharina in breathing exercises similar to the Lamaze exercises laboring women practice today, and she would have administered a number of medicinal remedies to ease the pain of contractions, some of which seem quite odd by modern standards. For example, a laboring woman was often given pepper or the evergreen flower hellebore to smell because it was believed that the act of sneezing hastened labor. The midwife also often lubricated the birth canal with duck fat, lily oil, or barleycorns saturated with saffron; applied a wool net soaked in a pungent oil made from evergreen leaves of rue; sprayed medicinal vapors (one of the more popular ones was made with dove dung) over the laboring mother; spread a variety of herbal poultices over the mother's belly; and administered medicinal teas and broths comprised of potent opiates and herbs. Rösslin also suggested that the midwife encourage and console the laboring mother "by telling her that the birth is going to be a happy one, and that she is going to have a boy."[15]

Once she delivered the baby, the midwife was also responsible for expelling any remaining afterbirth (popular remedies thought to hasten that process ranged from instructing the mother to hold her breath and push to warming her genital area with the "sweet vapors of burned donkey hoofs"),[16] tending to any bleeding, and stitching a lacerated birth canal or perineum. Katharina's midwife also likely bathed little Hans in warm water, along with a bit of milk or fragrant blossom sap (elder or peach) and a fresh egg (a symbol of fertility). Luther, who would have been allowed into the bedroom once Katharina had been tended to, may have slipped a silver coin into Hans's bathwater, both as a bonus for the midwife and a symbol of his pledge to care for his child.[17] Hans would have then been rubbed with nut or other oils to protect his skin, swaddled in a blanket, and placed at Katharina's left side, over her heart.[18]

At this point, as was the custom of the time, Katharina's housemaid probably went door-to-door in Wittenberg to declare the news of Hans's birth, while Luther penned announcements, such as the ones quoted earlier. In some German towns, an aptly named "joy maid" carried a bouquet throughout town to announce the birth of a girl; if a boy had been born, the joy maid carried an additional, larger bouquet in her hand, "attesting to the age's preference for male offspring."[19] Birthing not only a child but a son was the best news of all; Katharina had done well.

A Simple Baptism

The single most important duty of the midwife, after assisting with labor and delivery, of course, was to ensure that the infant was immediately baptized if death was thought to be imminent. Unbaptized children were considered defenseless against Satan and eternal damnation, and parents counted death of an unbaptized child among their greatest fears. Stillborn infants were sometimes rubbed vigorously by the midwife or mother until "a spark of life was perceived, or imagined, and a baptism, 'while alive,' quickly performed."[20]

Hans Luther, however, was born in good health, and thus, as was the custom of the time, was baptized the afternoon he was born, at the parish church in the presence of his godparents, who included Bugenhagen, as well as Justus Jonas, Lucas Cranach, the wife of the mayor of Wittenberg, Electoral Vice Chancellor Christian Baier, Mansfeld Chancellor Caspar Muller, and Strasbourg professor Nikolaus Gerbel.[21] Having given birth just hours before, Katharina was not present at her son's baptism.

The baptismal ceremony was laced with symbolism and ritual. Prior to the Reformation, the sacrament of baptism was as much an exorcism as a sacrament and a blessing. The priest typically began the service by blowing under the newborn's eyes and commanding the devil: "Flee from this child, unclean spirit, and make room for the Holy Spirit." In addition to the water poured over his head, the child also received the mark of the cross on his forehead and chest and a pinch of consecrated salt in his mouth, accompanied by the words: "Take the salt of [divine] wisdom, and may it atone for you in eternity." The priest dabbed a mix of his own spit and dirt in the child's nose and ears (symbolizing Christ's healing of the deaf-mute man in Mark 7 and the blind man in John 9) while pronouncing a double command—the first for the child, the second for the devil—"[Dear child] receive the sweetness of God. . . . Devil, flee, for the judgment of God is near." He then anointed the child's chest and shoulders with olive oil and placed a consecrated mixture of olive oil and balsam—called the *holy chrism*—on the crown of the infant's head. The final part of the baptism service was performed by one of the godparents, who clothed the naked, baptized child in the traditional white gown, called the *Westerhemd* or *Wester*, symbolizing purity and acceptance into the body of Christ. Finally, the father, or both parents if the mother was also present, accepted a lit candle as a symbol of the light of Christ.[22]

In his *Small Catechism*, Luther greatly simplified the baptismal ceremony by stripping away much of the formality and symbolism and focusing on the water, which he considered the sole biblical element of the sacrament. Everything else—the oil, the holy chrism, the candle, the white gown, and even the exorcism and many of the prayers—he considered unnecessary human additions. Yet because many people of the time were reluctant to part from the traditions they valued, Luther continued to allow Protestant congregations to keep these human additions to the baptismal ceremony, as long as the pastors emphasized the cleansing element of the water. We can assume, though, that with his own son's baptism, Luther stuck close to his own reforms. Hans's was undoubtedly a very simple baptism.

It's questionable, as well, whether Luther and Katharina participated in another popular ritual of the time. The "white bath" (or *Westerbad*) traditionally took place three days after birth and was the occasion on which the white baptismal gown was ceremonially removed. The infant was thus "bathed out of the *Wester*" and dressed in the clothes he would typically wear from then on.[23] Although the event was a popular one and often attended by friends and family and celebrated with a great feast, Luther never mentioned the "white bath" in any of his letters or *Table Talk* discussions. It's likely the Luthers decided to skip this ceremony with Hans and their other five children in order to emphasize the importance of the sacrament of baptism without the distraction of the other traditional rituals. Or perhaps they simply couldn't afford to host a banquet to celebrate the arrival of each child. Although the Luthers' financial situation was much improved with Katharina at the helm, the birth of each subsequent child meant another person to clothe, feed, and provide for in the increasingly crowded Black Cloister.

A Growing Family

Luther and Katharina eventually had six biological children along with as many as eleven foster children living with them under the roof of the Black Cloister. Eight months after Hans's arrival, Katharina became pregnant again. She gave birth to Elizabeth during an outbreak of the plague on December 10, 1527. Magdalene, nicknamed Lena, arrived on May 4, 1529, followed by Martin on November 9, 1531, Paul on January 28 or 29, 1533, and their last child, Margarete, named after Luther's mother, on December 17, 1534. Elizabeth and Lena both died in childhood, Elizabeth at eight months old and Lena at age thirteen. (It was not unusual during this time period for a family to lose more than one child. Approximately one-quarter of all babies born alive during the early modern period in Europe died in infancy, and another quarter died before reaching puberty. Nearly one child in two in early modern Europe failed to live to the age of ten.)[24] The Luthers' other four children lived into adulthood.

When Luther's sister and her husband died young, their six children—George, Cyriacus, Andreas, Fabian, Elsa, and Lena Kaufmann—came to live at the Black Cloister. Likewise, Luther's nephews Martin Luther and Hans Polner, along with Anna Strauss and Hanna von der Saale, poor relatives of Katharina, lived with the Luthers. So many people, in addition to the students, guests, and other boarders, made for a chaotic environment, and Luther and Katharina had their hands full managing some of their more rebellious foster children.

Andreas, for example, whom Luther called Enders, was terribly lazy and spent most of his time shirking his chores and napping in the clover fields outside the Black Cloister. He also got secretly engaged when he was still a student at Wittenberg University, which, for obvious reasons, infuriated Luther.[25]

Hans Polner studied theology at Wittenberg University, but he had a drinking problem and was prone to impulsive anger.[26] For a time he was Katharina's biggest headache when Luther was traveling, and several of Luther's letters mention Polner by name, along with advice for how to control his erratic behavior. Eventually Polner matured and became a schoolmaster and later an ordained minister.

Luther and Katharina's nieces, particularly Lena Kaufmann, were a handful as well. As a young teen, Lena set her heart on marrying another of Luther's houseguests, the young theologian Veit Dietrich, but Luther adamantly believed Lena was too young for marriage and refused to approve her engagement. She eventually married the widower Ambrosius Berndt, but when he died just four years later, Luther and Katharina took Lena back under their roof, where she took up with a twenty-year-old medical student. The two got secretly engaged, but Luther so vehemently opposed their union (he suspected the suitor was only interested in Lena's small fortune), they didn't dare marry until after Luther's death.[27]

In some ways, it sounds much more tumultuous than it actually was. With all those children and guests under one roof, life was hectic and chaotic to be sure, but as Ernst Kroker points out, "Based on the amount of material that has come down to us, we learn more of the exceptions than the regular routine of family life in the Black Cloister."[28] In other words, those gathered around the Luthers' table likely only recorded the extraordinary events and interactions, the ones that stood out—the arguments, the snarky comments, the sass—rather than the everyday, ordinary comings and goings and conversations of the Luther family. “If Luther had to punish or scold,” Kroker acknowledges, “they eagerly wrote that down and preserved the offense of the little sins for posterity.”[29] What’s more telling, says Kroker, are the numerous occasions in which Luther praised marriage as a blessed state and parenting as both a holy and a delightful endeavor, even in the midst of its challenges.[30] As we’ll see in the next chapter, the Luthers delighted in their children and truly enjoyed them, but they also believed that God had ordained them to be parents. Luther and Katharina approached child rearing as nothing short of holy work.

The Noblest, Most Precious Work

A circa 1875 oil painting by German artist Gustav Adolf Spangenberg titled *Luther Making Music in the Circle of His Family* hangs in the Leipzig Museum. The portrait depicts Luther sitting in a chair with Katharina next to him, a sleeping Margarete in her lap. Luther holds a lute in his hands, the stringed, guitar-like instrument popular during the time. Standing before the couple are their four older children, singing as Luther strums, while in the background, Melanchthon looks on, a slight smile on his face. It's a tender scene that conveys a quiet joy and comfort—the family together in the home, music filling the air.[1]

The scene portrayed in this painting may seem unrealistically idyllic, but this little musical quintet and its audience was, in actuality, a familiar occurrence at the Black Cloister.

Many evenings the family would gather in the dining room as the lilting notes of Luther's lute accompanied the sweet voices of his children. Martin and Paul were especially musical, little Margarete sang religious songs from the age of five, and every Christmas Eve the whole family participated in singing "From Heaven Above to Earth I Come," the Christmas hymn Luther composed in 1534 for his children.[2] Luther enjoyed nothing more than gathering his family around him for an evening of musical entertainment.

For a long time, contemporary historians assumed that parents who lived during the early modern period had a markedly different relationship with their children than we do today. It was thought that because of the high mortality rates of infants and children, parents distanced themselves from their offspring and limited their psychological involvement.[3] This assumption was based in large part on the work of British historian Lawrence

Gustav Spangenberg [Public domain], via Wikimedia Commons

This circa 1875 painting by Gustav Adolf Spangenberg is entitled *Luther Making Music in the Circle of His Family.*

Stone, who in 1977 published his seminal book, *Family, Sex and Marriage in England 1500–1800.*

Today, at least in industrialized countries, infant death is considered highly unusual, but this was not the case until well into the eighteenth century, when infant and child mortality rates finally began to decline. Prior to the eighteenth century, the most dangerous period in a person's life was infancy and early childhood. One out of every four or five infants failed to survive the first year.[4] Child mortality between the ages of one and five also remained very high; about 50 percent of early modern mortality occurred before age ten.[5] Children died; it was a brutal fact of life. Because of this, Stone claimed, parents couldn't risk getting too attached to their offspring.

Stone's theories about parental detachment have largely been disproved in recent years. Primary sources like letters and journals offer substantial evidence that parents were not only emotionally connected to their children but that they also genuinely enjoyed being around and spending time with them, despite the very real risk of losing them at a young age. Luther's letters and comments around the dinner table illustrate that he and Katharina were no exception.

Doting Parents

We hear the most about Hans. As is often the case with firstborns, when everything about the infant and parenting is brand-new, Luther couldn't help but gush over every little detail, boasting like a proud new father about many of his young son's milestones and accomplishments. We learn, for instance, that Hans was teething at seven months. Soon after he learned to stand, walk, and babble and was affectionately called "*homo vorax et bibax*"—"a little man who heartily gobbles and gulps."[6] Luther's letters even detailed Hans's escapades, including his naughtiness. In a letter to Justus Jonas on October 19, 1527, Luther reported that Hans had crawled around the entire room, as was evident by the unmistakable traces he'd left behind—alluding, perhaps, to a diaper malfunction, or simply to the fact that a crawling toddler leaves chaos and destruction in his wake.[7]

When Luther was away at the Diet of Augsburg he penned what became a famous letter to his son on Hans's fourth birthday, encouraging his "Hänschen" [Hansen] to "study hard, pray diligently, and be in good order" so that he would be invited into the imaginary fantasy world Luther described, a beautiful and cheerful garden complete with singing, dancing, merry children, and "nice ponies with golden reins and silver saddles."[8] The letter is sentimental, sweet, encouraging, and creative, and one can easily see how it would have delighted Luther's young son.

We see, too, how much Luther worried about his children's health and well-being. For example, he wrote about the twelve-day period during which Hans was bedridden from teething, unable to ingest anything but liquids.[9] Teething was thought to be dangerous for children, but in actuality, it was the popular remedies of the time—which included lancing, blistering, bleeding, and placing leeches on the gums—that caused the harm, sometimes even death from infection, rather than the physical process of teething itself.[10] Luther's mention of Hans's struggle with teething illustrates his awareness of the dangers associated with this childhood milestone, and he was genuinely relieved that Hans survived the ordeal largely unscathed.

Luther's love and affection for his children and his wife are clearly conveyed in the tender expressions peppered throughout his letters to Katharina. He often included a sweet sentiment and a prayer in the valediction of his letters: "Kiss the children for me. . . . With this I commend you to God, together with our young ones and all the members of our household. Amen."[11] He missed his family when he was away, and no matter how important the business matter at hand, he was always eager to return home. In 1530, when Luther was away for months in Coburg, working with his colleagues and officials on the Augsburg Confession, Katharina sent him a tiny portrait of Magdalena to ease his homesickness.[12] A few weeks later Luther's friend, Veit Dietrich, who was with him in Coburg, wrote to Katharina to tell her that the picture, which he had fastened near the table in the dining room, had lifted Luther's spirits.[13]

It's also clear from his letters that Luther doted on his children to the point of spoiling them. "I have for Hansen Luther a big fine piece of sugar [candy],"[14] he wrote to Katharina from Coburg. In the letter to Hans on his birthday, Luther promised to bring him home "a nice present from the fair" (literally translated as "bring along a beautiful fair for you," it's assumed Luther meant a gift from the fair, and not the entire fair itself).[15] On another occasion Luther complained to Katharina that he had been unable to buy any trinkets in the town he was staying in to send the children. He instructed his wife to purchase some gifts and have them ready for him to present to the children as his own when he returned home.[16]

We also know by how often they were mentioned in the comments recorded in *Table Talk* that the Luther children weren't removed from their parents' day-to-day activities but were very much present in the daily comings and goings at the Black Cloister. When they were old enough they often dined with Luther and Katharina's guests, and even as toddlers and young children, they were not sequestered in a nursery but were generally underfoot. Luther wrote about one instance in which Hans was playing and singing in the tower study as Luther tried in vain to work. In spite of his father's attempts to silence him (Luther, like most parents of young children, lost his patience from time to time), Hans continued to sing, albeit more quietly under his breath, glancing up at his father to gauge whether his singing was still annoying him.[17] The children were part of daily life, and Luther was an active and engaged participant in nurturing, disciplining, and raising them.

God and His Angels Are Smiling

Parenting during Reformation times was a surprisingly equitable affair. Luther himself declared more than once that fathers should not be mocked for participating in the holy work of parenting, no matter how menial the task. "Now you tell me, when a father goes ahead and washes diapers or performs some other mean task for his child, and someone ridicules him as an effeminate fool—though that father is acting in the spirit and in Christian faith—my dear fellow, you tell me, which of the two is most keenly ridiculing the other?" Luther declared in *The Estate of Marriage*. "God, with all His angels and creatures, is smiling—not because that father is washing diapers, but because he is doing so in Christian faith."[18] Whether Luther actually ever changed or washed a diaper himself we can't be sure, but there's something to be said for the fact that he championed a father's participation in such chores.

Traditionally mothers took the lead in parenting the child from infancy through toddlerhood. A major factor in a child's survival was whether a mother was able or willing to breast-feed. Despite the fact that medical experts touted the benefits of mothers nursing their own children, many upper-class women hired wet nurses, both so that they didn't have to be burdened with the chore of nursing and so they could get back to the business of producing heirs (nursing has a contraceptive effect, virtually preventing a new pregnancy for at least six months after a birth). A wet nurse was selected carefully, for it was thought that the quality of a woman's milk depended on both her physical health and her moral character, and that she passed some of her own qualities to the child through her milk.[19] However, because wet nurses were usually poorer than the families that hired them, and because they also regularly nursed their own child or other children at the same time, a child handed over to a wet nurse for feeding was much less likely to survive than a child breast-fed by his biological mother. Modern studies indicate that wet nursing doubled infant mortality in cities.[20] And cow's or goat's milk was absolutely out of the question. The survival of a child raised on cow's milk was considered a miracle, which is why that detail is often mentioned in the biographies of saints as a sign of their chosen status.[21]

Because the Luthers were not wealthy enough to hire a wet nurse, Katharina breast-fed each of her six children herself, in some cases well beyond the twelve months recommended by modern-day pediatricians. Luther was involved even in this aspect of child rearing, at one point offering Katharina advice on when to wean their daughter Magdalena. "I think it would be good if you want [to stop nursing her], [but] gradually," Luther wrote to Katharina in 1530, when Magdalena was just over a year old, "so that at first you omit one feeding per day, then two feedings per day, until [the child] clearly stops [nursing by herself].” Luther, it turned out, had been chatting with an acquaintance, Lady Argula von Grumbach, about parenting over dinner and passed on her advice to his wife.[22] It’s worth noting that Luther did not consider it beneath him to confer with a female friend on a topic typically relegated to the realm of women. At one point he even debated the merits of breast milk with his students and colleagues around the dinner table, concluding that infants benefited from long-term nursing; that a pregnant woman shouldn’t nurse an infant because a fetus draws all the nutrients, leaving little for the nursing baby; and that “large and flabby breasts cause unhappiness because they promise much but produce little.”[23] Katharina was surely present for this conversation, but her comments, if she indeed made any, were not recorded.

Like most fathers of the time, Luther’s involvement in day-to-day child rearing intensified as each of his children reached the age when they were considered capable of mortal sin and thus could also begin to respond to discipline (usually around six or seven years old).[24] Luther’s disciplinary measures aligned with the popular theories of the time; in other words, he was strict, and he also employed physical punishment if he felt circumstances necessitated it. Sixteenth-century moralists generally believed that too little discipline was more harmful than too much,[25] and thus, while the housefather books of the time (which were typically written by educators and moralists to offer child-rearing and disciplinary advice to the heads of households) considered corporal punishment a last resort, it was also not altogether unusual.[26] In his *Table Talk* comments Luther referred to a few incidents in which he punished his children and foster children, sometimes harshly. At one point he became so angry with Hans, he refused to see the boy for three days, even after

Hans had asked his father in writing for forgiveness. "I would rather have a dead son, than an ill-mannered one," he stubbornly declared when Katharina, Melanchthon, Jonas, and another friend interceded on Hans's behalf.[27] Another time he beat his nephew Andreas Kaufmann with a stick when the boy uttered a foul word at the table.[28] Likewise when Katharina's nephew Florian stole a knife from the Luthers' son Paul and then denied it, Luther ordered three days of corporal punishment for the boy at his boarding school.[29]

However, the parenting manuals of the day also instructed fathers to refrain from punishing to the point at which the child became terrorized, embittered, or moved to anger against the parent himself.[30] Likewise, city officials urged teachers to use moderation in the classroom. "Confine your punishment to words and a few strokes of the birch," instructed the governments of Strasbourg and Ulm. "Don't beat them about the head, never use your fist or bare hand on them, and don't pull them by the hair."[31]

As we've already seen, Luther had strong opinions about both parents' and teachers' use of corporal punishment. He was critical of his own parents and teachers for beating him as a child for what he considered minor infractions. More importantly, he argued that parents and teachers should understand a child's temperament before instituting punishment. "They weren't able to keep a right balance between temperament and punishment," Luther said about his own parents. "One must punish in such a way that the rod is accompanied by the apple. Whatever method that's used, it ought to pay attention to the difference in aptitudes and teach in such a way that all children are treated with equal love."[32] If the records are accurate, we can count on one hand the number of times Luther used corporal punishment with his children and foster children. Clearly, despite the fact that the moralists condoned its use, he was reluctant to use physical punishment as a disciplinary measure, preferring a more measured verbal scolding instead.

It's no surprise that Luther was also very involved in his children's spiritual growth. In fact, his *Small Catechism*, which was published in 1529 and is still used in Lutheran youth education and confirmation classes today, was compiled as a result of the religious instruction he led in his own home. "When I get up in the morning, I pray with the children the Ten Commandments, the Creed, the Lord's Prayer, and then some psalm," he said in a sermon in 1530.[33] He was the first to admit, "Here one forever remains a learner. Though I am a great doctor, I haven't yet progressed beyond the instruction of children."[34] Thus, Luther learned alongside his children, acknowledging that he still prayed the same prayers Hans and Lena did.[35]

Teaching his children to commit prayers, hymns, and psalms to memory was important to Luther because he believed ambiguity inevitably led to doubt.[36] "The delicate and untouched minds [of children]," he wrote to Nikolaus von Amsdorf in 1534, "must be shaped by simple, necessary, and undoubted doctrines which they can accept as certain truths. Before a beginner can learn anything, he must believe."[37] Repetition of prayers and Scripture, he believed, cemented one's faith. On Sundays he also led devotions with his family and visitors staying at the Black Cloister, which were later recorded, compiled, and published in 1544 as Luther's *House Postil*.[38] Later, when the children were older, they each read a few verses aloud from the Bible before every meal.

Luther understood parenting as nothing less than a holy calling. "The greatest good in married life, that which makes all suffering and labor worthwhile, is that God grants offspring and commands that they be brought up to worship and serve Him," he wrote in 1522, before he was married or had children of his own. "In all the world this is the noblest and most precious work, because to God there can be nothing dearer than the salvation of souls."[39] Luther believed the parent should be apostle, bishop, and priest to the child, and he considered there no greater or nobler authority on earth than that of parents over their children.[40] Yet the comments and stories sprinkled throughout *Table Talk*, the tender letters Luther penned to his wife, and the portraits depicting Luther and his family also reveal something obvious yet not often mentioned: Luther and Katharina had fun with their kids and enjoyed spending time with them. They delighted in their children's antics and their innocent comments and expressions. Love and joy were obviously abundant in the Luther household. Luther and Katharina deeply loved each of their children, and as we will see in the next chapter, there was no greater testament of that love than the depth of their grief.

16

In the Valley of the Shadow of Death

On the morning of September 20, 1542, Katharina awoke from a lovely dream. Later, when she told Melanchthon she had dreamt that two handsome young men had arrived at their home to take her daughter Magdalena to a wedding, he was deeply disturbed, but he didn't dare tell Katharina what he believed the dream meant. He feared the two handsome young men were angels who had descended to whisk the gravely ill Lena away to be united with Jesus in the kingdom of heaven.

The Spirit Is Willing, but the Flesh Is Weak

As he sat by his dying thirteen-year-old daughter, Luther vacillated, one moment surrendering to God's will, the next moment begging for his mercy. "I love her very much," he prayed. "But if it is thy will to take her, dear God, I shall be glad to know that she is with thee."[1] Later, weeping inconsolably at Magdalena's bedside, he admitted, "The spirit is willing, but the flesh is weak. I love her very much. I'm angry with myself that I am unable to rejoice from my heart and be thankful to God."[2] He acknowledged that he tried to sing a little and offer thanks to God, though the effort felt forced.

Luther and Katharina considered Magdalena a gift from God following the loss of their firstborn daughter. Magdalena was born less than a year after Elizabeth's death, and the Luthers struggled to comprehend why and how God could now take this precious daughter from them too. "I'd like to keep my dear daughter because I love her very much, if only our Lord God would let me," Luther lamented. "However, his will be done! Truly nothing better can happen to her, nothing better."[3]

Luther repeated this consolation again and again, reminding and perhaps trying to convince both Katharina and himself that their daughter's suffering and their grief was brief compared to the incomprehensible joy and peace of eternal life. When Katharina was overcome with weeping, Luther reminded her that their daughter was going to heaven: "Think where she's going. She'll get along all right. Flesh is flesh, spirit is spirit."[4] Yet it's clear from his grief-laced words that in the face of such devastating loss, Luther struggled to trust his own faith. "Dear Magdalene, my little daughter," he said, as he kneeled at her bedside, "You would be glad to stay here with me, your father. Are you also glad to go to your Father in heaven?"[5] At Magdalena's innocent, trusting answer—"Yes, dear Father, as God wills"—Luther was forced to turn away in anguish, unable to look his daughter in the eyes.[6]

Luther's only hope was that the arrival of her favorite brother, Hans, would rally her and in some way raise her from the depths of sickness. But it was no use. Despite the fact that Hans kept a constant vigil by his sister's bed from the moment he arrived home from boarding school, four days later, on September 20, 1542—the same day Katharina awoke from her startling dream—Magdalena died as Luther held her in his arms. At the moment of her death, he wept bitterly, beseeching God aloud to save her. Wittenberg student Caspar Heydenreich, who described the deathbed scene in his *Table Talk* notes, observed that although Katharina was in the room when her daughter died, her grief prevented her from keeping vigil at Lena's bedside.[7] Katharina was simply too overcome to gather herself together. She couldn't bear to witness the passing of her beloved daughter.

Magdalena Luther was barely a teenager. Katharina and Luther, who had already lost their eight-month-old daughter Elizabeth fourteen years before, were nearly destroyed by grief.

The Honorable Funeral

Prior to the Reformation, the rituals surrounding death—from the ministration of last rites and the petitioning of the saints to the requiem Mass and the purchase of indulgences—played a big part in what the Church saw as its role in the ushering of souls into salvation. As historian Diarmaid MacCulloch observes, the medieval church claimed "to be able to offer living humanity an active part in directing the fate of the dead."[8] Luther's affirmation of justification by faith alone, however, absolutely denied the involvement of anything or anyone—common man, priest, saint, or otherwise—in the salvation of a soul. Reformers believed that the spiritual relationship between two people was severed at the moment of death. Prayers for the dead, a central part of the Christian notion of salvation since the second century, were made obsolete by the Lutheran doctrine of salvation by faith alone. The "middle place" of purgatory was abolished, and the notion that the living could intercede on a soul's behalf, either to God himself or to the saints, was denounced. Salvation was determined by God and God alone and was dependent not on intercessory prayers or the number of indulgences purchased by loved ones, but simply on an individual's faith. "Everyone must fight his own battle with death by himself, alone," Luther preached in Wittenberg in 1522.[9]

This is why the deathbed statement of faith became so critical to early Protestants. Without the presence of a priest to minister last rites and declare the soul absolved of sin, and without the aid of the living to pray a wayward soul to salvation, it was up to the dying person to repent and acknowledge belief in God once and for all. Thus Luther's pointed question to his dying daughter—"Are you glad to go to your Father in heaven?"—and her concise answer, "Yes, as God wills it." Both Luther and Magdalena were following standard Reformation deathbed protocol. Knowing and believing that his young daughter's salvation was based on her faith while she lived, his question offered her the opportunity to state her convictions while she still had the chance. Though obviously distraught by this exchange, Luther and Katharina would have been comforted and relieved by Magdalena's declaration of faith. It was seen as a bad omen if a dying person experienced a particularly anxious or painful death or slipped into unconsciousness before making a final declaration of faith.

Early reformers stripped the funeral ritual down to its simplest form in order to deemphasize human involvement in a soul's journey to salvation. Burials were often held without clergy present and with little ceremony and were sometimes even conducted after dark, although nocturnal burials were usually reserved for those who died in disgrace, such as by suicide.[10] Likewise the tradition of the wake, or night watch, in which loved ones kept vigil next to the body of the deceased, was also abolished. The wake was traditionally a time for intercessory prayers for the dead; reformers' attempts to eradicate the wake sought to separate the bodies of the dead from the living.[11] By 1528 Saxony had done away with nocturnal burials, but several cities in Germany continued to relocate cemeteries outside the city walls to symbolize the distinct separation between the living and the dead.[12]

As the Reformation progressed, however, the funeral ritual began to be utilized as a way to remind the living of their own mortality. "For it is meet and right that we should conduct these funerals with proper decorum in order to honour and praise that joyous article of our faith, namely, the resurrection of the dead, and in order to defy Death, that terrible foe who so shamefully and in so many horrible ways goes on to devour us," wrote Luther.[13] The funeral procession, the tolling of the church and city bells, the hymns, and the burial in the communal cemetery were all elements of what was called "the honorable funeral" and were orchestrated with a dual purpose: to honor the dead *and* to remind the living of their mortality in order that they adequately prepare for their own deaths. "All [this] is done to spite the stinking and shameful death and to praise and confess the resurrection of the dead, in order to console those weak in faith and the sorrowful," Luther wrote.[14]

"I Sent a Saint to Heaven"

As they prepared for their daughter's funeral, Luther and Katharina struggled to accept that their precious daughter was indeed gone. Luther in particular had difficulty reconciling his immeasurable suffering with Lena's state of rest. He was especially disturbed to discover that his daughter's coffin was too small to accommodate her body. "The little bed is too small for her," he cried out, as he and Katharina prepared Magdalena's corpse for burial.[15] "The flesh doesn't take kindly to this," he observed. "The separation [caused by death] troubles me above measure. It's strange to know that she is surely at peace and that she is well off there, very well off, and yet to grieve so much!"[16] We don't get many details about Magdalena's funeral, but those that were shared, like the ill-fitting coffin, take one's breath away.

We can hardly imagine the parents' grief as they gazed at Lena's face. As he lowered his daughter's body into the coffin, Luther said, "You dear little Lena! How well it has turned out for you!"[17] Gazing at her young face one last time, he added, "Ah, dear child, to think that you must be raised up and will shine like the stars, yes, like the sun!"[18]

Funerals typically took place quickly, often on the same day as a person's death, or at most, the day following. The community was called together for the ritual of the honorable burial by the ringing of the church bell. Then, along with the pastor, the local schoolmaster and school choir led the procession of mourners in the singing of hymns as they walked to the cemetery. The use of coffins was rare even in the sixteenth century; typically the body of the deceased was laid directly on a bier and covered with a black or white shroud.[19] But we know from Luther's comments that Magdalena's body was likely wrapped in a shroud and laid in a coffin. The casket may have had a window carved into the lid which could be opened and shut as the mourners wished while they paid their respects. Katharina most likely wore a covering of white linen over her face as she walked to the cemetery, Luther a covering of black linen. As they walked with the other mourners behind the coffin in the funeral procession, they would have been guided by a servant, a family member, or a friend. At the cemetery, the bereaved may have laid rosemary, bay leaves, or other evergreens on the coffin to symbolize the soul's immortality.[20]

Detailed city ordinances cited specific funeral rituals, depending on the social class of the deceased. For example, bells were not typically rung for the death of a commoner; the body was simply accompanied by "the nearest neighbours to the grave."[21] When a member of the *Burgher*, or middle class, died, the family was instructed to summon the schoolmaster and the school choir, but a pastor was not present and the bells were not rung. When someone of "the distinguished people" died, the body was buried with a full procession, including the pastor, the schoolmaster and school choir, and the family and townspeople, and the "great bells" (i.e., the city bells, as opposed to the church bells) were tolled.[22] It was the number of bell tolls, or lack thereof, which signified the social status of the deceased. Given Luther's status, Magdalena's funeral was likely more elaborate and may have included bell tolls, a formal procession, and a ceremony, including a sermon, either at the church or at the cemetery preceding the burial.

Luther seemed to rally a bit at the funeral as he focused his attention on consoling the other mourners, reminding them that he had sent a living saint to heaven and acknowledging that his daughter was now safe from bodily suffering.[23] He also couldn't resist making a statement against the Catholic practice of the intercessory Mass. As the mourners sang the verse from Psalm 79, "Lord, remember not against us former iniquities," Luther interrupted, "O Lord, Lord, Lord, not only former iniquities but also present ones. . . . For fifteen years I read mass and conducted the abominations of the mass."[24] Luther acknowledged that he, too, had done his part in the recitation of intercessory Masses, a ritual he now considered an "abomination."

As was typical of the time, the mourners returned to the Black Cloister for a meal following the funeral. Again, Luther maintained his stoic reserve, stating matter-of-factly, "My daughter is now fitted out in body and soul. We know that it should and must be so, for we are altogether certain about eternal life."[25] Yet it's clear from his subsequent comments about Magdalena's death that Luther was merely putting on a brave face for the benefit of his fellow mourners. He may have yearned to believe the statements of faith he uttered so confidently at his daughter's funeral, but the truth was, his words were part of the funeral rhetoric of the time, words he felt obligated to utter but couldn't quite embrace himself. Luther didn't handle the loss well. The sting of Magdalena's death seared for months and even years after, and for a time threatened to undermine Luther's personal faith.

Grief in Their Hearts

In the wake of her daughter's death, Katharina found herself uneasy at the thought of her oldest son, Hans, returning to boarding school in Torgau, thirty-one miles away. When Hans departed, she urged him to return home immediately if he began to feel unwell. Perhaps Katharina was nervous that yet another child would be taken from her before his time. Perhaps she was simply reluctant to part with her firstborn so soon after such a devastating loss. At any rate, just three months later, Hans found himself consumed with homesickness and grief while away at school and wrote to his mother requesting to come home. Luther, however, intervened.

"I readily believe that my son turned soft through the words of his mother, in addition to mourning over his sister's death," Luther wrote to Hans's teacher, Marcus Crodel. "Order him, therefore, to curb that womanish feeling, to get accustomed to enduring evil, and to not indulge in that childlike weakness. For this is the reason that he has been sent away, namely, that he learn something and become hardened."[26] Luther followed up with a tough-love letter to Hans himself the next day. "You see to it that you overcome those tears like a man, so that you do not cause your Mother additional pain and worry, for she worries easily and becomes anxious," Luther wrote. "Mother was unable to write, and also thought it unnecessary. She says all that she said to you (that you should return if by chance you feel poorly), was meant to refer to an illness. . . . In addition she wishes you to put aside this mourning so that you may study in a happy and peaceful frame of mind."[27]

Despite their severity, Luther undoubtedly intended his words to help his son, as a means of jolting him out of the grief in which he was mired. Luther was also clearly worried about Katharina, whom he implied was suffering from anxiety; thus his "shape up and get yourself together" directive to Hans was issued as a means to protect his grief-stricken wife from further suffering. We also know that a hardened response to death was both appropriate social etiquette for the time and considered a sign of a person's faith. In the sixteenth century, "outward insensitivity to death, whether that of a child or an adult, was considered a moral and religious obligation, behavior every Christian should strive to achieve," German history and Reformation scholar Steven Ozment observes.[28] Yet in his strongly voiced words to his son, we can also infer the depth of Luther's own sorrow and his struggle to wrestle with his own overwhelming grief and splintering faith. It's almost as if, in speaking so harshly to his son, Luther was in fact speaking to himself.

A letter from Luther to Justus Jonas not long after Magdalena's death points to this very struggle. "I and my wife should only joyfully give thanks for such a felicitous departure and blessed end by which Magdalen has escaped the power of the flesh, the world, the Turk [referring to the territorial expansion of the Ottoman Empire; the "Turks" were a threat to the Holy Roman Empire], and the devil; yet the force of [our] natural love is so great that we are unable to do this without crying and grieving in [our] hearts, or even without experiencing death ourselves," Luther admitted. "For the features, the words, and the movement of the living and dying daughter who was so very obedient and respectful remain engraved deep in the heart; even the death of Christ is unable totally to take all this away as it should."[29] Luther then went on to ask his friend to pray and give thanks to God for them, as he and Katharina were unable to do so adequately themselves. Three years after his daughter's death, Luther continued to struggle with the loss, admitting, "It is an amazing thing how much the death of my Magdalena torments me. I cannot forget her."[30]

We don't know how the deaths of Elizabeth and Magdalena affected Luther and Katharina's marriage or their relationship as husband and wife. On one hand, couples were aware of the extraordinarily high rate of infant mortality and the risks associated with bringing children into the world. While shocking, their daughters' deaths would not have been entirely unexpected. On the other hand, we also know that parents who lived during early modern times were as attached to their children as parents today, and thus, the death of a child—and in the Luthers' case, two children—would have had a tremendous impact on them. The loss of a child often drives a wedge between couples, yet there is no evidence in correspondence, *Table Talk*, or any of Luther's writings of distance, bitterness, or resentment between Luther and Katharina following either daughter's death. In fact, we see ample evidence of the opposite: Luther attempted to comfort his distraught wife as Magdalena neared the end of her life, and he clearly communicated his concern for Katharina's welfare in letters to friends and to his son. It seems Luther and Katharina weathered the devastating loss of their daughters as they had other difficult circumstances and turmoil: together, through a mutual and steadfast love.

17

'Til Death Did Them Part

Although Luther continued to write, preach, and negotiate political situations in Wittenberg and beyond, Magdalena's death significantly dimmed his light. No longer the fiery, larger-than-life force he once was, the great Reformer grew noticeably weaker as the years passed. His health was more fragile than ever, and he suffered a variety of maladies, from gout and kidney stones to chest pains, headaches, and increasing melancholia. Overweight and frequently short of breath, Luther became less and less mobile and was eventually forced to rely on a horse and wagon to carry him even short distances around town.

Early on the morning of February 18, 1546, less than four years after Magdalena's death, Katharina was startled by a knock on the door. Luther had been gone for nearly a month on a trip to his hometown of Eisleben. Last she had heard from him, he planned to return home that week. He had been ill, but his most recent letter had been positive and optimistic. Luther relayed that "the stone" (kidney stone) was no longer bothering him. He was also sending along a trout, he reported, a gift from the Countess of Albrecht.[1] The letter was typical of Luther's correspondence to his wife: breezy, teasing, and full of tidbits and news. It contained no hint of ominous foreboding.

Still, Katharina had felt uneasy ever since Luther had departed Wittenberg weeks earlier. Concerned about his poor health, she had tried to convince her husband to stay home, but he had insisted on traveling to Eisleben to help solve a political dispute in person. He hadn't fared well during the journey and complained to Katharina that a frigid draft on the back of his neck had caused the vertigo and weakness he experienced en route. (In fact, Luther, who made anti-Semitic remarks throughout his lifetime and even wrote a treatise titled *On Jews and Their Lies*, noted to Katharina that perhaps the Jews in the town they'd passed through had blown the cold air upon him.)[2] Although he had recovered by the time he reached Eisleben, Katharina was not reassured. During the weeks he was away, she wrote him letter after letter expressing her anxiety and concern. Luther responded with his typical mix of humor and tenderness, joking about what a worrier she was, while at the same time endeavoring to console his wife and put her at ease.

As for Luther himself, it seems he didn't realize how gravely ill he really was until the very end. His last two letters, both written on February 14 (one to Katharina and one to Melanchthon), just four days before he died, were newsy and upbeat. In fact, in his letter to Katharina, Luther was more concerned about Justus Jonas's leg, which had become badly infected from a wound incurred when he bumped it on a piece of furniture.[3]

But soon after writing to his wife and his closest friend, Luther took a turn for the worse. He attended negotiations regarding the Eisleben dispute on February 16, but the next day he felt so poorly, his friends urged him to stay in bed. The final documents were stamped with his seal on February 17, but it's doubtful Luther was present to sign the paperwork himself.[4]

Luther's health spiraled quickly on February 17 and 18. While he had suffered myriad physical trials in the past, this one was a much different experience, not only because it was the end, but also because Katharina was not at his side as she had so often been in the past. Not able to console her in person or even write a proper farewell to her during his final hours, Luther was undoubtedly worried about Katharina and racked by his own sense of loss. Nonetheless, according to reports of those who kept vigil at his bedside, the Reformer, though physically in pain, was "mentally alert, spiritually composed, and steadfastly confessing the faith he had come to embrace," as was expected of him.[5]

Because of her persistent anxiety and the foreboding feeling she had experienced since Luther had departed Wittenberg three weeks earlier, Katharina wasn't entirely unprepared for bad news when she opened the door on the morning of February 18. Yet nothing could have readied her for the shocking revelation of Luther's death. The moment she saw Johannes Bugenhagen, Caspar Cruciger, and Philip Melanchthon on her doorstep, Katharina fell apart. "When she received the report of her husband's death, this poor woman was terribly frightened and became despondent," Melanchthon later reported. "She felt especially sad for their three sons who had been with the blessed Doctor at Eisleben, and she did not know how to provide for them after the father's death."[6]

Wave after wave of emotion converged on Katharina at once: sorrow, grief, and above all, fear—fear for her own livelihood and, most especially, fear for the well-being of her children. In addition to her utter devastation and anguish, Katharina was also well aware of the struggles that awaited her in the wake of Luther's death.

An Excellent Father Lost

The Count of Mansfeld wanted Luther's body to be buried in his hometown, but the Elector determined that Luther should be laid to rest in Wittenberg's Castle Church. Still, the people of Eisleben were determined to honor the great leader properly in his hometown. Luther's body was laid in a specially made pewter coffin and brought to St. Andrew's Church, where it lay in state in the chancel. Justus Jonas preached the funeral sermon (funeral services were expected to be held in a few of the larger towns along the way from Eisleben to Wittenberg), and the next morning, the procession, led by the Count and Countess of Mansfeld and followed by Luther's three sons, several of Luther's Eisleben relatives, and a large crowd of mourners, departed through the city gates toward Halle.

Bells tolled as the funeral procession passed through each village and town along the way, and by the time the crowd reached Halle, more than forty riders on horseback had joined the procession, along with hundreds of wailing, weeping mourners. The procession could be heard approaching from miles away. Progress was slow on account of the massive crowds, and the procession arrived too late in the evening for another funeral service to be held in Halle. Instead, the citizens kept vigil in the sacristy of the Church of Our Lady until six the next morning, when, bells tolling, the ever-growing group of mourners departed again.

Luther's body was expected to arrive in Wittenberg on February 21, but excessive crowds dramatically slowed progress. At Kemberg, less than ten miles from Wittenberg, the procession was forced to stop for the night. The final leg of the journey was completed early the next morning, February 22. Crowds thronged the streets of Wittenberg as the wagon carrying Luther's body made its way through town. Katharina had waited four long days for her beloved husband to be returned to her. She and her daughter Margarete were among the crowds gathered outside the Black Cloister as the procession approached.

Members of the clergy, professors, and students led the procession, followed by the electoral representatives, the Count and Countess of Mansfeld and their entourage, and various dignitaries, totaling sixty men on horseback. A four-horse wagon carried Luther's coffin; Katharina and Margarete rode in a carriage behind it, with sons Hans, Martin, and Paul, along with Luther's brother Jacob and his nephews George and Cyriacus Kaufmann, walking behind them. Luther's closest friends, including Chancellor Brück, Melanchthon, Jonas, Bugenhagen, Cruciger, and Jerome Schurf, along with councilmen, politicians, and more professors, brought up the rear. At the very end of the procession were hundreds of men, women, and children, most of them wailing and weeping loudly or otherwise singing Christian hymns as bells tolled constantly throughout the city. It was, in short, a spectacle like nothing Wittenberg had ever seen before.

The procession wound its way around the city, through the marketplace, along College Street, and down Castle Street to

Castle Church in Wittenberg, now named All Saints' Church, where Luther nailed the *Ninety-five Theses*. He is buried in front of the pulpit.

Castle Church, where Johannes Bugenhagen preached the sermon. Katharina and her four children stood next to Luther's casket while Melanchthon offered the memorial eulogy in Latin. At one point during the eulogy, Luther's longtime friend turned to Katharina and the children, acknowledging their shared suffering: "We are like poor orphans who had an excellent man as a father and lost him."[7] Finally the pallbearers lifted the casket and laid Luther's body to rest in a grave directly in front of the pulpit.

The Good Widow

A 1546 woodcut by Lucas Cranach the Elder titled *The Widow of Martin Luther in Mourning* depicts Katharina wrapped in a black fur cloak, a small prayer book clutched in her hands. A long white ribbon extending from her head covering wraps around her mouth before cascading to the hem of her robe.[8] The prayer book signified the widow's commitment to God; the ribbon binding her mouth symbolized the expectation that she would live out the remainder of her days quietly and humbly.

A widow during early modern times, especially an older widow like Katharina, who was forty-seven when Luther died,

By Jörg Scheller (Kupferstichkabinett Schloßmuseum Gotha) [Public domain], via Wikimedia Commons

This copy of the 1546 woodcut by Lucas Cranach the Elder depicts Katharina in mourning following Luther's death.

was expected to mourn her husband's death and, ideally, to live a life of quiet chastity, committed to God and largely withdrawn from day-to-day society. The German word for widow, *Witwe*, is derived either from the old Saxon *witgen*—meaning to lament, moan, or cry—or the lower Saxon *wedeweh*, which describes "a pitiful state in [the] life of poverty and sorrow."[9] The "good widow," according to early seventeenth-century English writer William Page, was the grieving woman who not only patiently and quietly endured her afflictions and grief, but who also considered her state of bereavement "an exceeding joy."[10] Along with this spirit of desolation, the widow was expected to practice certain spiritual exercises, including prayer, fasting, and solitude, and exhibit certain qualities, like taciturnity and meekness. "If every good woman should be like a snail hid within her house . . . then much more should my widow keep within doors," Page wrote in his treatise on widowhood, titled "Widdowe Indeed."[11] If all women should be quiet, Page argued, widows should be even more so. Talkativeness leads to "busyness" with men's affairs, Page concluded, and men's affairs were no place for a widow.[12] The danger posed by widows, as exemplified by the perception of them during the witch craze, stemmed from their independence and relative power. With potential inherited wealth, they were under no obligation to marry again.

Despite Cranach's artistic portrayal of Katharina as "the good widow," with her prayer book in her hands and her mouth bound to silence, in reality, Katharina couldn't have been further from the idealized model of the meek and silent widow. As her grief-stricken words to her sister-in-law illustrated, Katharina did deeply mourn the loss of her husband; yet she did not play the part of the quiet, withdrawn, snail-in-her-house widow. Instead, within weeks of her husband's death, Katharina suddenly found herself in a precarious social and financial position and was forced to defend herself. Without immediate action, she was at risk of losing not only her property, which was the source of her livelihood, but custody of her children as well. Katharina couldn't afford to be the good widow; she had too much at stake.

A Chair and a Spinning Wheel

Luther had experienced more than one brush with death in his sixty-three years, yet even after several close calls, he had been reluctant to draw up a will and testament. During his first serious illness, in July of 1527, he acknowledged that he had little to leave his wife and child. Instead, he asked Katharina to entrust herself to God's gracious will, and then he called young Hans to his bedside and commended him and his mother into God's faithful hands.[13] Luther reminded Katharina about the valuables they had in the house—a few silver tankards, gifts from nobles—but admitted they had little else. "Don't worry on my account!" Katharina reassured her anxious, ailing husband. "I entrust you to His divine will. God will certainly keep you."[14]

Luther recovered, but ten years later, while gravely ill with an attack of kidney stones in Smalcald, he was again riddled with anxiety about the welfare of his family. Katharina was miles away in Wittenberg, but Elector Johann Frederick visited Luther at his bedside and assured the Reformer that he would care for Katharina and his children as if they were his own. Still, Luther couldn't shake the memory of a conversation his friend Jerome Schurf had had recently with Katharina at the Black Cloister. "Does the house belong to you yet?" Schurf had asked Katharina.

When she responded no, Schurf urged her to make the proper arrangements. "Take it!" he advised. "And when someone offers you a pig, then hold open the sack! If Christ has been forgotten, then Luther will certainly be forgotten as well."[15] Despite this conversation and the anxiety it caused, Luther still delayed putting his affairs in order.

Not surprisingly, widowhood generally led to a decline in a woman's economic status unless she inherited substantial wealth. As Merry Wiesner points out, the poorest households in towns and villages were typically headed by elderly widows, and during times of increased economic hardship, crime by widows, mostly petty theft, increased.[16] In addition, widows were generally viewed with suspicion because they were "sexually experienced women not under the tutelage of a man."[17] For these reasons remarriage, especially for young widows, was often encouraged after the proper year of mourning.

However, remarriage was not a viable option for a widow like Katharina, who was older, beyond childbearing years, and already had four living children of her own. In addition, her status and class worked against her. Widows of merchants, for instance, frequently assumed management of the husband's business—at least until a son or son-in-law took over—and were able to sustain a viable income and live independently that way. On the other hand, pastors' widows were often able to eke out a living as maids, an option that, because of her status as Martin Luther's widow, was not available to Katharina. In short, Katharina was too important to seek menial labor, but not wealthy enough to sustain herself and her children and live independently.

Luther was well aware of the widow's plight. According to Saxon law, a widow was promised only the *Morgengabe*, the "morning gift"—that is, the gift given by the husband to his wife on their wedding night—and the *Gerade*, certain household items that typically included food, some furniture, clothing, and jewelry. The specifics of what was included in the *Gerade* varied from region to region.[18] A popular adage of the time summarized the law: "After the death of her husband, a married woman should be given a chair and a spinning wheel."[19] Luther argued that the law should be interpreted broadly according to common sense. After all, a servant or a beggar at the door would be given more than was accorded a widow. He claimed the "chair" should encompass the house and the yard, and the "spinning wheel" should include whatever would allow the widow an income, thereby assuring her independence (i.e., property, brewing rights, livestock, gardens, etc.).

Luther's interpretation of the law didn't matter, however; it was the law itself that counted in the end. And the law stated that the house and yard—along with everything that accompanied the property, from the livestock to the gardens to the brewing rights—belonged not to the widow, but to the heirs—either the children or, if there were no children, the nearest blood relatives. If the heirs were not old enough to manage the inheritance themselves, a guardian was appointed to oversee the inheritance and make business and financial decisions until the children came of age. In fact, by law, the guardian was responsible for the livelihood of the children overall, which often included determining their education (for boys) and where and with whom they would live.

There was a loophole, however. In advance of his death, a husband could assign to his wife the legal right to some of his property for her lifetime, and this is exactly what Luther finally did. On January 6, 1542, he wrote his testament, bequeathing to

Katharina a "widow's dower" that included the Zülsdorf estate; a small cottage in front of the Black Cloister that would serve as Katharina's and the children's residence; and the silver cups, medals, and jewelry, which had an estimated value of 1,000 *Gulden*.[20] Anticipating that Katharina would be the victim of vicious gossip and rumors after his death, Luther also stipulated that his friends protect her from malicious rumors and from those who would surely insist that she had hidden cash reserves from her own children.[21] Finally, Luther stated for the record that there was no such cash on hand, and that Katharina would be more than 450 *Gulden* in debt if Luther did not succeed in paying it off during his lifetime.[22] Predicting that Katharina would be accused of poor management, he also stated that the accounting books could be examined publicly as proof of what income had been received. Two years after writing his will, on February 1, 1544, Luther listed his bequests in the city record book, stating that, with the exception of the Black Cloister (which had been given to him as a gift by the elector), all his properties and the gardens within the city limits should go to Katharina upon his death.[23]

Unfortunately, Luther stubbornly overlooked one critical component of his will and testament. The law required that for it to be valid, the will not only had to be stated in writing, it also had to be notarized by a lawyer. Luther didn't care for lawyers (a distaste that perhaps stemmed from his father's vehement wish for Luther to pursue that profession), and thus he adamantly refused to have his will notarized by one. Instead, he asked Melanchthon, Cruciger, and Bugenhagen to sign the documents, banking on the expectation that their signatures would serve as a proper testament of the will's authenticity. In short, Luther trusted that his own signature and seal and the signatures of his friends would carry far more authority and weight than that of a lawyer's. He was wrong. Without the signature of an attorney, the will was not legally binding.

Luther's second error was that he did not designate a guardian for Katharina or his children, but instead confidently appointed Katharina, as the mother, the best guardian for their children.[24] "You bore the children, you nursed them; you will not manage their affairs to their disadvantage," he said. "I am opposed to guardians; they seldom do well."[25] Luther was centuries ahead of his time in granting his wife this responsibility. His decision signaled that their relationship consisted of more than attraction or compatibility, but at its core was based on mutual respect. At the same time, however, Luther's unconventional decision was also incredibly foolish and ultimately left Katharina in a terrible position. The fact was, a widow and her children were, by law, not allowed to live independently without a guardian. Katharina couldn't serve as a guardian to her children because as a widow, she was required to have a guardian herself. Luther knew this, yet in ignoring this critical detail, he put Katharina at risk to lose everything, including custody of her own children.

Where There's a Will, There's a Way

In the early days and weeks following Luther's death, Wittenberg and Saxony officials allowed Katharina and her children a respectful peace. The elector kept this promise to Luther, writing to Katharina to express his condolences and assure her that "for the sake of your husband we are ready to be at your and your children's disposal and will not forsake you."[26] Luther's friends rallied around the grieving widow and her children, sending money and supplies to help sustain them. However, it wasn't long before the tides began to turn. In particular, the elector's chancellor, Gregor Brück, formerly one of Luther's close friends, opposed Katharina's attempts to secure her own future and the future of her children.

Brück, it turned out, held a long-brewing grudge against Katharina. Years before she had counseled Luther on a decision that had negatively affected the chancellor, and he hadn't taken kindly to "the rib" meddling in political affairs. As a result, Brück was now determined to make life difficult for Katharina. He accused her of greed and mismanagement of her inherited funds and stymied her attempts to purchase the estate of Wachsdorf, ownership of which Katharina believed would secure her children's future. In addition, Brück suggested to the elector that Katharina send her two youngest boys away to boarding school (at twenty, Hans was considered an adult, so Brück didn't have as much control over his future), dispense of her property, and live with her daughter on a modest allowance provided by the elector. He announced that he intended to "break up Kate's extravagant household" and "take Luther's three sons away from their mother."[27] Finally, Brück suggested that Katharina and her children should be given separate guardians who would oversee their affairs.

Luther's friends didn't exactly rally to Katharina's cause, despite his stipulation in his will that they serve as his "dear Kate's witness and protect her from useless, evil, and envious tongues."[28] When Brück claimed that Martin and Paul would be in poor hands with their mother and better off at boarding school, neither Melanchthon nor Cruciger defended Katharina. In fact, Melanchthon suggested that all three boys should be separated from their mother and from each other. Hans should study at the electoral chancellery, he suggested, and the two younger boys should each board with their own tutor.

Melanchthon and Cruciger also refused to serve as Katharina's guardians. Their reasoning? Katharina would never heed their advice—an assumption probably grounded in experience. Ultimately the elector appointed Katharina's brother, Hans von Bora, and Erasmus Spiegel, the captain of the city guard, as her guardians, with Luther's brother Jacob, Wittenberg mayor Ambrosius Reuter, and electoral physician Matthew Ratzeberger as guardians for the children. Melanchthon and Cruciger were appointed secondary guardians, and even in that lesser, supporting role, Melanchthon still complained that Katharina pestered them relentlessly to keep her petitions moving forward.[29] In his and the other guardians' defense, working with Katharina and caught between her single-minded strong will and Brück's vengeful resistance couldn't have been an easy position.

The one person who did keep his word to Luther was Elector Johann Frederick. Ignoring Brück's suggestions, the elector ratified Luther's will, earmarked a generous sum to support Katharina and her two younger sons and daughter, and decreed that the purchase of the Wachsdorf estate be decided not by Brück but by Katharina's and her children's guardians. The only point on which he agreed with Brück was the subject of the guardians: the elector ordered separate guardians to be named for Katharina and her children, which, while not a decision with dire consequences, did slightly complicate Katharina's life.

After months of discussion between Katharina, Chancellor Brück, Elector Frederick, and the guardians, Katharina's strong will and savvy negotiating skills prevailed. Luther's properties, including the Black Cloister and the gardens, remained in her possession. She retained custody of her children—the younger boys continued to live with her and Margarete and were not sent off to boarding school. She was allowed to purchase the Wachsdorf estate, which would become the property of her sons when they came of age, and her children were granted an annual stipend of 1,000 *Gulden*, with an additional 5 percent added each year. Her only failure was that she was not allowed one guardian for the whole family, but Katharina knew when to quit pushing. In the most critical matters, she had won.

Katharina had exhibited relentless determination and resilience. She had pursued the business and financial decisions she thought would best benefit her children, and she had refused to be cowed by Brück's attempts to bully her into a position of powerlessness. Above all, Katharina had put her children and their future livelihood above all else, including her own reputation, and had proven herself a formidable opponent to some of the most powerful authorities in Wittenberg and Saxony. As Ernst Kroker points out, Katharina had the elector to thank more than the others, "but most of all she had herself to thank."[30]

Unfortunately, Katharina's victories were short-lived. War was on the horizon, and even greater challenges lay ahead.

By the fall of 1546, just months after Luther's death, Wittenberg had become a military zone. Men, armed with whatever weapons they could find—swords, spears, matchlock muskets, and even rocks—positioned themselves along the bulwark that surrounded the city and prepared for the attack of Emperor Charles V and his troops, which, bolstered by Hungarian reinforcements, were advancing toward Wittenberg. As news spread that the town of Zwickau, 128 miles south of Wittenberg, had been seized, Katharina and her children packed a wagon with as many valuables and necessities as they could fit and set their sights on Magdeburg, about fifty miles northwest of Wittenberg, one of the few remaining towns that had not been captured.

When it was finally safe to return home to Wittenberg in early spring of 1547, Katharina discovered that, while the Black Cloister was intact, her other properties in the country had suffered irreparable damage. Her fields and gardens had been ravaged, and her livestock was decimated, either stolen or butchered. She was on the verge of financial ruin.

There was no time, however, to begin the process of restoration. By late spring, Elector Johann Frederick was taken prisoner, and Charles V entered Saxony and conquered Wittenberg. Katharina and her children fled just in time. They hoped to make it all the way to Denmark, where King Christian III was a friend and ally. Instead, the refugees were forced to stop in Braunschweig, about sixty miles west of Magdeburg. It was too dangerous to travel any farther.

By June it was considered safe to return to Wittenberg, which was now under the control of Duke Moritz of Saxony, who had allied himself with Charles V. From her seat in the wagon during the long journey home, Katharina observed the utter destruction of the landscape, farms, and houses. Hardly a tree was left standing. Crops were ravaged, farmhouses destroyed, barns and stables ruined, and livestock stolen. Katharina's own rural properties in Wachsdorf, Zülsdorf, and Boos (where, beginning in 1539, she leased fifty-six acres of pasture land to supplement her cattle-breeding operation) were in ruins. Her cattle were gone, and many of the buildings and stables had been burned by the people of Wittenberg themselves to inhibit the enemy from settling in close to the city walls. She had worked tirelessly to retain and maintain the properties Luther had bequeathed her, all for naught. Katharina was more destitute than ever. She gathered what few silver cups and tankards she had left to pawn. And then, pen in hand, she begged.

Calling in Favors

A mere eight of Katharina's letters are extant, none of them addressed to Luther and all but one connected with economic or legal concerns. Her "official" letters, in which she negotiated her and her children's legal status, were preserved, pointing to an interesting observation made by historians Sandra Cavallo and Lyndan Warner: "The widow often becomes visible to the historian because she left traces of her new 'uncovered' legal status."[31] That is, as a married woman, Katharina didn't exist, at least legally—she was simply connected to her husband's legal status. But as a widow, her legal and patrimonial condition changed, and Katharina became more independent, at least comparatively.

For example, in one of her rare extant letters, Katharina secretly wrote to her godfather, the electoral treasurer Hans von Taubenheim, for help in leasing a rural property in Boos. "Please do not listen to those [such as Chancellor Brück] who maintain that I want to bring the estate, deceitfully, as an inheritance into my possession. I just ask that the Boos farm be leased to me for a year or two at a reasonable rent so I will [have a place] to keep my household and livestock more conveniently. Please do not let this petition get into anybody else's hand."[32] Likewise, several letters have survived in which Katharina requested financial aid from the elector and other authorities, which she did with increasing frequency during and following the Schmalkaldic War. In 1547, for example, Katharina wrote to King Christian III of

Denmark to express her gratitude for his financial assistance. "Since during this past year I had so much deep sorrow and suffering, with the death of my husband and then the dangerous wars and devastation of this land," she wrote, "it has been a great comfort to me to receive from Your Royal Highness 50 talers so I can better maintain myself and my children, and for this I want to give you my most humble thanks."[33]

After her second return home to Wittenberg in June of 1547, however, Katharina's letters grew increasingly desperate. Her appeals were eloquent and humble, but to the point, and she didn't hesitate to remind her benefactors of their relationship with Luther. For example, in the spring of 1549 she wrote to both thank and appeal to Duke Albrecht of Prussia, who had provided Hans with a scholarship to study at Königsberg. "I do not want to bother you with reminiscing about the great privation in my household after this last war and how hard it is to nourish and maintain myself and my children from my devastated and depredated properties," she wrote. "I do not doubt that Your Highness would, for the sake of my husband—a true prophet in these last dangers and restless times—also take me as Luther's surviving widow and my children under your gracious protection."[34]

In 1550, after she had remortgaged Zülsdorf and pawned her remaining silver, she wrote a humble plea to King Christian III of Denmark, noting, "As Dr. M. Luther's widow I am making this petition as I and my children are receiving less now and the restlessness of this time has laid many heavy burdens on me," and pleading, "Would Your Royal Highness please arrange such help for this purpose?"[35] She heard nothing in response. Finally, in 1552, she wrote her eighth and last of her extant letters, again to King Christian:

> Since my late dear husband has always loved Your Royal Highness and considered you a most Christian king, and you have always favored him with such an allowance, I am now constrained by my urgent need to humbly beseech Your Royal Majesty in my misery to have mercy on this unworthy widow, who is now forsaken by everybody, and graciously forward said allowance. More damage has been done to me by my friends than by my enemies. For these and other reasons, I am compelled to humbly petition Your Royal Highness to help me since everybody treats me like a stranger and no one has mercy on me.[36]

Katharina's desperation and despair are obvious. Impoverished, in deep debt, her property remortgaged to the hilt, Katharina was forced to rely on her late husband's famous name, call in favors, and even beg in order to ensure her survival and the survival of her children.

To make matters worse, her friends blamed her. Bugenhagen, for instance, insinuated that she wouldn't be poor if she knew how to manage her property properly.[37] Not only was his comment unkind, it was also unfair and untrue. Since Luther's death, Katharina had labored tirelessly to support herself and her children. In addition to attempting to maintain her properties and livestock in between fleeing and returning to war-torn Wittenberg, she also kept the Black Cloister open and welcomed boarders during the months she was living in town. To supplement that income, she also rented out two large rooms next to her living room for university professors to use as lecture halls.

Katharina was industrious and innovative, but her labors were not enough, even with financial assistance, to overcome the deep debt and the devastation her properties had incurred during the war. Given adequate time, she might have succeeded in digging herself out of the financial hole—she had certainly demonstrated savvy business skills and a seemingly endless determination in the past. Unfortunately, she didn't have adequate time to prove herself. During the summer of 1552 the plague descended upon Wittenberg, and by autumn, the disease had spread to the Black Cloister. In order to protect her family from the deadly illness, Katharina was forced to flee Wittenberg for a third time.

She didn't make it very far. Just outside Wittenberg, en route to Torgau with her two youngest children, Paul and Margarete, the horses pulling their wagon were startled. As they threatened to tip the heavy load, Katharina jumped to the ground, landing hard and tumbling into a ditch of dirty, cold water, where she lay injured and barely conscious until her children managed to get her back into the wagon.

By the time Paul and Margarete got their mother to Torgau, found adequate lodging, and located a physician to attend to her,

Katharina is buried in St. Mary's Church in Torgau, Germany.

Katharina was near death. Several factors likely contributed to Katharina's demise: the stress of living on the edge of financial ruin and poverty for the last six years; the violent fall from the wagon; the exposure and shock as she lay in the cold water while her two children frantically scurried to help; and perhaps even internal injuries that were never diagnosed.[38]

Katharina Luther's epitaph can still be seen in St. Mary's Church in Torgau, Germany.

She remained in that precarious state, slowly fading, sometimes conscious but often not, for three months, until finally, on December 20, 1552, at the age of fifty-three, Katharina Luther died. Melanchthon wrote a lengthy commemoration in Latin, in which he acknowledged Katharina's suffering by quoting the Greek playwright Euripides, who wrote, "No evil is so horrible for language to describe, No fate or God-imposed adversity, Which does not bring its burdens on mortals."[39] Because many of the university's professors and students were in Torgau to escape the plague, Melanchthon posted a public obituary and an invitation to Katharina's funeral on December 21. At three o'clock that afternoon, a surprisingly large crowd assembled and progressed to St. Mary's Church.

There, Katharina Luther was laid to rest beneath the loft of the boys' choir, as Hans, Martin, Paul, and Margarete stood alongside her grave.

Katharina Luther had not labored in vain. Thanks to her tireless efforts, the financial security of her children was assured, even after she was gone. A year after his mother's death, Hans married Elizabeth Cruciger, the daughter of his parents' close friend, Caspar Cruciger. He worked in Duke Albrecht of Prussia's chancery and died in the duke's service in 1575. Martin, who had studied theology but was unable to work as a pastor due to his ill health, married the daughter of Wittenberg's mayor and died in 1565 at the age of thirty-four. Paul became a highly respected doctor, professor, and personal physician and counselor to the duke in Jena, about one hundred miles south of Wittenberg. Later he served as the private physician for the electors of Brandenburg and Saxony. He married Anna von Warbeck and died in 1593. Margarete married the lord George von Kunheim in 1555, had nine children, and died in 1570.

18

A Chancy Thing

A man and woman, backpacks in hand, cameras slung around their necks, pose arm in arm in front of the doorway while a friend snaps their picture with a cell phone. When they are finished and have disappeared inside to tour the building, another couple steps up to the same spot. They sit opposite one another on the stone seats flanking the entrance and smile broadly at the camera. Then they, too, step across the threshold into Martin and Katharina Luther's home.

Tourists visiting the Black Cloister (called *Lutherhaus* today) often gather at this particular entrance, which opens from the former monastery into the courtyard. The intricately carved doorway is known as the *Katharinenportal* (Katharina's door) and was commissioned by Katharina as a gift for Luther on his fifty-seventh birthday. Designed in the late Gothic style, the sandstone carving arches elegantly over the original wooden door in a graceful gable, at the top of which is etched 1540, the year Katharina gave Luther the gift. On each side of the doorway a small stone seat is tucked beneath a stone awning. A portrait of Luther is carved into the underside of the left awning; under the right awning is carved the Luther coat of arms, which includes a rose, its petals encircling a heart and a cross. The letters V.I.V.I.T.—spelling "He lives" in Latin, referring to

Onnola, "Lutherstadt Wittenberg—Katharinenportal am Lutherhaus (1540)," https://www.flickr.com/photos/30845644@N04/13900958438

This carved doorway, called the *Katharinenportal*, was given by Katharina as a gift to Luther on his fifty-seventh birthday.

Christ—are engraved around the coat of arms. According to Luther, the letters also represent the first five words of his personal motto, which the Reformer took with him to his grave. Luther never revealed his personal motto to anyone, saying only that the five letters represented German words connected to faith and God. The words "Etatis sue 57," indicating Luther's age, are engraved around his portrait, along with Isaiah 30:15, one of Luther's favorite verses: "In quiet and hope will be my strength."[1] Katharina clearly put a great deal of thought into the doorway's design, which highlights elements of Luther's faith and personality in intricate detail. The doorway is a love letter of sorts, an intimate portrait of Katharina's devotion to her husband.

Martin Luther and Katharina von Bora each had an agenda when they crossed the threshold of the Black Cloister on June 13, 1525, to marry: Katharina to survive in a world hostile to women; Luther to put his theological beliefs about marriage, grace, and obedience into practice for the world to witness. We don't know if they walked through the doorway together with confidence or fear, with hope or despair, with excitement or dismay. What we do know is that their motives began to shift with each subsequent step over that threshold. As months and then years passed and their bond as a couple strengthened, Luther and Katharina turned away from their own personal interests and toward each other. As their respect, trust, and love for one another grew, their marriage flourished.

Luther saved Katharina. He rescued her from the convent, from a life she didn't choose for herself, and offered her security, stability, and a place in a society that regarded her very existence with suspicion. Marriage opened a life of relative freedom to Katharina. As Luther's wife, she was allowed a voice and a degree of autonomy unavailable to most women, as well as the opportunity to experience the gift of motherhood and to enjoy the status society offered her in that role. In Luther, Katharina also finally found the love, connection, and companionship she had yearned for since childhood.

What history has largely failed to acknowledge, however, is that Katharina saved Luther as well. She first came to him as a burden, a woman abandoned and unwelcome in the world. But what was once a burden grew into an unexpected grace that surprised and delighted Luther with the richness of its gifts.

Luther's commitment to Katharina began as a test of his charity and a practical expression of his theology. Not only was Katharina instrumental in helping Luther live out his theology, but in loving her, he came to understand how self-sacrifice, empathy, compassion, and love flowed freely out of his love for God. But even beyond that, Katharina was living proof that Luther's theology and beliefs weren't just intellectual, theoretical exercises, but real, attainable reforms grounded in human respect and love. Luther thrived as a reformer not only because Katharina served as an astute business, financial, and household manager, but also because she showed him again and again that a love for others, as much as a love for God, was at the core of his beliefs. The Protestant Reformation would have happened without the marriage of Luther and Katharina. But Luther would not have been the same Reformer without Katharina.

Martin and Katharina Luther are arguably the most famous couple in Christian history. A close look at their lives reveals a daily existence shockingly different from our own. Yet as remote as their world is from ours, and as different as they are from us, they also offer us a surprisingly accurate picture of ourselves. In Martin and Katharina we recognize how flawed we are. We see our own stubbornness, pride, self-righteousness, and fears. We recognize our loneliness, isolation, and brokenness; we realize how desperately we need the grace of God. At the same time, we also see in them our own capacity for connection, our triumphs and joys, the depth and breadth of our compassion, the potential within us to love others as well as we love our own selves, and our desire to live wholeheartedly as followers of Christ. In short, the lives of Martin and Katharina Luther point to a common humanity that spans time, distance, and difference.

Many years after he took his first step over the threshold as a husband, Luther acknowledged the challenges inherent in matrimony. "Marriage does not always run smoothly, it is a chancy thing," he admitted. "One has to commit oneself to it."[2] The day they walked through the doorway of the Black Cloister for the first time as husband and wife, neither Luther nor Katharina could have comprehended the dramatic and lasting impact their commitment would have on the world and on history. Together they changed the institution of marriage and left an enduring legacy as Christian leaders. Yet perhaps even more significantly, Martin and Katharina Luther were also real people not so unlike us—a man and a woman who committed to a "chancy thing" nearly five hundred years ago, and in doing so, continue to teach us much about faith, love, and life today.

APPENDIX

The following three letters are a small representation of Luther's correspondence to Katharina that spans the nearly twenty-one years of their marriage.[1] Although I quote from his letters extensively throughout this book, reading even a small sample of his correspondence in full offers a deeper perspective on the Luthers' relationship. The three letters included here represent three periods of their marriage: the early years (1529), the middle years (1540), and the last days (February 1546). Each of the letters also includes an explanatory paragraph that offers some context.

At the end of September 1529, Luther was invited by Landgrave Philip of Hesse to attend a conference in Marburg with Huldrych Zwingli, leader of the Reformation in Switzerland, and German theologian Johannes Oecolampadius to hash out differences of opinion and theology regarding the symbolic interpretation of the Lord's Supper. At the end of the conference, which was called the Marburg Colloquy, both sides declared victory. This letter illustrates Luther's willingness to talk candidly with Katharina about important and complicated theological and political matters.

To Mrs. Martin Luther
October 4, 1529
Marburg

To my kind, dear Lord, Catherine Luther, a doctor and preacher in Wittenberg:

Grace and peace in Christ, Dear Sir Katie! You should know that our amiable colloquy at Marburg has come to an end, and we are in agreement on almost all points, except that the opposition insists on affirming that there is only simple bread in the Lord's Supper, and on confessing that Jesus Christ is spiritually present there. Today the Landgrave is negotiating [to see] if we could be united, or whether, even though we continue to disagree, we could not nevertheless mutually consider ourselves brethren, and members of Christ. The Landgrave works hard on this matter. But we do not want this brother-and-member business, though we do want peace and good [will]. I assume that tomorrow or the next day we shall depart here and travel to our Gracious Lord in Schleiz/Vogtland, where His Electoral Grace has ordered us [to go].[2]

Tell Mr. Pomer[3] *that the best arguments have been, in Zwingli's case, that a body cannot exist without a location, therefore Christ's body is not in the bread, [and] in*

Oecolampadius' case, [that] this sacrament is a sign of Christ's body.[4] *I assume that God has blinded them so that they had nothing else to offer.*

I am very busy, and the messenger is in a hurry. Say "good night" to all, and pray for us! We are all still alert and healthy, and live like kings. Kiss Lenchen and Hänschen on my behalf.[5]

Your obedient servant,
Martin Luther

John Brenz, Andrew Osiander, [and] Doctor Stephen from Augsburg have also come here.[6]

The people here have become almost mad with fear of the English fever; about fifty people fell ill yesterday, of whom one or two have [already] passed away.[7]

This letter was written in July 1540, when Luther was summoned by Elector Johann Frederick to travel to Weimar, where Melanchthon had become gravely ill (Melanchthon had been en route to Hagenau to participate in reconciliation negotiations between Protestant and Roman Catholic theologians). After Melanchthon had recuperated, the two traveled with another friend, Caspar Cruciger, to Eisenach in order to find a solution to Landgrave Philip of Hesse's bigamy problem. Luther was away from Wittenberg for approximately six weeks. This letter to Katharina is indicative of Luther's often playful tone with her. It's also a testament of his trust in her, as he instructs her to assist with the interview process for a pastor in nearby Greussen.

To Mrs. Martin Luther
July 2, 1540
Weimar

To my dearly beloved Katie, Mrs. Doctor Luther, etc., to the lady at the new pig market:

Grace and Peace! Dear Maid Katie, Gracious Lady of Zölsdorf (and whatever other names Your Grace has)! I wish humbly to inform Your Grace that I am doing well here. I eat like a Bohemian and drink like a German; thanks be to God for this. Amen. The reason for this is that Master Philip truly had been dead, and really, like Lazarus, has risen from death.[8] *God, the dear father, listens to our prayers. This we [can] see and touch [with our hands], yet we still do not believe it. No one should say Amen to such disgraceful disbelief of ours.*

I have written to Doctor Pomer, the pastor, that the Count of Schwarzburg is asking that a pastor be sent to Greussen. As a wise woman and doctor, you, with Master George Major and Master Ambrose, might also give counsel to which of the three candidates I suggested to Pomer might be convinced [to go].[9] *It is not a bad parish. Yet you people are wise and will find a better solution [than I suggested].*

There at Arnstadt the pastor has driven a devil out of a young girl in a truly Christian way. Regarding this event we say: may the will of God, who is still alive, be done, even though the devil should be sorry about this.[10]

I have received the letters from the children, also the one from the baccalaureus (who is no child)—(Marushe [is] also not [one])—but from Your Grace I have received nothing.[11] *If it please God, then you might now, at least once, answer this, the fourth letter, with your gracious hand.*

I am sending along with Master Paul the silver apple which my Gracious Lord presented to me.[12] *As I previously said, you may divide it among the children and ask them how many cherries and apples they would wish in exchange for it; give them these at once, and you retain the stalk, etc.*

Give my heart greetings and good will to our dear boarders, especially to Doctor Severus or Schiefer, and tell them to help in all affairs of the church, school, house—wherever the need arises.[13] *Also [tell] Master George Major and Master Ambrose to help you around the house. By God's will we shall be here until Sunday, and then, with Philip, we shall travel from Weimar to Eisenach.*

With this I commend you to God. Tell our Lycaon not to neglect the mulberries by oversleeping; of course, he won't oversleep unless he forgets about it.[14] *Also, he should tap the wine at the right time. All of you be happy and pray. Amen.*

Martin Luther
who loves you from his heart

This letter, one of the last written to Katharina before Luther died on February 18, illustrates both his humor and his deep concern and care for his wife. He attempts to ease her anxieties by joking about the misfortunes that have befallen him in recent days, and he urges her to release her worries to God.

To Mrs. Martin Luther
February 10, 1546
Eisleben

To the holy lady, full of worries, Mrs. Catherine Luther, doctor, the lady of Zölsdorf, at Wittenberg, my gracious, dear mistress of the house:

Grace and peace in Christ! Most holy Mrs. Doctor! I thank you very kindly for your great worry which robs you of sleep. Since the date that you [started to] worry about me, the fire in my quarters, right outside the door of my room, tried to devour me; and yesterday, no doubt because of the strength of your worries, a stone almost fell on my head and nearly squashed me as in a mouse trap. For in our secret chamber mortar has been falling down for about two days; we called in some people who [merely] touched the stone with two fingers and it fell down. The stone was as big as a long pillow and as wide as a large hand; it intended to repay you for your holy worries, had the dear angels not protected [me]. [Now] I worry that if you do not stop worrying the earth will finally swallow us up and all the elements will chase us. Is this the way you learned the Catechism and the faith? Pray, and let God worry. You have certainly not been commanded to worry about me or about yourself. "Cast your burden on the Lord, and he will sustain you," as is written in Psalm 55[:22] and many more passages.

We are chipper and healthy, praise be to God, except that that affair is disgusting to us and that Jonas would also like to have a bad calf; and so he accidentally bumped into a chest. So great is human envy that he did not want me to have a bad calf all by myself.[15]

With this I commend you to God. We would gladly be free [of the matter] now and drive home, if God would will it. Amen.

Your Holiness' willing
servant,
Martin Luther

NOTES

Abbreviations Used in Notes

LW: Jaroslav Pelikan and Helmut T. Lehmann, gen. eds., *Luther's Works, American Edition*, 55 vols. (St. Louis: Concordia; Philadelphia: Fortress Press, 1955–1986).

WA: *D. Martin Luthers Werke*, 67 vols. (Weimar: Hermann Bohlaus Nachfolger, 1883–1997).

WA, TR [Table Talk]: *D. Martin Luthers Werke: Kritische Gesamtausgabe, Tischreden*, 6 vols. (Weimar: Hermann Bohlaus Nachfolger, 1912–1921).

WA, BR [Correspondence]: *D. Martin Luthers Werke: Kritische Gesamtausgabe*, Briefwechsel (Weimar: Hermann Bohlaus Nachfolger, 1930–1970).

Introduction

1. Martin Brecht, *Martin Luther: His Road to Reformation, 1483–1521*, trans. James L. Schaff (Philadelphia: Westminster Press, 1895), 3:376.
2. LW, vol. 50, 311; Letter from Martin Luther to Katharina Luther, February 14, 1546.
3. Ernst Kroker, *The Mother of the Reformation: The Amazing Life and Story of Katharine Luther*, trans. Mark E. DeGarmeaux (St. Louis: Concordia, 2013), 221.
4. LW, vol. 50, 291; Letter from Martin Luther to Katharina Luther, February 1, 1546.
5. LW, vol. 50, 302; Letter from Martin Luther to Katharina Luther, February 7, 1546.
6. Ibid.

7. Ibid.

8. LW, vol. 50, 305; Letter from Martin Luther to Katharina Luther, February 10, 1546.

9. Ibid.

10. Ibid.

Chapter 1 To the Cloister School

1. Moritz Meurer, *Katharina Luther geb. Von Bora*, 2nd ed. (Leipzig, Germany: Justus Naumann, 1873); quoted in an endnote in Rudolf K. Markwald and Marilynn Morris Markwald, *Katharina von Bora: A Reformation Life* (Saint Louis: Concordia, 2002), 204.

2. Martin Treu, "Katharina von Bora: The Woman at Luther's Side," *Lutheran Quarterly* XIII (1999): 157.

3. Merry Wiesner, *Gender, Church and State in Early Modern Germany: Essays by Merry E. Wiesner* (London: Addison Wesley Longman Limited, 1998), 116.

4. Ibid., 124.

5. Markwald and Markwald, *Katharina von Bora*, 15.

6. Kroker, *Mother of the Reformation*, 108.

7. Markwald and Markwald, *Katharina von Bora*, 14–17.

8. Ibid., 22.

9. Michelle DeRusha, *50 Women Every Christian Should Know: Learning from Heroines of the Faith* (Grand Rapids: Baker Books, 2014), 19.

10. Kroker, *Mother of the Reformation*, 10.

11. Ibid., 10–11.

12. C. H. Lawrence, *Medieval Monasticism: Forms of Religious Life in Western Europe in the Middle Ages* (London: Longman Group LTD, 1984), 216.

13. DeRusha, *50 Women Every Christian Should Know*, 61.

14. Charlotte Woodford, *Nuns as Historians in Early Modern Germany* (Oxford: Oxford University Press, 2002), 4.

15. Markwald and Markwald, *Katharina von Bora*, 27.

16. Ibid., 27.

17. The origin of the word *Cistercian* comes from the Latin name for Cîteaux; Dictionary.com, accessed December 21, 2015, http://dictionary.reference.com/browse/cistercian.

18. M. Basil Pennington, OCSO, "The Cistercians: An Introduction," The Order of St. Benedict, accessed November 11, 2015, http://www.osb.org/cist/intro.html.

19. Lawrence, *Medieval Monasticism*, 174–76.
20. Markwald and Markwald, *Katharina von Bora*, 27.
21. Ibid., 29–30.
22. Lawrence, *Medieval Monasticism*, 174–76.
23. Markwald and Markwald, *Katharina von Bora*, 28.
24. Kroker, *Mother of the Reformation*, 13.

Chapter 2 A Nun without a Choice

1. Julie Kerr, *Life in the Medieval Cloister* (New York: Continuum US, 2009), 58.
2. "Daily Life of a Nun in the Middle Ages," LordsAndLadies.org, accessed May 20, 2015, http://www.lordsandladies.org/daily-life-nun-middle-ages.htm.
3. Kerr, *Life in the Medieval Cloister*, 41.
4. Walter Map, *De Nugis Curialium*, ed. and trans. M. R. James, rev. C. N. L. Brooke / R. A. B. Mynors (Oxford: Oxford University Press, 1983), 77, as quoted in Kerr, *Life in the Medieval Cloister*, 38.
5. Kerr, *Life in the Medieval Cloister*, 55.
6. Ibid., 56.
7. Ibid., 55.
8. Ibid., 56.
9. Albrecht Thoma, *Katharina von Bora, Geschichtliches Lebensbild* (Berlin: Georg Reimer, 1900), 87, as quoted in Markwald and Markwald, *Katharina von Bora*, 81.
10. Markwald and Markwald, *Katharina von Bora*, 33.
11. Kroker, *Mother of the Reformation*, 19.
12. Markwald and Markwald, *Katharina von Bora*, 32.
13. Ibid., 30.
14. Kerr, *Life in the Medieval Cloister*, 47.
15. Ibid.
16. Ibid.
17. Bernard of Clairvaux, *The Letters of Bernard of Clairvaux*, ed. and trans. by B. S. James (Stroud: Sutton Publishing Ltd., 1998), 8, as quoted in Kerr, *Life in the Medieval Cloister*, 46.
18. William of St. Thierry, *The Golden Epistle: A Letter to the Brethren at Mont Dieu*, trans. by T. Berkeley (Kalamazoo, MI: Cistercian Publications, 1971), 44–45, as quoted in Kerr, *Life in the Medieval Cloister*, 47.

19. Bernard of Clairvaux, *St. Bernard's Apologia to Abbott William*, trans. by M. Casey (Kalamazoo, MI: Cistercian Publications, 1970), 57, as quoted in Kerr, *Life in the Medieval Cloister*, 47.

20. Kroker, *Mother of the Reformation*, 22.

21. Woodford, *Nuns as Historians*, 6–7.

22. Markwald and Markwald, *Katharina von Bora*, 32–33.

23. Thoma, *Katharina von Bora, Geschichtliches Lebensbild*, 192, as quoted in Markwald and Markwald, *Katharina von Bora*, 33.

Chapter 3 A Family Rift

1. The family name, a derivative of the Christian name *Lothar*, was often written *Luder*, as well as *Loder* and *Lotter*. It was only when he began to publish his writing that Martin Luther chose the form by which we know him today. From Richard Friedenthal, *Luther: His Life and Times* (New York: Harcourt Brace Jovanovich, Inc., 1967), 8.

2. Friedenthal, *Luther*, 15.

3. Ibid.

4. Ibid.

5. Luther's father had risen through the ranks of the mining business, so St. Anne, the patron saint of miners, held a place of importance in the Luther family.

6. WA, vol. 8, 574, as quoted in Richard Marius, *Martin Luther: The Christian between God and Death* (Cambridge, MA: Harvard University Press, 1999), 44.

7. Brecht, *Martin Luther: His Road to Reformation*, 1:5.

8. Marius, *Martin Luther*, 24.

9. Friedenthal, *Luther*, 8.

10. Peter Manns, *Martin Luther: An Illustrated Biography* (New York: The Crossroads Publishing Company, 1982), 15; James M. Kittelson, *Luther the Reformer: The Story of the Man and His Career* (Minneapolis: Augsburg, 1986), 31.

11. Marius, *Martin Luther*, 24.

12. Manns, *Martin Luther: An Illustrated Biography*, 15.

13. Ibid.

14. Friedenthal, *Luther*, 11.

15. Martin Marty, *Martin Luther: A Life* (New York: Viking Penguin, 2004), 2.

16. Marius, *Martin Luther*, 22.

17. Friedenthal, *Luther*, 11.
18. Kittelson, *Luther the Reformer*, 35.
19. Friedenthal, *Luther*, 11.
20. Heinrich Boehmer, *Martin Luther: Road to Reformation*, translated from the German by John W. Doberstein and Theodore G. Tappert (Cleveland: The World Publishing Company, 1957), 18.
21. Kittelson, *Luther the Reformer*, 37–38.
22. Friedenthal, *Luther*, 12.
23. Marius, *Martin Luther*, 23.
24. Erik H. Erikson, *Young Man Luther: A Study in Psychoanalysis and History* (New York: W.W. Norton, 1958), 77.
25. LW, vol. 54, no. 1559, 157.
26. LW, vol. 54, no. 3566A, 235.
27. Ibid.
28. Roland H. Bainton, *Here I Stand: A Life of Martin Luther* (Peabody, MA: Hendrickson, 1950), 23.
29. Robert Herndon Fife, *Young Luther: The Intellectual and Religious Development of Martin Luther to 1518* (New York: AMS Press, Inc., 1970), 111–12.
30. Friedenthal, *Luther*, 47.
31. Ibid.
32. LW, vol. 49, 319; Letter from Martin Luther to Philip Melanchthon, June 5, 1530.
33. Ibid.
34. Ibid.
35. Ibid.
36. WA, BR, vol. 5, 379, as quoted in a footnote in LW, vol. 49, 319.
37. Ibid.
38. Marius, *Martin Luther*, 21.

Chapter 4 The Good Monk

1. Marius, *Martin Luther*, 41.
2. Friedenthal, *Luther*, 22.
3. James M. Anderson, *Daily Life during the Reformation* (Santa Barbara, CA: ABC-CLIO, LLC, 2011), 32.
4. Marius, *Martin Luther*, 10.
5. "Plague: The Black Death," National Geographic, accessed August 17, 2015, http://science.nationalgeographic.com/science/health-and-human-body/human-diseases/plague-article/.

6. Giovanni Boccaccio, as found in "Black Death," History.com, accessed August 17, 2015, http://www.history.com/topics/black-death.

7. "Black Death," History.com, accessed August 17, 2015, http://www.history.com/topics/black-death.

8. Ibid.

9. Giovanni Boccaccio, as found in "The Black Death, 1348," Eyewitness to History, accessed August 17, 2015, http://www.eyewitnesstohistory.com/plague.htm.

10. Kittelson, *Luther the Reformer*, 34.

11. Mark Konnert, *Early Modern Europe: The Age of Religious War, 1559–1715* (Toronto: University of Toronto Press, 2008), 22.

12. Henry Kamen, *Early Modern European Society* (London: Routledge, 2005), 18.

13. Konnert, *Early Modern Europe*, 22.

14. Kittelson, *Luther the Reformer*, 34.

15. Kamen, *Early Modern European Society*, 18.

16. Ibid.

17. Michael Camille, *The Gargoyles of Notre-Dame: Medievalism and the Monsters of Modernity* (Chicago: University of Chicago Press), 14–17.

18. Marius, *Martin Luther*, 43.

19. Bainton, *Here I Stand*, 17.

20. Ibid., 18.

21. Friedenthal, *Luther*, 44.

22. Kittelson, *Luther the Reformer*, 51–52.

23. Ibid., 78–79, 83.

24. Marius, *Martin Luther*, 83.

25. Friedenthal, *Luther*, 83.

26. WA, vol. 51, 68, as quoted in Marius, *Martin Luther*, 83.

27. Martin Luther, as quoted in Bainton, *Here I Stand*, 26.

28. Marius, *Martin Luther*, 201.

29. Ibid., 59.

30. Ibid., 32.

31. Fife, *Young Luther*, 126.

32. Ibid.

33. Boehmer, *Martin Luther: Road to Reformation*, 40.

34. Kittelson, *Luther the Reformer*, 43.

35. Marius, *Martin Luther*, 487.

36. Brecht, *Martin Luther: His Road to Reformation*, 3:376.

37. Edith Simon, *Luther Alive: Martin Luther and the Making of the Reformation* (Garden City, NY: Doubleday and Company, Inc. 1968), 35.

38. Kittelson, *Luther the Reformer*, 56.

39. Ibid.

40. Bainton, *Here I Stand*, 34.

Chapter 5 The Road to Damascus and a Nail in the Door

1. Kittelson, *Luther the Reformer*, 63.

2. Bainton, *Here I Stand*, 33.

3. Kroker, *Mother of the Reformation*, 82.

4. Kittelson, *Luther the Reformer*, 63.

5. A prince-elector (the title was abbreviated to elector) was a member of the electoral college of the Holy Roman Empire. From the thirteenth century through the beginning of the nineteenth century, the electors were very powerful, as they were responsible for electing the person who would be crowned the Holy Roman Emperor by the pope. In 1519, seven electors selected Charles V as the Holy Roman Emperor after the death of his paternal grandfather, Maximilian I.

6. Marius, *Martin Luther*, 85.

7. Bainton, *Here I Stand*, 43.

8. "Catechism of the Catholic Church," Vatican, accessed July 30, 2015, http://www.vatican.va/archive/ENG0015/__P4G.HTM.

9. Enrico dal Covolo, SDB, "The Historical Origin of Indulgences," CatholicCulture.org, accessed July 30, 2015, http://www.catholicculture.org/culture/library/view.cfm?id=1054.

10. Bainton, *Here I Stand*, 54.

11. Ibid., 53.

12. Bainton, *Here I Stand*, 53, and Simon, *Luther Alive*, 65.

13. Bainton, *Here I Stand*, 53.

14. Ibid., 60–61.

15. Marius, *Martin Luther*, 135.

16. Ibid., 137.

17. Ibid., 139.

18. Martin Luther, *Works of Martin Luther, with Introduction and Notes*, vol. 1 (Philadelphia: A. J. Holman Company, 1915), 37.

19. Ibid., 30–32.

20. Bainton, *Here I Stand*, 62.

21. Marius, *Martin Luther*, 192.

22. WA, vol. 54, 186, as quoted in Marius, *Martin Luther*, 193.

23. Martin Brecht, "Luther's Reformation," *Handbook of European History, 1400–1600*, vol. 2, eds. Thomas A. Brady, Jr., Heiko A. Oberman, and James D. Tracy (Grand Rapids: Eerdmans, 1996), 133.

24. LW, vol. 48, 106; Letter from Martin Luther to George Spalatin, February 7, 1519.

25. John M. Todd, *Luther: A Life* (London: Hamish Hamilton Ltd., 1982), 160.

26. Ibid., 159.

27. "The Disputation of Tortosa," Jewish Virtual Library, accessed April 12, 2016, https://www.jewishvirtuallibrary.org/jsource/judaica/ejud_0002_0020_0_19966.html.

28. Marius, *Martin Luther*, 173.

29. Ibid., 179, 182.

30. Ibid., 187.

31. Friedenthal, *Luther*, 211.

32. Ibid.

33. Marius, *Martin Luther*, 234.

Chapter 6 Hear This, O Pope!

1. Friedenthal, *Luther*, 251.

2. Ibid.

3. The papal bull of excommunication was issued on June 15, 1520, but though Luther had heard rumors of it, the official bull didn't reach his hands until October 10, 1520. Sixty days later, when the period that was allowed for him to recant was up, he burned it, on December 10, 1520.

4. LW, vol. 44, 193.

5. Ibid., 163.

6. Ibid., 168.

7. Ibid., 169.

8. Marius, *Martin Luther*, 265.

9. Ibid., 266.

10. Martin Luther, "The Freedom of a Christian," in *Selected Writings of Martin Luther, 1520–1523*, ed. Theodore C. Tappert (Philadelphia: Fortress Press, 1967), 35.

11. Ibid., 40–43.

12. Ibid., 42.

13. LW, vol. 48, 188.

14. Simon, *Luther Alive*, 12–13.

15. Marius, *Martin Luther*, 294.

16. LW, vol. 32, 112–13. Footnote for the last sentence of this passage notes: "These words are given in German in the Latin text upon which this translation is based. There is good evidence, however, that Luther actually said only: 'May God help me!' Cf. *Deutsche Reichstagsakten*, Vol. II: *Deutsche Reichstagsakten unter Kaiser Karl V* (Gotha, 1896), p. 587."

17. Todd, *Luther: A Life*, 203.

18. Marius, *Martin Luther*, 295.

19. Todd, *Luther: A Life*, 204.

20. LW, vol. 48, 222; Letter to George Spalatin, May 14, 1521.

Chapter 7 The Risks of Freedom

1. Markwald and Markwald, *Katharina von Bora*, 38–39.

2. Ibid., 39.

3. Ibid., 40.

4. LW, vol. 44, 291.

5. Heiko A. Oberman, *Luther: Man between God and the Devil* (New York: Doubleday, 1992), 272.

6. Martin Luther, *Against the So-called Spiritual Estate of the Pope and the Bishops*, LW, vol. 39, 297.

7. Merry Wiesner-Hanks, ed., *Convents Confront the Reformation: Catholic & Protestant Nuns in Germany* (Milwaukee: Marquette University Press, 1998), 45–47.

8. Ibid., 47.

9. Ibid., 49.

10. Ibid.

11. Ibid., 61.

12. Amy Leonard, *Nails in the Wall: Catholic Nuns in Reformation Germany* (Chicago: University of Chicago Press, 2005), 31.

13. Ibid., 50.

14. Wiesner-Hanks, *Convents Confront the Reformation*, 12.

15. Ibid., 13.

16. Merry E. Wiesner, *Gender, Church and State in Early Modern Germany: Essays by Merry E. Wiesner* (London: Addison Wesley Longman Limited, 1998), 60.

17. Leonard, *Nails in the Wall*, 53.

18. Ibid., 51.

19. Ibid.

20. Merry E. Wiesner, "Nuns, Wives, and Mothers: Women and the Reformation in Germany," in *Women in Reformation and Counter-Reformation Europe: Private and Public Worlds*, ed. Sherrin Marshall (Bloomington: Indiana University Press, 1989), 10.

21. Caritas Pirckheimer, as quoted in "The Nuremberg Abbess: Caritas Pirckheimer," in Katharina M. Wilson, ed., *Women Writers of the Renaissance and Reformation* (Athens, GA: University of Georgia Press, 1987), 298–300.

22. Caritas Pirckheimer, *Caritas Pirckheimer: A Journal of the Reformation Years 1524–1528*, trans. Paul A. MacKenzie (Rochester, NY: Boydell & Brewer Ltd., 2006), 93.

23. Ibid.

24. Ibid.

25. Ibid.

26. Ibid., 179.

27. Wiesner-Hanks, *Convents Confront the Reformation*, 35.

28. Ibid., 37.

29. Wiesner, *Gender, Church and State in Early Modern Germany*, 119.

30. Ibid., 118.

31. Leonard, *Nails in the Wall*, 83.

32. Ibid., 19–20.

33. Wiesner, *Gender, Church and State in Early Modern Germany*, 123.

34. Ibid., 139–40.

35. Ibid., 139.

36. Ibid., 140.

37. Ibid.

38. Ibid., 139.

39. Ibid.

40. Merry Wiesner, *Women and Gender in Early Modern Europe* (Cambridge: Cambridge University Press, 2000), 45.

41. Ibid., 44.

42. Ibid., 76.

43. Boehmer, *Martin Luther: Road to Reformation*, 14.

44. Wiesner, *Women and Gender in Early Modern Europe*, 56.

45. Ibid.

46. LW, vol. 7, 76.

47. Wiesner, *Women and Gender in Early Modern Europe*, 57.

48. WA, vol. 2, 166–71, 1519, quoted in *Luther on Women: A Sourcebook*, ed. and trans. Susan C. Karant-Nunn and Merry E. Wiesner-Hanks (New York: Cambridge University Press, 2003), Kindle edition, 91.

49. Wolfgang Breul, "Celibacy—Marriage—Unmarriage: The Controversy over Celibacy and Clerical Marriage in the Early Reformation," in *Mixed Matches: Transgressive Unions in Germany from the Reformation to the Enlightenment*, ed. David M. Luebke and Mary Lindemann (New York: Berghahn Books, 2014), 33.

50. Martin Luther, *Against the So-called Spiritual Estate of the Pope and the Bishops*, LW, vol. 39, 296.

Chapter 8 Escape

1. Markwald and Markwald, *Katharina von Bora*, 42.
2. Ibid.
3. Ibid.
4. Martin Luther, *Dr. Martin Luther's Sammtliche Schriften*, 2nd ed., ed. Johann Georg Walch (St. Louis: Concordia, 1881–1910), 19:1669–71, as quoted in Markwald and Markwald, *Katharina von Bora*, 43.
5. Markwald and Markwald, *Katharina von Bora*, 45.
6. Margaret A. Currie, *The Letters of Martin Luther* (London: MacMillan and Company, Limited, 1908), 111; Letter from Martin Luther to Wenzel Link, April 8, 1523.
7. Markwald and Markwald, *Katharina von Bora*, 46.
8. Simon, *Luther Alive*, 327.
9. Kroker, *Mother of the Reformation*, 34.
10. Ibid.
11. Ibid., 35.
12. Currie, *Letters of Martin Luther*, 111; Letter from Martin Luther to Wenzel Link, April 8, 1523.
13. Luther, *Dr. Martin Luther's Sammtliche Schriften*, 21a:497, as quoted in Markwald and Markwald, *Katharina von Bora*, 52.
14. Florentina von Oberweimar, *Ein Geschicht, wie Gott Einer ehrbarn Klosterjungfrauen ausgeholfen hat* (Strasbourg: J. Pruss, 1524), fol. viii, as quoted in Leonard, *Nails in the Wall*, 54.
15. Leonard, *Nails in the Wall*, 54.
16. Luther, *Dr. Martin Luther's Sammtliche Schriften*, 21b:1896, as quoted in Markwald and Markwald, *Katharina von Bora*, 57.

17. Beatus Rhenanus, *Briefwechsel* (Leipzig: B.G. Teubner Verlag, 1886), 319, as quoted in Roland Bainton, *Women of the Reformation in Germany and Italy* (Minneapolis: Augsburg, 1971), 24.

18. Kroker, *Mother of the Reformation*, 39.

19. Steven Ozment, *When Fathers Ruled: Family Life in Reformation Europe* (Cambridge, MA: Harvard University Press, 1983), 25.

20. Kroker, *Mother of the Reformation*, 56.

21. Currie, *Letters of Martin Luther*, 129; Letter from Martin Luther to Hieronymus Baumgartner, October 12, 1524.

22. Kroker, *Mother of the Reformation*, 57.

23. Markwald and Markwald, *Katharina von Bora*, 61.

24. Ibid.

25. Eva Zeller, *Die Lutherin Spurensuche nach Katharina von Bora* (Berlin: Langenscheidt, 1982), 480, as quoted in Markwald and Markwald, *Katharina von Bora*, 62.

Chapter 9 Marriage Makeover

1. Luke Dysinger, OSB, "History of the Sacrament of Matrimony," adapted from *The New Commentary on the Code of Canon Law, "Title VI-Marriage [canons. 1055–1165], Historical Overview,"* eds. John P. Beal, James A. Coriden, and Thomas J. Green (Mahwah, NJ: Paulist, 1998), accessed August 28, 2015, http://www.ldysinger.com/THM_544_Marriage/05_Hist_Devt/001_hist-sum.htm.

2. Diarmaid MacCulloch, *The Reformation* (New York: Viking, 2003), 612.

3. Joel F. Harrington, *Reordering Marriage and Society in Reformation Germany* (New York: Cambridge University Press, 1995), 171.

4. Ozment, *When Fathers Ruled*, 25.

5. Ibid.

6. Harrington, *Reordering Marriage*, 30.

7. Ozment, *When Fathers Ruled*, 25.

8. Harrington, *Reordering Marriage*, 177.

9. LW, vol. 36, 96.

10. Harrington, *Reordering Marriage*, 184.

11. Ibid.

12. Ibid.

13. Steven Ozment, *Flesh and Spirit: Private Life in Early Modern Germany* (New York: Penguin Books, 1999), 45.

14. Ibid.

15. Ibid.

16. Harrington, *Reordering Marriage*, 188.

17. LW, vol. 46, 268.

18. Harrington, *Reordering Marriage*, 187–88.

19. LW, vol. 44, 8.

20. Martin Luther, "The Estate of Marriage," 1522, LW, vol. 45, 17–49, quoted in Karant-Nunn and Wiesner-Hanks, *Luther on Women*, 100–101.

21. Oberman, *Luther: Man between God and the Devil*, 273.

22. WA, vol. 18, 275, 19–28, as quoted in Oberman, *Luther: Man between God and the Devil*, 273.

23. Francis and Joseph Gies, *Women in the Middle Ages* (New York: HarperCollins, 1978), 53.

24. Ibid.

25. Harrington, *Reordering Marriage*, 51.

26. Ibid.

27. Leonard, *Nails in the Wall*, 1.

28. LW, vol. 1, 35.

29. WA, vol. 18, 277, 26–36, as quoted in Oberman, *Luther: Man between God and the Devil*, 272–73.

30. Oberman, *Luther: Man between God and the Devil*, 274.

31. LW, vol. 39, 298; from Martin Luther's *Against the So-Called Spiritual Estate of the Pope and the Bishops*.

32. LW, vol. 45, 44; from Martin Luther's *The Estate of Marriage*.

33. Ibid.

34. Luebke and Lindemann, *Mixed Matches*, 15.

35. Karant-Nunn and Wiesner-Hanks, *Luther on Women*, 137–38.

36. Simon, *Luther Alive*, 345.

37. Markwald and Markwald, *Katharina von Bora*, 63.

38. Currie, *Letters of Martin Luther*, 129; Letter from Martin Luther to George Spalatin, November 30, 1524.

39. LW, vol. 49, 104–5; Letter from Martin Luther to George Spalatin, April 16, 1525.

40. Ibid., 105.

41. Markwald and Markwald, *Katharina von Bora*, 61.

42. Ernst Kroker, "Luthers Werbung um Katharina von Bora," in *Lutherstudies zur 4, Jahrhunderfeier der Reformation* (Weimar: H. Bohlaus, 1917), 142, as quoted in Markwald and Markwald, *Katharina von Bora*, 61.

43. Ibid.

Chapter 10 Tying the Knot

1. Kroker, *Mother of the Reformation*, 64–65.

2. "German Peasants' Revolt," New World Encyclopedia, accessed January 8, 2016, http://www.newworldencyclopedia.org/entry/German_Peasants'_revolt.

3. LW, vol. 49, 111; Letter from Martin Luther to John Rühel, May 4, 1525.

4. Johann Georg Walch, ed., *Dr. Martin Luther's Sammtliche Schriften*, 20:1156, as quoted in Markwald and Markwald, *Katharina von Bora*, 70.

5. WA, BR, vol. 3, 479–82, no. 860, as quoted in Markwald and Markwald, *Katharina von Bora*, 69.

6. LW, vol. 49, 117; Letter from Martin Luther to Nikolaus von Amsdorf, June 21, 1525.

7. Ibid.

8. Ibid.

9. WA, TR, vol. 5, no. 4787, 503–5, as quoted in Karant-Nunn and Wiesner-Hanks *Luther on Women*, 132.

10. Brecht, "Luther's Reformation," *Handbook of European History, 1400–1600*, 2:132.

11. Ibid.

12. Martin Luther, "The Freedom of a Christian," in *Reformation Writings of Martin Luther*, trans. Bertram Lee Woolf (New York: Philosophical Library, 1953), 357.

13. Marius, *Martin Luther*, 269.

14. Luther, "The Freedom of a Christian," in Woolf, *Reformation Writings of Martin Luther*, 376.

15. Lyndal Roper, *The Holy Household: Religion, Morals and Order in Reformation Augsburg* (Oxford: Clarendon Press, 1989), 143–44.

16. Ibid.

17. Kroker, *Mother of the Reformation*, 71.

18. Markwald and Markwald, *Katharina von Bora*, 81.

19. Kroker, *Mother of the Reformation*, 66.

20. G. Kawerau, ed., *Der Briefwechsel des Justus Jonas*, vol. 1 (Halle: O. Hendel, 1884), no. 90, 94, 3–9, as quoted in Oberman, *Luther: Man between God and the Devil*, 282.

21. Markwald and Markwald, *Katharina von Bora*, 71–72.

22. Kroker, *Mother of the Reformation*, 66.

23. Simon, *Luther Alive*, 307.

24. Roper, *Holy Household*, 151.
25. Ibid., 152.
26. Ibid., 153.
27. Ibid., 154.
28. Currie, *Letters of Martin Luther*, 141; Letter from Martin Luther to Johann von Doltzig, Electoral Chancellor, June 21, 1525.
29. WA, BR, vol. 3, 537, as quoted in Kittelson, *Luther the Reformer*, 201.
30. Simon, *Luther Alive*, 331.
31. Marius, *Martin Luther*, 438.

Chapter 11 Backlash

1. Simon, *Luther Alive*, 331.
2. WA, TR, vol. 2, no. 1657, 165, and WA, TR, vol. 3, no. 3179a-b, 312, as quoted in Markwald and Markwald, *Katharina von Bora*, 71.
3. Marjorie Elizabeth Plummer, "Nothing More than Common Whores and Knaves: Married Nuns and Monks in the Early German Reformation," in Luebke and Lindemann, *Mixed Matches*, 47.
4. Ibid.
5. Breul, "Celibacy—Marriage—Unmarriage," in Luebke and Lindemann, *Mixed Matches*, 34.
6. Ibid., 46.
7. Plummer, "Nothing More than Common Whores and Knaves," in Luebke and Lindemann, *Mixed Matches*, 59.
8. Claudia Jarzebowski, "The Meaning of Love: Emotion and Kinship in Sixteenth-Century Incest Discourses," in Luebke and Lindemann, *Mixed Matches*, 166.
9. Plummer, "Nothing More than Common Whores and Knaves," in Luebke and Lindemann, *Mixed Matches*, 55.
10. Ibid., 57.
11. Ibid., 46.
12. Simon, *Luther Alive*, 331.
13. Jeanette C. Smith, "Katharina von Bora through Five Centuries: A Historiography," *Sixteenth Century Journal* 30, no. 3 (Autumn 1999): 757.
14. Ibid.
15. Markwald and Markwald, *Katharina von Bora*, 78.
16. Kroker, *Mother of the Reformation*, 73.
17. Markwald and Markwald, *Katharina von Bora*, 78.
18. Marius, *Martin Luther*, 438.

19. Oberman, *Luther: Man between God and the Devil*, 278.

20. Simon, *Luther Alive*, 331.

21. Smith, "Katharina von Bora through Five Centuries: A Historiography," 756.

22. Friedenthal, *Luther*, 437.

23. Ibid.

24. MacCulloch, *Reformation*, 544.

25. Hans Peter Broedel, *The* Malleus Maleficarum *and the Construction of Witchcraft* (Manchester: Manchester University Press, 2003), 19.

26. Alan C. Kors and Edward Peter, eds., *Witchcraft in Europe 1100–1700: A Documentary History* (Philadelphia: University of Pennsylvania Press, 1972), 121.

27. Ibid., 126–27 and 117.

28. Ibid., 127.

29. Broedel, *The* Malleus Maleficarum *and the Construction of Witchcraft*, 26.

30. Ibid., 27.

31. Smith, "Katharina von Bora through Five Centuries: A Historiography," 766.

32. Katharina Schütz Zell, *Church Mother: The Writings of a Protestant Reformer in Sixteenth-Century Germany*, ed. and trans. Elsie McKee (Chicago: University of Chicago Press, 2006), 62.

33. Ibid., 77.

34. Ibid., 78–79.

35. Letter from Johann Hasenberg, quoted in Markwald and Markwald, *Katharina von Bora*, 79.

36. Ibid.

37. Ibid.

38. Letter from Joachim von der Heyden, in Markwald and Markwald, *Katharina von Bora*, 78.

39. Markwald and Markwald, *Katharina von Bora*, 78–79.

Chapter 12 Hausfrau Extraordinaire

1. Kroker, *Mother of the Reformation*, 82.

2. Kroker, *Mother of the Reformation*, 79.

3. BBC News, "Luther's Lavatory Thrills Experts," October 22, 2004, accessed September 23, 2015, http://news.bbc.co.uk/2/hi/europe/3944549.stm.

4. "Toilet Where Luther Strained to Produce the Reformation," *Sydney Morning Herald*, October 23, 2004, accessed September 23, 2015, http://www.smh.com.au/articles/2004/10/22/1098316865171.html.

5. Kroker, *Mother of the Reformation*, 82.

6. Ibid., 95.

7. Simon, *Luther Alive*, 335.

8. Markwald and Markwald, *Katharina von Bora*, 81.

9. Bainton, *Here I Stand*, 299.

10. John Fitzherbert, *Boke of Husbandry* (London, 1525), as quoted in Anderson, *Daily Life during the Reformation*, 122–23.

11. Terence Scully, *The Art of Cookery in the Middle Ages* (Woodbridge, UK: Boydell Press, 1995), 78.

12. Ibid., 233.

13. All three recipes from ibid., 233–35.

14. Ibid., 120.

15. Ibid., 42.

16. Ibid., 102.

17. Anderson, *Daily Life during the Reformation*, 174.

18. Ibid., 101–2.

19. Ozment, *Flesh and Spirit*, 89.

20. Instructions for beer making from "Alcoholic Drinks of the Middle Ages: How Beer Is Made," accessed September 25, 2015, http://myplace.frontier.com/~mshapiro_42/cbeer.html#how beer is made.

21. WA, TR, vol. 1, no. 798c, 379, as quoted in Markwald and Markwald, *Katharina von Bora*, 137.

22. WA, TR, vol. 2, no. 2757a, 638, as quoted in Markwald and Markwald, *Katharina von Bora*, 136.

23. Elaine Leong and Alisha Rankin, eds., *Secrets and Knowledge in Medicine and Science: 1500–1800* (Burlington, VT: Ashgate Publishing Company, 2011), 23.

24. Markwald and Markwald, *Katharina von Bora*, 165.

25. Ibid.

26. Mary Lindemann, *Medicine and Society in Early Modern Europe* (Cambridge: Cambridge University Press, 1999), 217.

27. Ibid., 219, and Anderson, *Daily Life during the Reformation*, 181.

28. Anderson, *Daily Life during the Reformation*, 179.

29. Ibid., 215.

30. Linda Pollock, *With Faith and Physic: The Life of a Tudor Gentlewoman, Lady Grace Mildmay, 1552–1620* (London: Collins and Brown, 1993), as quoted in Lindemann, *Medicine and Society in Early Modern Europe*, 215.

31. Anderson, *Daily Life during the Reformation*, 173.

32. Friedenthal, *Luther*, 447–48.

33. The History Learning Site, "Health and Medicine in Medieval England," accessed September 28, 2015, http://www.historylearningsite.co.uk/medieval-england/health-and-medicine-in-medieval-england/.

34. Markwald and Markwald, *Katharina von Bora*, 165.

35. Johann Georg Walch, *Dr. Martin Luthers Sämmtliche Schriften*, 2nd ed., 20:2030–32, as quoted in Markwald and Markwald, *Katharina von Bora*, 166.

36. Ibid.

37. Kroker, *Mother of the Reformation*, 77.

38. WA, TR, vol. 3, no. 2835a, 13, as quoted in Markwald and Markwald, *Katharina von Bora*, 87.

39. William J. Petersen, *Martin Luther Had a Wife* (Wheaton: Tyndale, 1985), 14.

40. Markwald and Markwald, *Katharina von Bora*, 88.

41. Kroker, *Mother of the Reformation*, 93.

42. Ibid.

43. Ibid.

44. Simon, *Luther Alive*, 335.

45. Marius, *Martin Luther*, 437.

46. Elsie McKee, "Teaching Katharina Schütz Zell (1498–1562)," in *Teaching Other Voices: Women and Religion in Early Modern Europe*, eds. Margaret L. King and Albert Rabil Jr. (Chicago: University of Chicago Press, 2007), 138.

Chapter 13 Two Pigtails on the Pillow

1. LW, vol. 44, 8–9; Martin Luther, *Sermon on the Estate of Marriage*.

2. Martin Luther, *Sermon No. 59*, WA, vol. 10, 3, as quoted in Karant-Nunn and Wiesner-Hanks, *Luther on Women*, 92.

3. Markwald and Markwald, *Katharina von Bora*, 56.

4. LW, vol. 49, 117; Letter from Martin Luther to Nikolaus von Amsdorf, June 21, 1525.

5. Oberman, *Luther: Man between God and the Devil*, 281.

6. Marius, *Martin Luther*, 438.

7. LW, vol. 49, 117; Letter from Martin Luther to Nikolaus von Amsdorf, June 21, 1525.

8. Brecht, *Martin Luther: His Road to Reformation*, 2:413; as quoted in Markwald and Markwald, *Katharina von Bora*, 89.

9. Bainton, *Women of the Reformation in Germany and Italy*, 37.

10. WA, TR, vol. 1, no. 255, 107, as quoted in Markwald and Markwald, *Katharina von Bora*, 136.

11. WA, TR, 3835; as quoted in Bainton, *Women of the Reformation in Germany and Italy*, 37.

12. Markwald and Markwald, *Katharina von Bora*, 143.

13. Bainton, *Women of the Reformation in Germany and Italy*, 37.

14. Meurer, *Katharina Luther geb. Von Bora*, 71, as quoted in Markwald and Markwald, *Katharina von Bora*, 135.

15. WA, TR, vol. 4, no. 4918, 580, as quoted in Markwald and Markwald, *Katharina von Bora*, 134.

16. Bainton, *Women of the Reformation in Germany and Italy*, 37.

17. Karant-Nunn and Wiesner-Hanks, *Luther on Women*, 16.

18. Martin Luther, *Lectures on Genesis*, LW, vol. 1, 69, as quoted in Karant-Nunn and Wiesner-Hanks, *Luther on Women*, 26.

19. WA, TR, vol. 1, no. 12, 5–6, and no. 103, 40, as quoted in Karant-Nunn and Wiesner-Hanks, *Luther on Women*, 28.

20. Martin Luther, *Sämmtliche Werke* (Erlangen and Frankfurt: 1826–57), vol. XX, 84, as quoted in Wiesner, *Women and Gender in Early Modern Europe*, 9.

21. Karant-Nunn and Wiesner-Hanks, *Luther on Women*, 9.

22. WA, TR, vol. 1, no. 55, 19, as quoted in Karant-Nunn and Wiesner-Hanks, *Luther on Women*, 28.

23. WA, TR, vol. 2, no. 1555, 130, as quoted in Karant-Nunn and Wiesner-Hanks, *Luther on Women*, 29.

24. LW, vol. 54, *Table Talk* no. 2847b, 174–75.

25. WA, TR, vol. 1, no. 1046, 528, as quoted in Karant-Nunn and Wiesner-Hanks, *Luther on Women*, 123.

26. Markwald and Markwald, *Katharina von Bora*, 131.

27. Bainton, *Women of the Reformation in Germany and Italy*, 29, 37.

28. Karant-Nunn and Wiesner-Hanks, *Luther on Women*, 122.

29. Susan C. Karant-Nunn, "The Masculinity of Martin Luther: Theory, Practicality, and Humor," in *Masculinity in the Reformation Era*, eds. Scott H.

Hendrix and Susan C. Karant-Nunn (Kirksville, MO: Truman State University Press, 2008), 178.

30. Martin Luther's introduction to Johannes Freder, *Ein Dialogus dem Ehestand zu ehren geschrieben*, WA, vol. 54, 174–75, as quoted in Karant-Nunn and Wiesner-Hanks, *Luther on Women*, 122.

31. Karant-Nunn, "The Masculinity of Martin Luther," in *Masculinity in the Reformation Era*, 178.

32. WA, TR, vol. 2, no. 1658, 166, as quoted in Karant-Nunn and Wiesner-Hanks, *Luther on Women*, 125.

33. LW, vol. 54, *Table Talk* no. 5659, 470.

34. Kroker, *Mother of the Reformation*, 160.

35. LW, vol. 49, 154; Letter from Martin Luther to Michael Stifel, August 11, 1526.

36. LW, vol. 49, 236; Letter from Martin Luther to Katharina Luther, October 4, 1529.

37. LW, vol. 49, 236, footnote 10.

38. Ibid.

39. Marius, *Martin Luther*, 442.

40. Currie, *Letters of Martin Luther*, 146; Letter from Martin Luther to George Spalatin, November 11, 1525.

41. LW, vol. 49, 403; Letter from Martin Luther to Katharina Luther, August 15, 1530.

42. Markwald and Markwald, *Katharina von Bora*, 109.

43. LW, vol. 54, *Table Talk* no. 49, 7.

44. WA, TR, vol. 1, no. 1110, 554, as quoted in Markwald and Markwald, *Katharina von Bora*, 130.

45. WA, BR, 3253, as quoted in Bainton, *Women of the Reformation in Germany and Italy*, 26.

46. Bainton, *Women of the Reformation in Germany and Italy*, 26.

47. LW, vol. 50, 290; Letter from Martin Luther to Katharina Luther, July 2, 1540.

48. LW, vol. 54, *Table Talk* no. 1461, 153.

49. Meurer, *Katharina Luther geb. Von Bora*, 46; as quoted in Markwald and Markwald, *Katharina von Bora*, 84.

50. Karant-Nunn, "The Masculinity of Martin Luther," in *Masculinity in the Reformation Era*, 185.

51. LW, vol. 50, 290; Letter from Martin Luther to Katharina Luther, July 2, 1540.

52. LW, vol. 50, 168; Letter from Martin Luther to Katharina Luther, February 27, 1537.

53. LW, vol. 50, 302; Letter from Martin Luther to Katharina Luther, February 7, 1546.

54. Kroker, *Mother of the Reformation*, 222.

55. Ibid.

56. Markwald and Markwald, *Katharina von Bora*, 91–92.

57. Ibid., 92.

58. Simon, *Luther Alive*, 336.

Chapter 14 A Family Affair

1. WA, BR, 932, as quoted in Bainton, *Women of the Reformation in Germany and Italy*, 34.

2. Markwald and Markwald, *Katharina von Bora*, 93.

3. Ozment, *Flesh and Spirit*, 71.

4. Roper, *Holy Household*, 233.

5. Martin Luther, *Lectures on Genesis*, LW, vol. 5, 331, as quoted in Karant-Nunn and Wiesner-Hanks, *Luther on Women*, 70.

6. LW, vol. 5, 355, as quoted in Karant-Nunn and Wiesner-Hanks, *Luther on Women*, 71.

7. LW, vol. 49, 152; Letter from Martin Luther to John Rühel, June 8, 1526.

8. Ibid., 154; Letter from Martin Luther to Michael Stifel, August 11, 1526.

9. Lindemann, *Medicine and Society in Early Modern Europe*, 24.

10. Wiesner, *Women and Gender in Early Modern Europe*, 79.

11. Ibid., 81.

12. Ozment, *When Fathers Ruled*, 101.

13. Ibid.

14. Ibid., 108–12.

15. Ibid., 108.

16. Eucharius Rösslin, "Rosengarten" (1513), in *Alte Meister der Medizin und Naturkunde in Facsimile-Ausgaben und Neudrucken nach Werken des* 15–18. *Jahrhunderts*, II, *Begleit-Text* by Gustav Klein (Munich, 1910), F 3 a-F 4 a/pp. 44–46, as quoted in Ozment, *When Fathers Ruled*, 110.

17. Ozment, *Flesh and Spirit*, 76.

18. Ibid.

19. Ibid., 76–77.

20. Ibid., 78.
21. Kroker, *Mother of the Reformation*, 122–23.
22. All baptism ceremony details from Ozment, *Flesh and Spirit*, 78.
23. Ibid., 85.
24. Konnert, *Early Modern Europe*, 22; and Kamen, *Early Modern European Society*, 18.
25. Kroker, *Mother of the Reformation*, 145–46.
26. Ibid., 151.
27. Ibid., 146–49.
28. Ibid., 152.
29. Ibid.
30. Kroker, *Mother of the Reformation*, 152–53.

Chapter 15 The Noblest, Most Precious Work

1. "Luther Als Musiker: Protestlieder und Psalmgesänge," Luther 2017, accessed January 11, 2016, http://www.luther2017.de/en/reformation/und-kultur/musik/protest-songs-and-the-singing-of-psalms-luther-as-a-musician/.
2. "The Hymns of Martin Luther," Zion Evangelical Lutheran Church, accessed April 13, 2016, http://atlanta.clclutheran.org/bibleclass/Hymns%20of%20Martin%20Luther.pdf.
3. Lawrence Stone, *Family, Sex and Marriage in England, 1500–1800* (New York: Harper & Row, 1977), 57, as quoted in Ozment, *When Fathers Ruled*, 116.
4. Lindemann, *Medicine and Society in Early Modern Europe*, 23.
5. Ibid.
6. Kroker, *Mother of the Reformation*, 123.
7. Ibid.
8. LW, vol. 49, 324 and 323; Letter from Martin Luther to Hans Luther, about June 19, 1530.
9. Kroker, *Mother of the Reformation*, 123.
10. Ann Dally, "The Lancet and the Gum-Lancet: 400 Years of Teething Babies," *The Lancet* 348, no. 9043 (Dec. 1996): 1710–11, accessed October 22, 2015, http://www.thelancet.com/journals/lancet/article/PIIS0140-6736(96)05105-7/fulltext.
11. LW, vol. 50, 81; Letter from Martin Luther to Katharina Luther, July 29, 1534.

12. LW, vol. 49, 312; Letter from Martin Luther to Katharina Luther, June 5, 1530.

13. LW, vol. 49, 312, footnote no. 6, quoting letter from Veit Dietrich, June 19, 1530.

14. LW, vol. 49, 419; Letter from Martin Luther to Katharina Luther, September 8, 1530.

15. LW, vol. 49, 323; Letter from Martin Luther to Hans Luther, about June 19, 1530.

16. LW, vol. 50, 50; Letter from Martin Luther to Katharina Luther, February 27, 1532.

17. Kroker, *Mother of the Reformation*, 134–35.

18. Martin Luther, *The Estate of Marriage*, 1522, LW, vol. 45, 39–41, as quoted in Karant-Nunn and Wiesner-Hanks, *Luther on Women*, 107–8.

19. Heidi Wunder, *He Is the Sun, She Is the Moon: Women in Early Modern Germany* (Cambridge, MA: Harvard University Press, 1998), 19.

20. Ozment, *When Fathers Ruled*, 118.

21. Wunder, *He Is the Sun, She Is the Moon*, 19.

22. LW, vol. 49, 311; Letter from Martin Luther to Katharina Luther, June 5, 1530.

23. LW, vol. 54, *Table Talk* no. 4105, 320–21.

24. Ozment, *When Fathers Ruled*, 132.

25. Ibid., 146.

26. Two popular housefather books during Luther's time were Otto Brunfels's *On Disciplining and Instructing Children* and Erasmus's *Behavior Befitting Well-Bred Youth*. Both were published in Latin and German so they could be read by scholars and common people alike. From Ozment, *When Fathers Ruled*, 136.

27. Kroker, *Mother of the Reformation*, 139.

28. Ibid., 138.

29. Ibid., 139.

30. Ozment, *When Fathers Ruled*, 148.

31. Gerald Strauss, *Luther's House of Learning: Indoctrination of the Young in the German Reformation* (Baltimore: Johns Hopkins University Press, 1978), 181.

32. LW, vol. 54, *Table Talk* no. 3566A, 235.

33. Kroker, *Mother of the Reformation*, 135.

34. LW, vol. 54, *Table Talk* no. 81, 9.

35. Ibid.

36. Strauss, *Luther's House of Learning*, 154.

37. WA, BR, vol. 7, no. 2093; Letter from Martin Luther to Nikolaus von Amsdorf, March 1534, as quoted in Strauss, *Luther's House of Learning*, 154.

38. Kroker, *Mother of the Reformation*, 135.

39. Martin Luther, *The Estate of Marriage*, LW, vol. 45, 45–47, as quoted in Karant-Nunn and Wiesner-Hanks, *Luther on Women*, 108.

40. Paraphrased from *The Estate of Marriage*, LW, vol. 45, 45–47.

Chapter 16 In the Valley of the Shadow of Death

1. LW, vol. 54, *Table Talk* no. 5494, 430.
2. Ibid.
3. LW, vol. 54, *Table Talk* no. 5497, 432.
4. LW, vol. 54, *Table Talk* no. 5491, 428.
5. LW, vol. 54, *Table Talk* no. 5494, 430.
6. Ibid.
7. LW, vol. 54, *Table Talk* no. 5496, 431.
8. MacCulloch, *Reformation*, 557–58.
9. WA, vol. 10, 3:1–2, as quoted in Craig M. Koslofsky, *The Reformation of the Dead: Death and Ritual in Early Modern Germany, 1450–1700* (New York: St. Martin's Press, 2000), 3.
10. MacCulloch, *Reformation*, 558.
11. Koslofsky, *Reformation of the Dead*, 96.
12. MacCulloch, *Reformation*, 557–58.
13. LW, vol. 53, 326–27, as quoted in Koslofsky, *Reformation of the Dead*, 93.
14. Ibid.
15. LW, vol. 54, *Table Talk* no. 5498, 432.
16. Ibid.
17. Ibid.
18. Ibid.
19. Koslofsky, *Reformation of the Dead*, 97.
20. Anderson, *Daily Life during the Reformation*, 131.
21. Koslofsky, *Reformation of the Dead*, 99.
22. Ibid., 100.
23. LW, vol. 54, *Table Talk* no. 5499, 432–33.
24. Ibid., 433.
25. LW, vol. 54, *Table Talk* no. 5500, 433.
26. LW, vol. 50, 239; Letter from Martin Luther to Marcus Crodel, December 26, 1542.

27. LW, vol. 50, 240–41; Letter from Martin Luther to John Luther, December 27, 1542.

28. Ozment, *When Fathers Ruled*, 169.

29. LW, vol. 50, 238; Letter from Martin Luther to Justus Jonas, September 23, 1542.

30. Kroker, *Mother of the Reformation*, 143.

Chapter 17 'Til Death Did Them Part

1. LW, vol. 50, 312; Letter from Martin Luther to Katharina Luther, February 14, 1546.

2. Ibid.

3. Ibid.

4. LW, vol. 50, from the epilogue, 318.

5. Ibid.

6. Markwald and Markwald, *Katharina von Bora*, 173.

7. Thoma, *Katharina von Bora, Geschichtliches Lebensbild*, 215, as quoted in Markwald and Markwald, *Katharina von Bora*, 176.

8. Dagmar Freist, "Religious Difference and the Experience of Widowhood in Seventeenth- and Eighteenth-Century Germany," in *Widowhood in Medieval and Early Modern Europe*, eds. Sandra Cavallo and Lyndan Warner (New York: Pearson Education, Inc., 1999), 164.

9. Ibid.

10. William Page, as quoted by Barbara J. Todd, "The Virtuous Widow in Protestant England," in Cavallo and Warner, *Widowhood in Medieval and Early Modern Europe*, 72.

11. Ibid., 73.

12. Ibid.

13. Kroker, *Mother of the Reformation*, 225.

14. Ibid.

15. Ibid., 226.

16. Wiesner, *Women and Gender in Early Modern Europe*, 90.

17. Ibid., 90–91.

18. Kroker, *Mother of the Reformation*, 226.

19. Ibid., 227.

20. Markwald and Markwald, *Katharina von Bora*, 178; Kroker, *Mother of the Reformation*, 228.

21. Markwald and Markwald, *Katharina von Bora*, 178.

22. Kroker, *Mother of the Reformation*, 228.

23. Ibid., 228–29.
24. Thoma, *Katharina von Bora, Geschichtliches Lebensbild*, 230–31, as quoted in Markwald and Markwald, *Katharina von Bora*, 181.
25. Kroker, *Mother of the Reformation*, 228.
26. Thoma, *Katharina von Bora, Geschichtliches Lebensbild*, 213, as quoted in Markwald and Markwald, *Katharina von Bora*, 174.
27. Kroker, *Mother of the Reformation*, 181.
28. Markwald and Markwald, *Katharina von Bora*, 178.
29. Kroker, *Mother of the Reformation*, 232.
30. Ibid., 238.
31. Sandra Cavallo and Lyndan Warner, "Introduction," in Cavallo and Warner, *Widowhood in Medieval and Early Modern Europe*, 3.
32. Thoma, *Katharina von Bora, Geschichtliches Lebensbild*, 82–83, as quoted in Markwald and Markwald, *Katharina von Bora*, 180.
33. Thoma, *Katharina von Bora, Geschichtliches Lebensbild*, 244, as quoted in Markwald and Markwald, *Katharina von Bora*, 186.
34. Thoma, *Katharina von Bora, Geschichtliches Lebensbild*, 251–53, as quoted in Markwald and Markwald, *Katharina von Bora*, 188.
35. Meurer, *Katharina Luther geb. Von Bora*, 115–16, as quoted in Markwald and Markwald, *Katharina von Bora*, 189.
36. Thoma, *Katharina von Bora, Geschichtliches Lebensbild*, 256–57, as quoted in Markwald and Markwald, *Katharina von Bora*, 190–91.
37. Kroker, *Mother of the Reformation*, 247.
38. Markwald and Markwald, *Katharina von Bora*, 191.
39. Ibid., 254.

Chapter 18 A Chancy Thing

1. Kroker, *Mother of the Reformation*, 78.
2. WA, TR, vol. 3, no. 3675, 514–15, as quoted in Karant-Nunn and Wiesner-Hanks, *Luther on Women*, 129.

Appendix

1. Letters reprinted with permission of Augsburg Fortress.
2. Elector Johann Frederick.
3. Luther's nickname for Johannes Bugenhagen.
4. Both Zwingli and Oecolampadius rejected the idea of the real presence of Christ in the elements, claiming the words "This is my body" and "This

is my blood" were symbols or metaphors for Christ's presence. Luther disagreed, arguing that Christ was physically present in the bread and the wine.

5. Luther's nicknames for his children, Magdalene and Hans.

6. These two sentences were added as a postscript following Luther's signature. Brenz was a German theologian and the Protestant Reformer of the Duchy of Württemberg. Osiander was the chief preacher at Nuremberg's St. Lawrence Church. Stephen Kastenbauer, or Agricola, was a lesser known participant in the Reformation.

7. The English fever, which was brought by English sailors to Germany at the beginning of the sixteenth century, was feared by people perhaps even more than the plague. Because of the outbreak in Marburg, Landgrave Philip of Hesse was forced to abort negotiations before reaching the consensus between Luther and Zwingli that he had hoped for.

8. Philip Melanchthon.

9. George Major and Ambrose Berndt were friends of Luther and professors at the University of Wittenberg.

10. Arnstadt was in Greussen, the district Luther had just written about. When Luther says the devil was driven out of the girl in "a truly Christian way," he means the pastor did not use the dramatic papal rite of exorcism, but the simpler practice of exorcism advocated by Luther.

11. "The baccalaureus" refers to Luther's oldest son, Hans, who had graduated in 1539 with a bachelor of arts from the University of Wittenberg. It's not clear who "Marushe" refers to—perhaps it is an allusion to Luther's daughter Margarete, whom he occasionally called "Marussala."

12. Paul Eber, Latin professor at Wittenberg University and a close friend of Melanchthon, had traveled with Luther to Weimar to visit his gravely ill friend.

13. Doctor Severus or Schiefer refers to Wolfgang Schiefer, who was originally from Austria and had been a student at Wittenberg University. He lived with the Luthers for at least a year.

14. Lycaon was Luther's nickname for his servant, Wolfgang Seberger—named after Lycaon the Wolf in Greek mythology.

15. Luther is referring to a treatment he underwent from time to time, in which he used an abrasive stone to make and keep an open wound in his left calf, which by oozing was supposed to offer relief from numerous ailments, including headaches and high blood pressure. His friend Justas Jonas had injured his own leg, which Luther jokes was an intentional ploy for attention.

SELECTED BIBLIOGRAPHY

The following is a partial list of sources, organized thematically, that were used in researching this book. This bibliography does not include any works by Martin Luther; those are listed in the endnotes.

Biographies of Martin Luther

Bainton, Roland. *Here I Stand: A Life of Martin Luther*. Peabody, MA: Hendrickson, 1950.

Boehmer, Heinrich. *Martin Luther: Road to Reformation*. Translated from the German by John W. Doberstein and Theodore G. Tappert. Cleveland: World Publishing Company, 1957.

Currie, Margaret, trans. *The Letters of Martin Luther*. London: MacMillan and Company, 1908.

Fife, Robert Herndon. *Young Luther: The Intellectual and Religious Development of Martin Luther to 1518*. New York: AMS Press, Inc., 1970.

Friedenthal, Richard. *Luther: His Life and Times*. New York: Harcourt Brace Jovanovich, Inc., 1967.

Karant-Nunn, Susan C., and Merry E. Wiesner-Hanks, eds. and trans. *Luther on Women: A Sourcebook*. New York: Cambridge University Press, 2003. Kindle edition.

Kittelson, James M. *Luther the Reformer: The Story of the Man and His Career*. Minneapolis: Augsburg Publishing House, 1986.

Manns, Peter. *Martin Luther: An Illustrated Biography*. New York: Crossroads, 1982.

Marius, Richard. *Martin Luther: The Christian between God and Death*. Cambridge, MA: Harvard University Press, 1999.

Oberman, Heiko A. *Luther: Man between God and the Devil*. New York: Doubleday, 1992.

Ozment, Steven. *The Serpent and the Lamb: Cranach, Luther, and the Making of the Reformation*. New Haven: Yale University Press, 2012.

Simon, Edith. *Luther Alive: Martin Luther and the Making of the Reformation*. Garden City, NY: Doubleday, 1968.

Biographies of Katharina von Bora

Bainton, Roland. *Women of the Reformation in Germany and Italy*. Minneapolis: Augsburg Publishing House, 1971.

Kroker, Ernst. *Mother of the Reformation: The Amazing Life and Story of Katharine Luther*. Translated by Mark E. DeGarmeaux. St. Louis: Concordia, 2013.

Markwald, Rudolf K., and Marilynn Morris Markwald. *Katharina von Bora: A Reformation Life*. St. Louis: Concordia, 2002.

Smith, Jeanette C. "Katharina von Bora through Five Centuries: A Historiography." *Sixteenth Century Journal* 30, no. 3 (1999): 745–74.

Treu, Martin. "Katharina von Bora: The Woman at Luther's Side." *Lutheran Quarterly* XIII (1999): 157.

Daily Life in Early Modern Germany

Albala, Ken. *Cooking in Europe: 1250–1650*. Westport, CT: Greenwood Press, 2006.

Anderson, James M. *Daily Life during the Reformation*. Santa Barbara, CA: ABC-CLIO, LLC, 2011.

Gordon, Bruce. *The Place of the Dead: Death and Remembrance in Late Medieval and Early Modern Europe*. New York: Cambridge University Press, 2000.

Roeck, Bernd. *Civic Culture and Everyday Life in Early Modern Germany*. Leiden: Brill, 2006.

Singman, Jeffrey L. *Daily Life in Medieval Europe*. Westport, CT: Greenwood Press, 1999.

Marriage and Family Life

Harrington, Joel F. *Reordering Marriage and Society in Reformation Germany*. New York: Cambridge University Press, 1995.

Karant-Nunn, Susan. *The Reformation of Ritual: An Interpretation of Early Modern Germany*. New York: Routledge, 1997.

Miller, Naomi J., and Naomi Yavnew, eds. *Gender and Early Modern Constructions of Childhood*. Burlington, VT: Ashgate Publishing Company, 2011.

Ozment, Steven. *Flesh and Spirit: Private Life in Early Modern Germany*. New York: Penguin Books, 1999.

———. *Magdalena and Balthasar: An Intimate Portrait of Life in 16th-Century Europe Revealed in the Letters of a Nuremberg Husband and Wife*. New Haven: Yale University Press, 1986.

———. *When Fathers Ruled: Family Life in Reformation Europe*. Cambridge, MA: Harvard University Press, 1983.

Roper, Lyndal. "Going to Church and Street: Weddings in Reformation Augsburg." *Past and Present* 106 (Feb. 1985): 62–101.

———. *The Holy Household: Religion, Morals and Order in Reformation Augsburg*. Oxford: Clarendon Press, 1989.

Strauss, Gerald. *Luther's House of Learning: Indoctrination of the Young in the German Reformation*. Baltimore: Johns Hopkins University Press, 1978.

Wiesner, Merry E. "Family Household and Community." In *Handbook of European History, 1400–1600*, vol. 1, edited by Thomas A. Brady Jr., Heiko A. Oberman, and James D. Tracy. Grand Rapids: Eerdmans, 1996.

Medicine

Leong, Elaine, and Alisha Rankin, eds. *Secrets and Knowledge in Medicine and Science, 1500–1800*. Burlington, VT: Ashgate Publishing Company, 2011.

Lindemann, Mary. *Medicine and Society in Early Modern Europe*. Cambridge: Cambridge University Press, 1999.

Siraisi, Nancy G. *Medieval and Early Renaissance Medicine: An Introduction to Knowledge and Practice*. Chicago: University of Chicago Press, 1990.

Women in the Middle Ages, the Reformation, and Early Modern Europe/Germany

Cavallo, Sandra, and Lyndan Warner, eds. *Widowhood in Medieval and Early Modern Europe*. New York: Pearson Education Limited, 1999.

Gies, Frances, and Joseph Gies. *Women in the Middle Ages*. New York: Harper-Collins, 1978.

Marshall, Sherrin, ed. *Women in Reformation and Counter-Reformation Europe: Public and Private Worlds*. Bloomington, IN: Indiana University Press, 1989.

Wiesner, Merry E. *Gender, Church and State in Early Modern Germany: Essays by Merry E. Wiesner*. London: Addison Wesley Longman Limited, 1998.

———. *Women and Gender in Early Modern Europe*. Cambridge: Cambridge University Press, 2000.

———. *Working Women in Renaissance Germany*. New Brunswick, NJ: Rutgers University Press, 1986.

Wilson, Katharina, ed. *Women Writers of the Renaissance and Reformation*. Athens, GA: University of Georgia Press, 1987.

Monastic Life

Burton, Janet, and Julie Kerr. *The Cistercians in the Middle Ages*. Woodbridge, Suffolk, UK; Rochester, NY: Boydell Press, 2011.

Hamburger, Jeffrey F., and Susan Marti, eds. *Crown and Veil: Female Monasticism from the Fifth to the Fifteenth Centuries*. New York: Columbia University Press, 2008.

Kerr, Julie. *Life in the Medieval Cloister*. New York: Continuum US, 2009.

Lawrence, C. H. *Medieval Monasticism: Forms of Religious Life in Western Europe in the Middle Ages*. London: Longman Group LTD, 1984.

Leonard, Amy. *Nails in the Wall: Catholic Nuns in Reformation Germany*. Chicago: University of Chicago Press, 2005.

Luebke, David, and Mary Lindemann, eds. *Mixed Matches: Transgressive Unions in Germany from the Reformation to the Enlightenment*. New York: Berghahn Books, 2014.

Pirckheimer, Caritas. *A Journal of the Reformation Years, 1524–1528*. Rochester, NY: D. S. Brewer, 2006.

Plummer, Marjorie Elizabeth. "'Partner in His Calamities': Pastors' Wives, Married Nuns and the Experience of Clerical Marriage in the Early German Reformation." *Gender and History* 20, no. 2 (August 2008): 207–27.

Wiesner-Hanks, Merry, ed. and introduction. *Convents Confront the Reformation: Catholic and Protestant Nuns in Germany*. Milwaukee: Marquette University Press, 1998.

Woodford, Charlotte. *Nuns as Historians in Early Modern Germany*. Oxford: Oxford University Press, 2002.

Medieval/Reformation History

Barstow, Anne Llewellyn. *Witchcraze: A New History of the European Witch Hunts*. San Francisco: HarperCollins, 1994.

MacCulloch, Diarmaid. *The Reformation*. New York: Viking, 2003.

Mackay, Christopher. *The Hammer of Witches: A Complete Translation of the* Malleus Maleficarum. New York: Cambridge University Press, 2009.

Makinen, Virpi, ed. *Lutheran Reformation and the Law*. Leiden: Brill, 2006.

Tentler, Thomas N. *Sin and Confession on the Eve of the Reformation*. Princeton, NJ: Princeton University Press, 1977.

Wandel, Lee Palmer. *The Reformation: Towards a New History*. New York: Cambridge University Press, 2011.

Michelle DeRusha is the author of *50 Women Every Christian Should Know* and the memoir *Spiritual Misfit*. She writes a monthly column about religion and spirituality for the *Lincoln Journal Star*, as well as a weekly blog at www.MichelleDeRusha.com. She lives with her husband and their two boys in Lincoln, Nebraska.

Meet Michelle!

MichelleDeRusha.com

Michelle M. DeRusha

@MichelleDeRusha

Michelle DeRusha

@MichelleDeRusha